P9-AOZ-573

LANGLEY HALL LIBRARY

Understanding Consciousness

Understanding Consciousness

Its function and brain processes

Gerd Sommerhoff

SAGE Publications
London • Thousand Oaks • New Delhi

© Gerd Sommerhoff 2000

First published 2000

All rights reserved. No part of this publication may be
reproduced, stored in a retrieval system, transmitted or
utilized in any form or by any means, electronic, mechanical,
photocopying, recording or otherwise, without permission
in writing from the Publishers.

SAGE Publications Ltd
6 Bonhill Street
London EC2A 4PU

SAGE Publications Inc
2455 Teller Road
Thousand Oaks, California 91320

SAGE Publications India Pvt Ltd
32, M-Block Market
Greater Kailash – I
New Delhi 110048

British Library Cataloguing in Publication data
A catalogue record for this book is available from the British
Library

ISBN 0 7619 6774 5
ISBN 0 7619 6775 3 (pbk)

Library of Congress catalog card number available

Typeset by Keystroke, Jacaranda Lodge, Wolverhampton
Printed in Great Britain by Athenaeum Press, Ltd.,.
Gateshead, Tyne & Wear.

CONTENTS

ACKNOWLEDGEMENTS

Of the many who have offered me their opinions, I am especially indebted to the following for their stimulating discussions or their comments on drafted sections of this manuscript: Roger Carpenter, Rodney Cotterill, Thomas Forster, Geoff Kendall, Klaus Kieslinger, Ray Paton, Nils Schweckendiek, Ed Scofield, Gysbert Stoet and Chris Town. Special thanks are also due to Nigel Harris for his valuable advice in the development of my IT and computer facilities.

For permission to reproduce copyright material I am indebted to the MIT Press (Figure 2.3), Blackwell Scientific Publications (Figure 2.4), John Wiley & Sons (Figure 4.1), and World Scientific Publishing (Figure 9.3). Also to the Cambridge University Press for the passage quoted from Blakemore (1977) in Chapter 6, to Vintage for that quoted from Rosenfield (1992) in the same chapter, and to Ulric Neisser for that quoted from Neisser (1976) in Chapter 8.

PREFACE:
PROBLEMS OF SUBSTANCE AND
OF PRESENTATION

The problem of consciousness, of what it is, what it does, why it evolved, and how it arises in the brain, has been described as the least understood of all the fundamental problems still facing the life sciences. The philosopher Daniel Dennett has called it 'just about the last remaining mystery and the one about which we are still in a terrible muddle' (Dennett, 1991, p. 22). It is a serious issue, not only because the relation between mind and brain can never be fully understood until the nature of consciousness is understood, but also because of the large number of academic disciplines that are directly or indirectly affected by our perceptions of the nature of consciousness.

In the many multidisciplinary conferences and new publications on consciousness that have occurred since Dennett's words were written, new technologies have produced a wealth of new empirical data, but at the theoretical level one still meets almost as many different views about consciousness as there are contributors to the discussion. There is not even the beginning in sight of a consensus about what kind of property we are actually here talking about, or where this property is to be found. According to some views, only humans have consciousness, while at the opposite extreme one even meets the belief that any system interacting with the environment has consciousness, e.g. a thermostat but not a thermometer. Again, while some authors regard consciousness as an essential product of neural activities, in the eyes of others it is no more than an inessential by-product of such activities and a mere spectator in the brain. A few regard the problem as insoluble and textbooks on cognitive science tend to play safe by not mentioning the topic at all. It is indeed a terrible muddle.

There is no way out of this muddle except by way of definite decisions, foremost a decision about what shall be understood by consciousness in the context of a scientific investigation. And these decisions must offer rewards and conceptual clarifications that can persuade others to go along with them. In this book I propose and follow up three main steps and hope to convince the reader of their rewards. The first step concerns the meaning of the word and I shall come to that in a moment. My second step is to regard consciousness as a biological property that has evolved in consequence of the function it performs. And my third is to proceed from this basis with an imaginative search for the most powerful and yet simplest empirically supported hypotheses that can explain the nature of this property, why it evolved and how it is implemented in the brain. At the same time I have taken into account that consciousness can be viewed either *objectively* as a particular faculty of the brain, or *subjectively* as particular qualities of experience, often called the 'qualia'. And I have held that a scientific model of consciousness needs to cover both.

The model I have arrived at does indeed do so, yet stands out by its basic simplicity. For it is formulated in terms of just *two key concepts*, and just *four propositions* – all accurately defined. Two of these propositions are hypotheses, fully supported by the empirical evidence. One postulates the existence of neural processes in the brain that perform certain specified representational functions. The other subjects these to capacity limitations. The remaining two propositions explain the objective and subjective aspects of conscious experience in terms of these underlying brain processes. The two key concepts relate to two different senses in which the term 'representation' is to be understood in the context of the theory. In fact, until second thoughts prevailed, the title I adopted for this book was *The Biological Simplicity of Consciousness*.

This simplicity is not achieved by trimming the meaning of consciousness, as the reader may at first have suspected. On the contrary, the notion of consciousness on which I have settled goes well beyond most theories by embracing all of the following facets of consciousness: awareness of the surrounding world, of the self as an entity, and of such things as thoughts and feelings. And it covers them both from the objective and the subjective perspective, explaining at the same time why we have subjective experience in the first place.

However, with an eye on both the evolutionary context and common perceptions, I have taken consciousness to be a property that can in principle be possessed also by creatures lacking a language faculty, such as the prelinguistic infant, the deaf-mute and our animal cousins. Hence in human consciousness I deal only with the subverbal levels of awareness. I call this the *primary* consciousness and argue that the most fundamental questions about the nature of consciousness and the mind–brain relation can be answered if this primary consciousness is understood. Chapter 5, for example, begins with a number of basic questions that are answered by my model.

I have to add two further warnings. First, most of my definitions are *functional*, and this may worry readers who happen to be acquainted with the long-drawn-out philosophical disputes about 'functionalism'. The issues that occupied these disputes are irrelevant here. Since mine is a biological approach, brain processes are quite rightly defined in terms of the role they play in meeting the organism's needs. The biological science of physiology, for example, is exclusively concerned with functional explanations.

Second, in view of the strong interest in consciousness found in many quarters in which a knowledge of the brain cannot be taken for granted, including among computer scientists, robotics engineers and students of artificial intelligence (AI), I have attempted to write in a language addressed to the general reader (without loss of precision where it mattered), and have added an extensive glossary. However, now and then I have also simplified where this seemed permissible. In my sketches of brain sections, for example, I have entered only those details that are relevant to the issues under discussion. I have had to make similar decisions as regards the bibliography. In view of the wide-ranging topics discussed in this book, a complete list of references to work done in the various fields would have been far beyond my capacity, and probably also beyond that of any single author. With an eye also on the general reader, I have confined myself in most cases to just a single key reference – leaving it to the bibliography of that publication to point readers to related work, should they want to follow up the topic in question.

There may be occasions when this economy will tax the patience of the professionals. I can only hope that this will not deter them from what they may stand to gain overall from the conceptual clarifications and new perspectives the book has to offer, as well as its specific answers to (*inter alia*) the questions of what consciousness is, what it does, why it evolved and how it arises in the brain.

Square brackets refer readers to other sections in the book, the use of bold type for a brain-related term directs them to the glossary. (This applies only at the term's first occurrence and as an occasional reminder.)

PART I

CONSCIOUSNESS EXPLAINED IN SIMPLE, FUNCTIONAL TERMS

1

A METHODICAL BIOLOGICAL APPROACH AND ITS CONCLUSIONS

1.1. Overview

The 'mystery' of consciousness

What is consciousness? What does it do? Why did it evolve? And how does it arise in the brain? It is the least understood part of human life. As I have mentioned in the Preface, the philosopher Daniel Dennett has called it 'just about the last remaining mystery and the one about which we are still in a terrible muddle' (Dennett, 1991, p. 22). In this book I aim to show how a top-down biological approach, conducted at the right level of abstraction and conceptual precision, can offer an explanation of consciousness that unlocks the mystery, slices through the muddle and is compressed into just four propositions. Despite this simplicity it covers the three main facets of consciousness: awareness of the surrounding world, of the self as an entity, and of one's thoughts and feelings. And it covers these divisions of awareness both as subjective experience and as objective representational processes in the brain distinguished by their functional architecture.

Other mysteries, Dennett says, such as those remaining in atomic physics or cosmology, may not have been solved, but at least they have been tamed. Physicists and cosmologists are agreed on what they are talking about and what questions need to be answered. They speak the same language. Not so in the case of consciousness. Anyone looking at the range of books on the nature of consciousness or the mind–brain relation on offer today – and there are quite a few to choose from[1] – is bound to notice one gaping hole: the lack of a common focus, of a clear and shared perception of what we are actually talking about when talking about consciousness. None of the contributions from even the most eminent of authors seems to converge with others towards a common view of the beast itself.

The importance of the problem

These are not trivial issues. Without a clearly defined perception of the nature of consciousness and the structure of the underlying brain processes there can be no full understanding of how the mind works, no clear perception of the conditions a brain event must satisfy to become a conscious experience, nor of the intrinsic nature of memory recall and of the general relation between mental events and brain events, between 'mind' and brain. This, in turn, touches on the larger question of the relation between 'mind' and 'matter' that has divided philosophers since the days of Plato and Aristotle. And, of course, a failure to understand the nature of consciousness leaves a large blank in our understanding of what sort of creatures we really are on the biological scale of life.

Although brain research, psychology and psychiatry are most immediately affected, other disciplines are also touched. Baars and Banks (1992) have listed more than 40 fields of investigation carried out under labels that imply such things as conscious experience, voluntary control and self-awareness. Moreover, the progress of AI (Artificial Intelligence), artificial neural networks, computer simulations and robotics has also brought a growing interest in all aspects of brain function from these quarters. I know this from the approaches I have received, especially over the last couple of years.

The recent revival of interest

Serious scientific interest in consciousness is a comparatively recent phenomenon. Between the two world wars and right into the 1960s, the rule of behaviourism virtually barred consciousness as a respectable topic for scientists. In its laudable, but fatally flawed attempts to integrate psychology with the natural sciences, this school of psychology rejected as a fit subject for scientific inquiry any concept that hinted at subjectivity and unobservability. It was founded in 1913 by J.B.Watson and inspired by Pavlov's famous experiments in conditioned reflexes – for example, the demonstration that if the presentation of food to a dog is regularly preceded by the sound of a bell, the animal soon begins to salivate merely at the sound of that bell. From this reflexology grew the behaviourist vision of psychology as a truly scientific discipline, devoted to the study of lawful and conditionable associations between observable stimuli and observable responses. Consciousness clearly did not fit this picture. B.F. Skinner, the high priest of the movement, even claimed that consciousness was a non-existing entity invented solely to provide spurious explanations. All of that has since changed dramatically. The need for a science of consciousness is rarely questioned today.

This revival of interest in consciousness has indeed been nothing short of explosive. Books and conferences on the subject have mushroomed and new journals have been dedicated to it. And it has been explosive not just in the range of experimental data reported to these conferences as somehow relevant to the problem, but also in the bewildering variety of theoretical frameworks the authors introduce in accordance with their own professional fields. Since these fields can range from the biochemical, neurological, physiological, evolutionary, computational, quantum theoretical, psychological, psychophysical and psychiatric to the philosophical, the sheer multitude of approaches, and the uneven quality of the concepts they introduce, is such that one can understand those who turn their backs on the whole problem. Indeed, for every researcher who feels drawn into the debate, you may also find one who scrupulously avoids it.

The present state of confusion and discord

How deep these divisions can run may be illustrated by the conflicting beliefs still met among theorists about the question of where consciousness is to be found. Leaving out of account the panpsychism of those who, following Leibniz or Whitehead, believe that consciousness may permeate all levels of being in the universe, we find at the one extreme writers who believe that only humans have consciousness. Daniel Dennett, for example, sees consciousness as just a cultural product. The psychologist Julian Jaynes goes even further and credits only *modern* humans with consciousness, denying it to Homer's Greeks and the Hebrews of the Old Testament (Jaynes, 1976). At the opposite extreme, the psychologist Susan Blackmore attributes consciousness to any system that interacts with the environment, hence thermostats but not thermometers (Blackmore, 1992). In between we meet all shades of opinion about the extent to which animals can be said to have consciousness.[2] Most biologists recognize it as a problem, but also tend to avoid it. The same applies to neuroscientists. You may look in vain for textbooks on the brain, or even cognitive science, that have a chapter on consciousness, or even mention consciousness in the index. It is no doubt true to say that most scientists regard consciousness as an effective function of the brain. But there are also some who regard it as something right outside the brain or as a mere spectator in the brain; others who deny the very usefulness of the concept in science; and again others who disagree with this but deny the possibility of ever finding a solution to the problem. In Section 5.12 I shall take a brief look at different philosophies of mind.

In *The Macmillan Dictionary of Psychology*, the entry under 'consciousness' concludes with the words: 'Consciousness is a fascinating but elusive phenomenon: it is impossible to specify what it is, what it does or why it evolved. Nothing worth reading has been written on it' (Sutherland, 1989). As you may have gathered from my opening remarks, I dispute every part of this entry except the fascination of the topic itself.

The need for decisions

All this discord may seem odd. We all experience consciousness directly and should we not be agreed, therefore, on what we are talking about? Should it not be superfluous to be more specific, as, for example, Sigmund Freud believed? The answer is no. Our own experience gives us merely a subjective, 'first-person' view of consciousness, whereas science needs to occupy a detached and objective 'third-person' standpoint, and that requires *decisions* about the sense in which consciousness is to be understood for the purposes of scientific investigations. To meet most closely what is expected of a scientific account of consciousness, these decisions should try to capture as much as possible of what is commonly meant by that word (for example, what we hope a patient will recover who has lost consciousness in an accident).

To come closest to the common usage of the word, I fall back on the dictionaries of the English language [1.2] and posit as the three main facets of consciousness *an awareness of the surrounding world, of the self as an entity, and of one's thoughts and feelings*. Hence I take these to be the three main divisions of awareness any explanation needs to cover. As you wake up from a deep sleep you meet their return as subjective experience, but from the detached standpoint of science this is the operational return of a set of representational functions of the brain of which science still lacks a clear conception. To say this is to make a *theoretical* statement. But this is unavoidable. Since 'consciousness' is a fuzzy notion, a precise concept of consciousness can only be the product of a *theory* of consciousness. Attempts to avoid this by searching for a scientific definition of consciousness exclusively in terms of observable behaviour patterns, have always fallen far short of the mark. Hence the failure of behaviourism to cope with consciousness.

In the same spirit, and also with an eye on the evolutionary context, I understand consciousness in a sense that enables it in principle to be possessed by creatures lacking a language faculty, such as the prelinguistic infant, the deaf-mute and our animal cousins. A scientific theory of consciousness that begins with a notion of consciousness which allows only humans to have feelings, strays too arbitrarily from the common notion and also ignores the evolutionary story. Hence this book concentrates exclusively on the subverbal level of human awareness, which I call the *primary consciousness*. It is a basic level of awareness in the sense that it is likely to be the level from which human consciousness has evolved and in which it is still grounded. Moreover, for answers to many of the most fundamental questions commonly asked about the nature of consciousness and the mind–brain relation, it suffices to understand the nature of this primary consciousness [5.1].

Human awareness of the world is greatly influenced by the knowledge that is brought to bear on what the eyes see and by the thoughts this knowledge stimulates. Much of this is in a verbal and propositional form – a kind of silent speech – but by no means all. Many thoughts consist of images rather than words, as when you visualize the goal of some activity, recall an accident you have witnessed, wonder how a new carpet might fit your room, or imagine a scene described in a novel. And, as Philip Johnson-Laird (1983) has shown, even in our logical reasoning we tend to fall back on mental models. Since the present theory is confined to the primary consciousness, the only thoughts it covers belong to this nonverbal category.

The need for conceptual clarity

It is my belief that the more intricate a problem is, the more precise need to be the concepts in terms of which it is analysed. It also helps if one can keep the number of key concepts to a minimum. As mentioned in the Preface, and as you will see below, the basic model of the primary consciousness presented in this book needs only two key concepts. Only one other will have to be introduced when, in Part II, we come to discuss the brain's implementation of this model. This is the concept of *expectation*. It relates to the power of the brain to anticipate a course of events either in real time or in the imagination. It will be accurately defined in functional terms, and will prove to be of prime importance. Without it we cannot understand the composition of the brain's internal model of the surrounding world, nor the essential role that motor information plays in the processes of sensory perception.

The history of science bears out the need for conceptual precision. Indeed, the level of abstraction from which my account of consciousness derives its simplicity owes everything to the precision of the concepts it introduces. I recently heard a neuroscientist complain that he finds the notions that some philosophers and psychologists introduce when trying to analyse the notion of consciousness to be no clearer than the notion they set out to clarify. I know exactly what he meant and have often felt the same, although I have no doubt that these notions helped to answer questions posed in the minds of the authors concerned.

One of my philosophy tutors at Oxford was Gilbert Ryle. He belonged to the school of linguistic philosophy and was thus mainly concerned with the analysis of concepts and linguistic structures, elegantly conducted in his *The Concept of Mind* (1949). One point troubled me about this school, namely the cycles in which its members seemed to become engaged. Typically an author would pick up a concept about which he felt unhappy and analyse it in terms of concepts about which he felt happier. But as the latter concepts now gained in prominence, they would in turn be questioned and further analyses be called for. And so the analytical process would continue without the promise of ultimate satisfaction and agreement. Even so, I learnt a lot from him and also owe to him my interest in the relation between mind and brain.

The need for a biological approach

We are all biological creatures, and in that sense consciousness is a biological property. Modern evolutionary theory leaves little room for doubt that *Homo sapiens* is the product of a continuous biological development and the faculty of consciousness is part of that product. If this is accepted, then it follows that if we are to properly understand the nature of consciousness it needs to be seen in its biological context. Thus my model sees the roots and rationale of consciousness in needs arising out of an organism's interactions with the external world. It is no coincidence that the development of a nervous system has been confined to actively moving (non-sessile) organisms.

Whereas the responses of the lower orders of life are stereotyped and genetically programmed to suit their ecological niche, the higher orders have learning capacities that enable them to adapt to a variety of worlds and contingencies. They discover the properties of those worlds primarily through the experienced consequences of their actions. This is a dynamic aspect of sensory perception in which self-paced movements play a crucial role and which is too often neglected in the contemporary studies of sensory perception, especially visual perception [7.2].

A second source of information for them lies in the *observation* of what leads to what in the external world. The child observes as well as explores its world. We can describe these two sources jointly as what-leads-to-what experiences that result in the corresponding what-leads-to-what expectancies as part of the brain's internal representation of the properties of the external world. When this point is reached in our discussion I shall introduce a functional definition of a state of expectancy which characterizes this state in terms of two separate components. Later it will be suggested that at the neural level one of these components is shared by mental images.

The need for hypotheses

As I said above, a precise concept of consciousness (primary or otherwise) can only be the product of a *theory* of consciousness. And scientific theories rest on hypotheses. In the present case these need to cover the three main divisions of awareness mentioned earlier. They also need to be:

1. formulated with the precision required by science generally, and consonant with the conceptual framework of the particular sciences concerned, in this case the biological sciences;
2. demonstrably able to explain the phenomena concerned – in this case the kinds of awareness I have named; and
3. supported by the empirical evidence.

Let me here forestall a misconception. Scientific hypotheses need not be inductive inferences from the known data. They need not be generalizations from the particular to the universal. Science does not progress just by grinding out generalizations from its observations. Contrary to what some experimenters seem to assume tacitly, inductive inference is not the only way of arriving at fruitful hypotheses. Science also progresses (and has done so startlingly in modern cosmology) by way of purely imaginative conjectures – lateral jumps, as it were. Indeed, you could regard Proposition 1 formulated below [1.4] as such a jump. Computer simulations, too, can suggest new hypotheses, and I shall return to this point in Section 4.11.

It is sometimes said that to arrive eventually at a scientific explanation of consciousness we merely have to go on diligently expanding the empirical base. That is a mistake. You cannot find out how a TV set works by patiently watching the pictures on the screen while at the same time recording voltages, currents and temperatures at numerous locations in the set. At some point you have to jump to inspired hypotheses (or be told) about the functional architecture of the set, about the modular functions being performed on the incoming signals to produce the observed pictures. Nor can the seat of consciousness in the brain be discovered just by finding what brain structures are essential to it. As Richard Gregory once put it, removal of a single resistor in our TV set may cause the picture to vanish, but does not, of course, warrant the conclusion that this component is part of the circuits in which the picture is encoded. An area of the **visual cortex**, labelled V2 and largely involved in intravisual associations, is a case in point. Semir Zeki (1993) found this area to be indispensable for vision, but acknowledges that this does not prove it to be actually part of the structures in which the perceived scene is encoded. (At the same time he confesses that consciousness is 'the most severe problem' that his research strategies meet, but also one that neurologists generally avoid discussing.)

Summary of the proposed explanation of consciousness

I claim that with precise concepts at our disposal, the nature of conscious-ness – what it is, what it does, why it evolved and how it arises in the brain – can be explained in terms of just two key concepts, and just four propositions, all accurately defined. Two of these propositions are hypotheses about the representational brain functions underlying con-sciousness, and two are statements that identify consciousness with the brain functions and processes specified in the two hypotheses. They will be introduced later in this chapter [1.4]. Despite this stark simplicity, the explanation covers the three main divisions of awareness listed above. Moreover, it covers them both as objective faculties of the brain and as subjective experience. By the latter I mean the qualitative dimensions of experience, the so-called 'qualia', the 'what it is like' to have this or that conscious experience. I know of no other scientific model of consciousness that satisfies all of these conditions, let alone with so few assumptions and at the same level of conceptual precision.

Since we are dealing here with representational functions of the brain, the notion of 'representation' needs to be defined in precise and objective terms. This is done in Section 1.5, when a distinction will also be drawn between two senses of the word, a *structural* sense and a *functional* one.

How much can be explained by so little will become fully apparent in Chapter 5. Together with several sections of other chapters, this is devoted to a wide range of fundamental questions relating to consciousness that now have an answer in terms of the basic perceptions outlined above, or will at least be seen in a new perspective.

Chapters 2–4 enlarge on these perceptions, while Chapters 6–9 are devoted to how these representations are implemented in the brain. Jointly they explain in general terms both the *why* and the *how* of the primary consciousness.

The empirical evidence

Several subsections in these chapters examine the empirical evidence supporting this explanation of consciousness. Evidence is drawn from behavioural studies, neuroscientific data, brain imaging and the effect of brain lesions or of brain stimulation applied through inserted micro-electrodes.

Further comments

Since behaviourism convincingly demonstrated that consciousness cannot be defined in terms of observable behaviour patterns, you may well have initially wondered how else an *objective* account of consciousness could be arrived at. The answer lies in objective *functional* explanations – one of the key features of the biological sciences. Most of my leading concepts are defined in functional terms, and my explanation of consciousness and its implementation is given in terms of the functional fabric of the underlying brain processes – in other words, in terms of the jobs the brain does in producing the kinds of awareness that distinguish a conscious person from one in a deep sleep or a coma.

Functional relationships and their internal structures or 'architecture' are among the key concepts of the biological sciences. An entire branch is devoted to their study. It is called *physiology*. Later in this volume we shall consider what precisely is meant by a functional relationship [4.8]. Let me just say at this point that to describe the function of an organic process or structure is to describe the *developmentally established* part it plays in the performance of the organism as a whole, as when we describe the 'function' of the heart as the circulation of the blood. Like all functional approaches this is a 'top-down' approach. By this is meant an approach in which the properties or needs of the system as a whole are the ultimate frame of reference. My analysis, too, follows such a top-down approach, albeit at a more abstract level of thought than that of the physiological sciences and specifically neurophysiology.

Even after we have examined in Part II how these functions are implemented in the brain, this model still leaves us some distance removed from the ultimate goal of brain research, namely to discover the concrete neural activities and mechanisms in which consciousness 'resides'. It merely gives us the functional composition of the underlying brain processes. And it gives the location of these processes in the brain only to the extent to which existing knowledge enables them to be associated with specific anatomical structures or regions of the brain. Nevertheless, the model should be important for all researchers whose eyes remain firmly fixed on that ultimate goal, for it clarifies what needs to be explained in terms of concrete neural mechanisms, and it points research in specific directions.

Some readers may be interested in new theories only to the extent that these suggest new experiments. The present theory does not suggest new experiments in the sense a dedicated experimentalist may have in mind, but it does so in a different sense. For example, it suggests connections, e.g. feedback loops, that may not so far have shown up in the existing evidence, but which neuroscientists are now invited to look out for. It may direct attention to known connections in the brain whose functions have so far remained a mystery. By highlighting the dominant role of anticipatory reactions in the brain's model of the world it invites brain research to keep an eye open for them. And by elaborating the role of movement in sensory perception it invites research to focus on the required mechanisms for integrating the sensory and motor information, and adding the result to the brain's internal model of the external world.

1.2. The three facets of consciousness that need to be covered

For the reasons I have given above, the notion of the 'primary' consciousness was introduced to denote levels of awareness below those at which verbal thoughts make their contribution. It is certainly true that the ability to put things into words creates a deeper and richer sense of conscious reality. However, to make these linguistic capacities a condition for consciousness as such, is to deprive the word of a great deal of relevance and strays too far from the common meaning of the term. But what is this common meaning?

I have turned here to the dictionaries of the English language. If we strip away such entries as 'consciousness: the state of being conscious' we find a fair agreement that 'consciousness' is commonly used mainly in one of three senses: (1) *awareness of the surrounding world*, (2) *awareness of the self as an entity* and (3) *awareness of one's thoughts and feelings*.[3] I have therefore taken these three divisions of awareness as the most distinctive features of consciousness. And weighing them individually I have concluded that one cannot be satisfied with a scientific theory of the nature of consciousness that does not cover all three. Moreover, one conclusion of our analysis will be that they have an underlying unity.

Confusingly, 'awareness' is often used synonymously with 'consciousness'. 'I was aware of being followed' and 'I was conscious of being followed' are often used interchangeably. Indeed, whereas some people talk about the mystery of *consciousness*, others talk about the mystery of *awareness*, and essentially they mean the same mystery. Among well known authors, Lawrence Weiskrantz uses awareness as synonymous with consciousness. Some authors add to the confusion by *explaining* consciousness in terms of awareness, which, of course, does not take us any further. For these various reasons, the above dictionary definitions cannot be accepted by us as useful definitions of the phenomena that need to be explained. But they are still of crucial importance in telling us what *domains of experience* a scientific theory of consciousness needs to cover if it is to reach the heart of what we commonly mean by consciousness.

If we ignore the first of the three divisions mentioned, *awareness of the surrounding world*, we make nonsense of the difference between being asleep and being awake. For the state of sleep is precisely one in which the organism suspends its interactions with the surrounding world and its model of that world, devoting itself instead to internal adjustments and the restoration of its energies. In view of the biological importance of the sleep/wake cycle it should be clear, therefore, that in any biological approach this facet of consciousness must rank as a crucial one. Thus it came as some surprise to me that Weiskrantz (1997) confined the problem of consciousness to that of self-awareness, conceived by him as a set of open or silent self-reporting 'commentaries'. In his eyes the ability to make a 'commentary' is what it means to be aware and what gives rise to it. This is true enough at his chosen metaphorical level, but covers considerably less than the model presented in this volume. The same applies to Nicholas Humphrey's identification of consciousness with having sensations (Humphrey, 1992) and to David Rosenthal's identification of it with having thoughts about thoughts (Rosenthal, 1993).

If we ignore the second facet of consciousness, *awareness of the self as an entity*, we would ignore *inter alia* what is happening in self-reports like 'I feel a tingle' or 'I see a red spot'. Self-reports like these are of particular significance in view of the common laboratory practice to accept that a subject is conscious of a stimulus if he or she can report it.[4] We would also ignore the fact that what you consciously do with your arm is always done in awareness, however inattentively, of the fact that it is *your* arm you are moving, and not a foreign object. (By contrast, when the **afferent** nerve fibres of an arm are cut, the limb will be experienced as a foreign object.) Furthermore, we would ignore the very basis of our personal sense of identity and of the brain's autobiographical capacities.

Finally, if we ignore *awareness of one's thoughts and feelings*, we would certainly ignore something that is indisputably part of conscious experience, and is already implied in the possibility of self-reports. We are reminded here of John Locke's definition of consciousness as 'the perception of what passes in a man's own mind'.

There are also the two perspectives to be considered which I have already mentioned: awareness viewed as a particular set of the brain's cognitive powers, and awareness viewed as subjective experience. To confine ourselves to just either one of these would be telling only half the story.

One sense of 'consciousness' has not so far been mentioned: the now obsolete *social* sense in which it means shared knowledge. The very origin of the word (from *con* and *scius*) springs from the notion of shared knowledge. We still meet something similar in reference to shared attitudes, as in 'class consciousness' or 'national consciousness'. But these are semantic questions that must not blind us to the fact that consciousness has an important social function. Some authors put this at the front of their analysis. The Cambridge physiologist Horace Barlow, for example, sees the biological rationale of consciousness entirely in its social function, declaring consciousness to sit at the interface between the individual and the society of which he or she is a part (Barlow, 1987). Julian Jaynes (1976) and Daniel Dennett (1991), too, regard the social context as the true source of consciousness. This social function is genuine enough. However, before consciousness can exercise this social function, the individuals concerned must have that awareness of the surrounding world, of the self as an entity and of their thoughts and feelings, listed above as the three main facets of consciousness. It follows that any theory of consciousness must begin at this end. Nor do we want *a priori* to deny consciousness to non-social species – any more than we want to deny it *a priori* to creatures lacking a language faculty.

1.3. The two perspectives that need to be covered

As stated above, in all discussions of consciousness, primary or otherwise, two perspectives or standpoints need to be distinguished, and both need to be taken into account by a scientific theory of consciousness.

The first-person perspective, the perspective of the experiencing subject

'Awareness' here means the subjective experience of, say, perceiving a red rose, tasting the milk or having a toothache. It means *what it is like* to have this or that experience, the 'raw feel' of the experience, also known as the 'phenomenal experience' or 'sentience'. It cannot be ignored in a scientific account of consciousness. Philosophers have introduced the term 'qualia' ('quale' in the singular) for this first-order qualitative dimension of experience, and I have accepted this as a convenient shorthand.

The third-person perspective

This is the perspective of the detached scientific investigator or observer, such as the nurse or clinician looking for signs of a comatose patient beginning again to respond to stimuli or even becoming aware of his or her surroundings. From this standpoint consciousness means a particular set of the brain's operational powers. A scientific explanation of consciousness must be based on this third-person standpoint, but that does not mean that it can ignore the first-person experience and qualia. It needs to explain not only how these qualitative differences in our experiences come about, but also why we should have subjective experience in the first place.

1.4. Four propositions that jointly cover both requirements

The requirements that have been spelt out in the last two sections can be covered jointly by just four propositions. The first two are conjectures, for which the support will be reviewed in the next chapter, while the remainder are interpretations of a kind that may for brevity be called 'identity statements'. You will meet them presently.

Proposition 1

The first conjecture:

> *The brain forms an extensive internal representation of the current state of the organism which includes representations of the total situation facing the organism both in the* outer *and the* inner *world.* For brevity, I call this the brain's **Integrated Global Representation** or **IGR**.

The precise sense in which 'representation' is here to be understood is defined in Section 1.5 below. I shall then also point out the feedback loops which the existence of particular representations suggests and brain research may have to be warned about. The questions of why and how these representations come to be formed will occupy us extensively later in this volume.

The elements relating to the *inner* world are here assumed to include (1) physiological and motivational stimuli, such as pain, hunger, thirst, most of which are represented in the brain by the activities of a set of neural structures known as the **limbic system** about which much more will be said later; (2) current mental events, such as memories relating to the recent or distant past, and thoughts about the future. At the subverbal level of the primary consciousness the products of the imagination, which I call *imaginative representations*, form the most important category of thoughts. A typical example would be the brain's internal representation of the goal of an intended action.

The elements relating to the *outer* world are assumed to comprise representations of the properties and current constitution of the surrounding world which the brain is able to infer from its current sensory inputs on the basis of past experience and other prior knowledge. I call this the brain's **Running World Model** or **RWM**. It is a representation of the here and now in the external world, including the body posture, body movements and body surface.

The IGR's extensive internal representation of the current state of the organism thus brings together as an integral whole the main elements that the organism needs to take into account to produce actions that are correctly related to the current situation, given the current needs of the organism. It is easy to see the benefits organisms derive from this representation as the basis of the brain's decision-making processes, and also how these benefits could in turn account for the gradual evolution of this whole system of representations. There are four main fields of IGR activity to be looked at especially:

1. top-level action planning;
2. top-level control of attention, essentially a control over the priority given to specific sensory or representational inputs in a given situation – although attention can also be captured outside IGR control [6.2];
3. top-level mobilization and co-ordination of imaginative representations, such as those occurring in mental images and pictorial thought; and
4. memory retrieval.

Proposition 2

The second conjecture:

> *The IGR, however, is subject to capacity and/or access limitations.*

According to this assumption, there is a limit to what the brain regions responsible for creating and updating the IGR can be given to handle. *Hence not all of the total situation facing the organism, both as regards the outer and inner world, will enter the IGR.* Note, therefore, that according to this assumption not all of the RWM will be included in the IGR, nor all of the brain's current emotive or motivational stimuli and imaginative representations. However, this does not mean that the items which here fail to enter the IGR remain without influence. At their subliminal level they may still participate powerfully in the brain's ongoing processes.

There is nothing startling in this proposition – not, at any rate, so far as it relates to the operations of the **cerebral cortex** (which for brevity I shall often just call 'the cortex'). It is widely accepted that much about the organization of the brain points to the cerebral cortex as an organ limited in its capacity to accommodate all the functions it might handle with profit. There is a notable tendency in the brain to relieve the cortex whenever possible without loss of efficiency. For example, the acquisition of a new motor skill typically begins as a sequence of deliberate steps under cortical control. But with practice, and as the routine becomes established, associations are formed at subcortical levels which gradually cause these steps to be superseded by a smooth semi-automatic performance – as in learning to type, for instance.

Proposition 3

The first identity statement:

The primary consciousness is the IGR.

On this assumption, brain events become *conscious* experiences only to the extent to which they become part of the IGR. It follows from Propositions 2 and 3 that *not all of the RWM will be conscious, nor all of the brain's current emotive and motivational stimuli and imaginative representations.*

Proposition 3 is the most incisive step of the theory and the most important after our first conjecture. It also implies that to find the location of consciousness in the brain we need to find the location of the IGR. This will be followed up in Chapter 9.

In plain terms, it identifies the primary consciousness with the set of brain processes defined in Proposition 1. In so doing, it tells us what the primary consciousness is, what it does and why it evolved. It tells us that consciousness is not just a redundant by-product of evolution. It clarifies the relation between consciousness and behaviour as well as the unique significance of consciously made decisions.

Since 'willed' or 'voluntary' actions are generally understood to be actions produced by *conscious* decisions, Proposition 3 enables us to identify them with actions based on the IGR. And, since the retrieval of memories means bringing something back into consciousness, Proposition 3 establishes this as bringing it back into the IGR – as I have already anticipated in my list of the four main IGR activities we shall look at.

Since the IGR is a representation of the current state of the organism, all stimuli and representations which become part of it also become part of this function. They acquire what for brevity I shall call *self-reference*. Proposition 3 thus establishes self-reference as an integral part of every conscious experience. This is an important feature to keep in mind.

William James, whose *Principles of Psychology* (first published in 1890 but revised several times later) has remained a classic, put the same insight into these words: 'Whatever I consciously experience is experienced in a special way as belonging to myself' – and more specifically:

> Our own bodily position, attitude, condition, is one of the things of which some awareness, however inattentive, invariably accompanies the knowledge of whatever else we know. We think; and as we think we feel our bodily selves as the seat of our thinking. (James, 1890, p. 242)

This account of self-reference forms the basis of my account of the main senses in which 'self-awareness' can be understood [3.1]. A bonus point is that this account of self-awareness does not require the brain to 'loop back on itself', as other theorists have had to assume [3.2].

Proposition 4

The second identity statement:

> *The subjective or qualitative aspects of conscious experience, the qualia, consist of those components of the overall effect an event has on the organism which are included in the IGR and, according to Proposition 3, thus become part of our conscious experiences.*

By the 'overall effect' is here meant the total repercussions the event has throughout an organism, the total impact it has on the organism. This includes both the physiological and the mental level. The latter, for example, could consist of the mental associations which the event conjures up. What 'included in the IGR' means in neural terms will be explained in Sections 2.5 and 2.6.

Every conscious experience has both a 'feeling aspect' and a 'cognitive' aspect – to use William James' phrases. The feeling aspect relates to the qualia, to the 'what it is like' to have this or that experience. It is covered by our Proposition 4. The cognitive aspect is covered by Propositions 1 and 3. It has two main levels: (a) the IGR as a representation of the current state of the organism and (b) the RWM as a representation of the current state of the surrounding world.

Figure 1.1 depicts the main inputs to the IGR, hence to the primary consciousness. Note that the levels shown here are *functional* levels and not anatomical ones. Each of the representations shown will have subcortical as well as cortical components. As regards the three main facets of the primary consciousness on which we concentrate, the figure is readily seen to cover awareness of the surrounding world (the part of the RWM that enters the IGR), awareness of the self as an entity (since the IGR is an internal representation of the current state of the organism), awareness of one's thoughts (in the form of imaginative representations and recalled memories that enter the IGR) and partly also awareness of one's feelings (the motivational factors shown to enter the IGR). It also symbolizes the division of the IGR into the attended and non-attended fields – a division which I shall later call the 'foreground' and 'background' consciousness. It is here shown to be determined by the motivational inputs. However, as regards awareness of one's feelings, the figure only covers the outputs of the limbic system, since I could find no way of symbolizing the qualia in their entirety. Willed actions are shown to be determined by the attended portions of the IGR.

From the biological standpoint, a scientific explanation of subjective experience needs to do no more than explain its distinctive properties and its biological function. Its distinctive properties are its *intrinsicness, privacy* and *uniqueness*. By *intrinsicness* is here meant the fact that this subjective 'feel' of an experience is an inherent part of each and every conscious experience. The *privacy* is obvious, for there is no way in which anyone can look into my feelings; nor is there a way in which my feelings, the hurt of

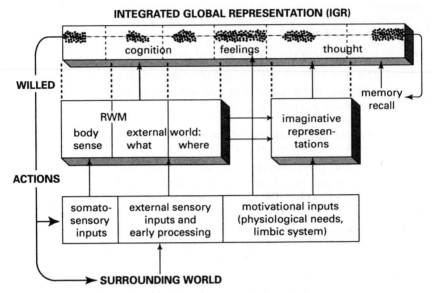

Figure 1.1   *Gross functional architecture of the IGR and primary consciousness. Speckled patches symbolize the currently dominant, i.e. attended fields of the IGR which jointly form the foreground of consciousness, and are shown to be determined by the current motivational state of the subject. Structured representations are shown shaded.*

   For definitions see the text. Note that not all of the RWM enters the IGR, hence consciousness. Nor do all imaginative representations. Note also that the levels shown are functional *and not* anatomical *levels.*

my pain, for example, can be conveyed to a third party to produce a true copy in the mind of that party. We cannot truly share experiences. My words or demeanour can at best enable others to identify my feelings with something they have experienced themselves, or could imagine experiencing. But that is as far as it goes. The *uniqueness* is no less characteristic. What it feels like to have a certain experience will depend on a whole variety of highly individual factors, even on the very history of the person's life. Strictly speaking, no experience can feel quite the same as a previous one even for the same person, since that person will have changed in the interval and so will the total effect which that experience has on the person.

   These three properties are fully accounted for by our fourth proposition by virtue of the fact that the overall effect of an event on the organism is a wholly individual thing, the singular product of the individual's current motivational state, cultural influences and past experiences.

   In this way, then, the theory covers both the objective and subjective sense in which consciousness may be understood. It also gives us an insight into the *function* of subjective experience, and why this subjective component of conscious experience should have evolved in the first place. For it is obviously of benefit to have this overall effect on the organism (or as much of this as can be accommodated in the IGR) included in the basis on which decisions can be made that fully serve the organism's current needs.

I shall return to the IGR and RWM in the next chapter, and will then also give a preview of some of the conclusions reached in Part II of the book about the manner in which these representations are implemented in the brain. First of all, however, I must clarify the notion of 'internal representation' in the two senses in which it will be used.

1.5. The structural and functional senses of 'representation'

In common usage 'representation' is far too fuzzy a notion to be left undefined in the present context. The readings of a speedometer can be called a representation of the speed of the vehicle; an ambassador can be said to represent his or her country; photographs and paintings can be called representations of their subjects; Arabic and Roman numerals may be described as different ways of representing numbers, and this book can be said to represent my beliefs about consciousness. So when the present theory asserts that the brain forms internal representations of, say, the surrounding world, it needs to be made quite clear in what sense or senses 'representation' is here to be understood. For the purposes of the theory I shall define two such senses, which I shall call the *structural* and *functional* respectively.

Consider the simple case in which you are looking at the table in front of you on which there are a number of objects, including, say, a glass of wine. Then somewhere in the brain there will be formed a representation of that table and its objects, of their perceived features and their mutual relations, including the spatial relations of the whole layout. Since the perceived scene is a highly structured complex I call representations of this kind *structural* representations. They will be in the form of some specific constellation of neural activities.

Now you may not respond to this perception of the table. On the other hand, you may be attracted by the glass of wine and decide to pick it up. In that case your motor control centres will take their cues from this structural representation. They will be 'looking at' the neural activities constituting that representation as a 'stand-in' for the actual table and its contents. The structural representation of that table and its contents has now become also a *functional one*.

Serious confusion can result if one fails to realize that this 'looking at' has a concrete neural correlate. Indeed, I have known a case where the referee of a cognitive science paper actually recommended its rejection because it used the word 'representation'. 'This is venerable nonsense', he wrote, 'since every representation implies a little man or humunculus who looks at that representation'(!). There is no little man implied in my present account.

In short, it is important to make it quite clear in what sense or senses, 'representation' is to be understood in the context of this and the following chapters. I shall begin with the structural sense. Structural representations may also be described as *analogue* representations, in contrast with the *symbolic* representations that will be mentioned later.

Definition of the structural sense

Kenneth Craik (1943) was the first to formulate in modern terms the general idea that the behaviour of the higher orders of life can be explained only on the assumption that the brain forms a working model of the surrounding world. And he took this model to cover not just the spatial relationships between objects or events, but also the features and properties by which they are recognized as belonging to particular kinds.

An obvious point of importance is the sense in which such representations can be said to 'model' the features of the referents and their mutual relations. According to Craik the brain's internal representation of the properties of objects *imitate* those properties; according to the philosophers Berkeley and Hume they *resemble* them; according to Dennett (1991) they 'mirror' them; according to Fodor (1975) they are 'mechanisms' that 'covary with the environment'. Finally, according to Pinker (1997), representations are 'a set of symbols corresponding to aspects of the world'. Clearly we need more definite concepts for the purposes of the present theory, especially since we shall also be dealing with representations of merely imagined objects, events or situations.

Definition

> *The activity of a set N of neurons constitutes a* structural representation *of an entity X, if and only if it maps the structure of X – where 'mapping' is here to be understood as a one-to-one or many-to-one (but not all to one) correspondence.*

The entities concerned may be *real* or *imagined* objects, events or situations, or any of their structured features, properties or relationships. The perceived contour of an object is a typical example of a structured feature that brain processes may be able to map in one form or another. This need not be a spatial projection. For example, it could be mapped in terms of expectancies relating to the eye movements occurring in tracking this contour. Other properties of objects may similarly be mapped in terms of expectancies – for example, expectancies relating to the way the object reacts when handled in one way or another.

What about imagined objects, events or situations? Where does the correspondence lie in such mental images? Suppose you are imagining a unicorn, or a house you would like to build. In all such cases you are creating something 'before your eyes' that has to satisfy a particular set of conditions, such as having the body of a horse but a large horn on its forehead. The resulting imaginative representations will map the stipulated conditions by satisfying them. We shall see later that such mental images can actually be scanned by the 'inner eye' [8.1].

Definition of the functional sense

In the case of a functional internal representation of an object we are dealing with a set of neural activities which (in the sense I have explained) 'stands in' for the object when the brain has to produce responses that are correctly related to the nature of that object. It is an important relationship, because in all goal-directed activities we are dealing with activities that need to be correctly related to the nature of the objects on which they act.

It follows from the notion of this 'stand in' that the activity of a set of neurons becomes a functional representation of an object or event, if the brain *uses* it as such. This is illustrated by the fact that what the brain accepts as a representation of, say, an external object, may, in fact, be a *mis*representation. The dim figure which on a dark night you take to be a man, may, in fact, be a small tree. Yet, this misinterpretation of the sensory inputs still *functions* as a representation of the object concerned, because the brain treats it as such: you respond to the apparition as being that of a man.

Definition

The activity of a set N of neurons constitutes a functional representation *of an entity X, if and only if responses that need to be correctly related to X in some particular way are treated by the brain as responses that need to be correctly related to the activity of N in some particular way.*

In the metaphorical terms which I have already used above, we could say that, in dealing with X, the brain 'looks at' the activity of N as the relevant basis for its responses to X. In the various cases we shall come to consider, the represented entities may be external objects, events, or situations, *real* or *imagined*, or any of their features, properties or relationships, especially spatial relationships. The mental image of the goal of an activity would be an example of an imagined situation to which a response needs to be correctly related, given the circumstances in which it is performed. Here, therefore, a structural representation becomes a functional one by virtue of it being *used*. What about my mental image of a unicorn? In what sense could this imaginative representation become functional? That mental image becomes a functional representation if what follows in the mind has to be correctly related to it in some particular way and the brain then 'looks at' the respective neural activities in bringing this about.

Since functional representations may in fact be *mis*representations, they raise the question of the feedback loops required to check or correct them. Figure 1.2 illustrates this for the internal representation R(O) of an external object O to which some goal-directed action has to relate in some specific way if it is to be successful. As would most commonly be the case, the action is assumed to be a *learnt* response, hence open to correction if it fails. Now, a failure of the action could be due either to a faulty representation of object O, or to a faulty response made to the existing representation (or both). The figure shows the respective feedback loops. What correction the brain in fact will make (if any) depends on the total context. The point to keep in mind is that when one deals with acquired functional representations in the brain, there are feedback loops to look out for. In specific cases this may be something worth following up by the researchers.

Note that we can have

1. *structural representations that are not functional representations.* This is obvious from what has gone before. Sometimes there are also structural relationships within a functional representation that are mapped in the brain but do not assume a functional role themselves since they are not relevant in the given context, or have indeed never been experienced as relevant. Some of the 'a's on this page, for example, may form a triangle. This will be duly reproduced in the retinal image of the page, but does not enter my brain processes in any functional capacity.

2. *functional representations that are not structural representations.* An important example is the case of *symbolic* representations. By definition the structure of a symbolic representation does not map that of the represented entity. A schoolbook example is the crown as a symbol of royalty. All letters, words, phrases and mathematical formulae belong to this category. Again, names do not map the objects named. In the visual system typical examples would be the so-called 'feature detectors' in the primary visual

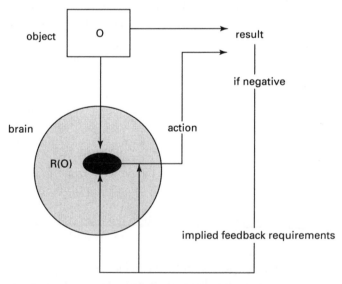

Figure 1.2 *Functional internal representation of an object.*
R(O) is the functional representation of object O. If the action fails, either R(O) or the action which it elicits needs changing. What feedback the brain will need to arrive at the right corrections depends on the case in question.

cortex, neurons that have been found to respond selectively to the mere presence of certain basic features in visual images, such as blobs, bars or line segments in specific orientations. Although these feature detectors are merely symbolic representations of the features that activate them, they can still have an important functional role. On the other hand, the brain needs much more than merely symbolic representations of the features that can be detected in the visual field. It needs representations of the *meaning* of those symbols, in other words of the physical reality of what the symbols stand for, that is to say, its causal properties and behavioural relevance [4.11].

I was once asked how one tells a representation when one sees one. Of course, it is a nonsense question because functional relationships are not *perceptible* entities. It is true, though, that the definitions given above tell us nothing about what kind of structures in the brain can support a full representation. This will be a topic for Part II of the book.

A universally important type of representation

One important type of representation will occupy us extensively because it is closely involved in the RWM. It has already been mentioned in passing. I mean the kind of representation which the brain forms of properties of the outside world that are discovered through the experienced consequences of our actions, as when we discover the weight of a chair by lifting it and the elasticity of a rubber band by stretching it. With familiarity such *act–outcome experiences* become *act–outcome expectancies* through the formation of the corresponding associations in the brain. In this manner the weight of that chair may come to be represented in the brain by the effort expected to lift it and the elasticity of the rubber band by the effort expected to stretch it. According to our definition, these associations form a structural representation of those particular properties. They become functional representations to the extent that they become actively involved in the ongoing processes of the brain. I have mentioned this type of representation in order to explain why our two definitions of internal representations are formulated in rather more general terms than may have been wished by the reader. Expectancy-based representations of one kind or another are exceedingly common, and my definitions had to be general enough to accommodate them. A functional definition of a 'state of expectancy' will be given in Section 2.3 and discussed in greater detail in Section 7.1.

1.6. The validity of the basic model

Support for the model

The truth of Proposition 1 is demonstrated for the human case by our ability to report our sensations, perceptions, feelings, etc. Every statement of the type 'I see a red spot' or 'I feel a tingle' presupposes the existence of an internal representation of the fact that the experience in question is part of the current state of the speaker. The trustworthiness of such self-reports is irrelevant in this particular context. In conjunction with Proposition 3 it receives further support from the fact that we regard a subject's ability to report a stimulus as evidence that the subject was conscious of that stimulus. Apart from this, you will find empirical evidence for these basic concepts cited in several chapters of this book, notably Chapters 6 and 9.

As regards Proposition 2, I have already mentioned as widely accepted that cortical functions are subject to capacity and/or access limitations. I cited as evidence the way the brain seems to be geared up to relieve the cortex whenever possible.

Propositions 3 and 4 are in a different category altogether. They are *interpretations* whose virtue lies in the precise scientific conceptualization of consciousness which they offer, while yet covering the main modes of awareness I have listed and from the subjective as well as the objective angle. Moreover, they make biological sense. To the best of my knowledge, this is the only scientific conceptualization on offer today which covers so much and does so in terms of such few propositions and key concepts.

How could the model be falsified?

The empirical nature of science demands that hypotheses should, in principle at least, be falsifiable by empirical evidence. For Proposition 1 that is undoubtedly possible in principle. However, it is difficult to see how in mature humans any experimental evidence could in practice achieve more than show the IGR to be more limited in scope than might be claimed for it. There is far too much evidence for the existence in mature humans of *some* internal representation of the IGR type, as we shall see later in this volume. Proposition 2 is not in question, while Propositions 3 and 4 are axiomatic and as such exempt from the test of falsifiability. They could be contested only on the grounds that they critically misrepresent what is commonly meant by consciousness and subjective experience. But that, of course, would not falsify them. It would merely disappoint what the public is entitled to expect from a scientific account of consciousness.

Checking hypotheses by computer simulations

As the power of computers has increased year by year, so has our power to check hypotheses by computer simulations. And since the development of networks of artificial neurons with high learning capabilities, these, too, can sometimes be applied to test a theory. The popularity of these methods has become such that there are indeed scientists who claim that they will not look at any model of brain function unless it has been checked by a computer simulation or modelled by an artificial neural network. In Section 4.11 I shall examine to what extent this can be applied in our case.

Notes

1 Notably those by Baars (1988), Churchland & Sejnowski (1992), Cotterill (1998), Crick (1994), Damasio (1994), Dennett (1991), Edelman (1992), Greenfield (1998), Hameroff (1994), Humphrey (1992), Jackendoff (1987), Johnson-Laird (1983), Kinsbourne (1995), McGinn (1991), Penrose (1994), Perner (1991), Pinker (1997), Searle (1997), Weiskrantz (1997) and Zeki (1993). Most of these authors will be referred to later.

2 Throughout this book I shall use 'animals' in the colloquial sense of nonhuman animals.

3 *Collins English Dictionary* combines all three: consciousness 'denoting or relating to a part of the human mind that is aware of a person's self, environment and mental activity, and that to a certain extent determines its choice of action'.

4 A robust degree of self-awareness can also occur in the dream state, in *lucid* dreams, so-called dreams in which you are aware that you are dreaming. Some people therefore claim that one is conscious during lucid dreams. I shall return to this point in Chapter 5.

AWARENESS OF THE SURROUNDING WORLD

2.1. The Running World Model (RWM)

In this chapter we look at the first of the three divisions of awareness which our model of the primary consciousness covers, namely awareness of the surrounding world, hence the RWM. I shall concentrate on those aspects that are highlighted by our biological approach – such as the key role of movement in the processes of sensory perception – and I shall confine myself to the most powerful of the senses contributing to the brain's world model, namely the *visual* perception of the world, our main window on the world. This will suffice for the main issues to be discussed. It is also the most important modality in the brain's RWM. Recent research has shown, for example, that when the brain pinpoints the source of an external sound, it stores its location as where it would have been *seen* if it had been a flash of light (Ducom, 1999). In all of this the following fact needs to be kept firmly in mind: *what we normally understand by 'vision' or 'visual perception' consists of the conscious components of the contributions which the eyes currently make to the RWM.* As Semir Zeki has put it: 'There is no colour unless I see it; I cannot see it unless I am conscious' (1993, p. 346). (One implication of this is only rarely appreciated fully by vision theorists: the physiology of vision cannot be fully understood until the physiology is understood of both the RWM and the basic brain processes underlying conscious awareness.)

Some of the ground I shall cover really belongs to Part II of the book, since it deals with the manner in which representations like the RWM are implemented in the brain. It is anticipated here because it will add flesh to the bones of some of the matters that will be discussed. I must stress in this connection that the validity of any hypotheses added in Part II in no way affects the validity of the basic model of the primary consciousness that was defined in Chapter 1 by our four main propositions [1.4].

* * *

The theory presented in the last chapter [1.4] includes two main statements:

- In the light of its sensory inputs, and on the basis of past experience and other prior knowledge, the brain forms an internal representation of the current external situation. For brevity I have called this the brain's *Running World Model*, or *RWM*;
- It follows from our main propositions, and as illustrated in Figure 1.1, that not all of the RWM enters the IGR, hence not all of it is conscious.

The following statements will help to clarify the notion of the RWM as it is here conceived. A more detailed discussion of the composition of the RWM is left to Chapters 6 and 7.

1. By definition the RWM relates strictly to the *current* point in time, to the here and now. As such, it forms the advancing front of what is generally known as the 'working memory' [8.5].

2. The RWM is a *functional* representation in the sense defined in Chapter 1. That is to say, an operative RWM denotes a state of the brain in which responses that need to be correctly related to the current state of the external world (or some aspect thereof) are processed by the brain as responses that need to be correctly related to the RWM (or the corresponding aspect thereof). Needless to say, the RWM would not be of much use unless it also formed a *structural* representation of the features of the world it covers.

3. The word 'model' has been chosen precisely because the RWM is so much more than just a snapshot of the surrounding world. If in a street scene one stationary car is half obscured by another, for example, it will appear in the RWM as one whole car behind another, and not as half a car located beyond the nearby one. Moreover, in the RWM either car will be more than just a pretty shape. It will be represented as an object expected to have certain properties: to be solid, mobile, controllably self-propelling, etc. We shall return to this again below and in Chapter 7. As I look around me, the brain constructs its model of the surrounding world from what is perceived in the different directions. By also taking into account the movements of the eyes that caused the different perceptions, it is able to construct this as a *stable* scene, that is to say, one that does not dance about as the eyes move in their sockets [7.2].

4. Since the RWM does not imply consciousness (not all of it being embraced by the IGR), the existence of an RWM of broadly the kind I have described can be assumed for creatures without implying that they have consciousness. A simple form of RWM is the so-called 'cognitive map', an internal representation of the local geography. Its existence has been demonstrated for a number of animal species, often in the form of an internal representation of the animal's location relative to some set of outstanding landmarks [6.4]. The question of animal consciousness will be taken up in Section 5.10.

5. In our biological approach, the living organism is viewed as a dynamic system interacting with the environment and drawing vital information about the properties of the surrounding world from the experienced consequences of its actions. This applies quite generally to our direct encounters with the physical properties and relations in the external world. I gave two elementary examples in Chapter 1 when I mentioned how we discover the weight of an object by lifting it and the elasticity of a rubber band by stretching it. As Roger Carpenter (1996) reminds us, a lot of simple properties, such as softness, resilience, roughness, stickiness and the like, rely on knowledge of what forces are being applied to the surfaces in question. Through the formation of the corresponding associations in the brain such *act–outcome experiences* become *act–outcome expectancies* which are representative of the properties concerned. A functional definition of 'states of expectancy' will be introduced below. It is our third key concept.

6. We also discover things about the causal structure of the world through mere observation or by being told about them. We may learn about the brittleness of a china cup by seeing one fall and disintegrate, or we may simply be told that this is what would happen. Hence what has been said above about act–outcome expectancies can be extended to the more general notion of *what-leads-to-what expectancies*. However, inasmuch as things derive their ultimate meaning from personal experience, the act–outcome experiences occupy a special position.

7. A not uncommon notion is that the brain constructs some kind of model of the surrounding world and from this derives expectations about what leads to what. This is an unnecessary multiplication of entities and a defiance of **Occam's razor**. There is a simpler and biologically more plausible answer: the relevant parts of the model actually consist of such acquired what-leads-to-what expectancies. In other words, the elasticity of a rubber band *is actually represented in the brain* by expectancies about the effort that would be required to stretch it, and the weight of an object by the expected effort of lifting it.

8. Act–outcome experiences also enter the most basic processes of sensory perception. For example, we discover the physical or 'causal' nature, hence behavioural relevance, of the spatial relations in the visual field through the eye movements required to shift fixation from one point of interest to another. Hence act–outcome expectancies relating to such eye movements can act as internal representation of the spatial relationships concerned.

9. Given that the ultimate aim of sensory perception is to furnish the brain with an effective internal representation of the current state of the external world, these considerations highlight two important facts about the RWM: (a) the importance of self-paced movements as the source of act–outcome experiences, and (b) the potential of the resulting act–outcome expectancies to function as internal representations of the features and properties of the world, hence as components of the RWM. Unfortunately, both aspects are

difficult to fit into the now widely favoured computational approach to cognitive functions [4.11]. But it would be fatal to ignore them on that account.

10. As regards the location of the RWM, it follows that to the extent to which the RWM consists of acquired what-leads-to-what expectancies, its location in the brain is distributed over those sites at which the underlying associations are formed, e.g. the act–outcome associations. Since these expectancies form a hierarchy that ranges from the simplest (e.g. the expected changes in the visual field that follow a movement of the eyes) to the most complex (e.g. the expected consequences of manipulating objects in one way or another), this distribution is obviously a very wide one. We shall see later that it extends over both the frontal and posterior regions of the cerebral cortex.

11. In the human case there is no shortage of empirical evidence for the existence of an RWM. The RWM is, after all, merely a precise and objective concept to cover what in loose cognitive terms would be described as an individual's (explicit and implicit) beliefs about the current constitution and state of the surrounding world. Although it is difficult to explore the full extent of an individual's RWM, its limits can be explored by virtue of the expectancies the RWM contains. Events beyond these limits come to the individual as *unexpected* events, and in contexts in which they are significant they tend to elicit characteristic reactions of 'surprise'. These can be explored in the laboratory in respect of both their conscious and unconscious manifestations [7.1].

2.2. The visual contribution

Vision is our main window to the world, and that goes for many other species as well. A review of 34 primate species made by Robert Barton of the University of Durham has shown that increases in brain size were mainly increases in areas to do with vision (*New Scientist*, 7 November 1998).

Two distinct cortical processing networks

The RWM covers both the features of external objects and their spatial relations, or, as we may conveniently put it, both the *what* and the *where*. To a considerable extent these are processed in different regions of the brain. In the cerebral cortex, the discrimination of specific features in the visual inputs begins at an elementary level in the visual cortex, which contains the primary cortical receiving area of optical inputs (Figure 2.1A). That of more complex or abstract features then broadly follows along two distinct, though linked, multistage pathways: (1) the *occipito-temporo-frontal* or **ventral** pathway that runs through the ventral **temporal lobe** with projections to the frontal lobe, and (2) the *occipito-parieto-frontal* or **dorsal** pathway, that runs through the **parietal lobe** with further projections to the frontal areas. Broadly speaking, the first deals with vision-driven object identification and the second with vision-driven actions. Apart from what the parietal lobe receives from the visual cortex, it is also the main cortical processing area for the **proprioceptive** impulses from muscles, tendons and joints, thus is deeply implicated in mapping the body's current posture and movement and in the control of reaching and grasping actions. It is also involved in the so-called **saccades**, the rapid jumps the eyes make when moving from one point of fixation to another – essential elements in the internal representations of the spatial relationships in the visual field (see note 8 [2.1]).

The general importance of movement information in the detection and internal representation of spatial relationships thus causes the dorsal pathway to be distinctly more deeply involved in the *where* than in the *what*. A patient with lesions in this pathway might quickly identify a postage stamp held within the visual field, but be unable to point to its location, while another with lesions in the ventral pathway might fail to recognize a postage stamp but readily point to its location. However, since object identification also depends to some extent on vision-driven action (such as the scanning of the contours of a shape), close integration must obviously occur. Some of this already occurs at the earlier cortical levels. For example, orientation-sensitive cells in the monkey visual cortex (area V3, Figure 2.4) have been found to be gaze-locked: they only respond to a particular orientation if the monkey gazes in a particular direction (Zeki, 1993).

Integration also occurs at subcortical levels, and here I need to mention the **thalamus** (Figure 2.1B). This is a cluster of **nuclei** of great importance in the brain's cognitive functions. Most of these nuclei are associated with particular cortical regions and may, for example, act as afferent relay stations in the transmission to the cortex of sensory inputs, with reverse projections from the cortical regions concerned. Other nuclei have more general projections and regulate the general level of cortical activity [9.2]. The close links between the nuclei bestow considerable integrating powers.

Since the RWM and IGR incorporate both the what and the where, they clearly have to draw on both these sources of information processing, as I have symbolized in the figure. In addition (but not shown) there are direct projections from the occipital visual areas to the frontal eye fields (shown), the regions that control the voluntary movements of the eyes.

Consider a simple willed action like my picking up a glass of water from the table in front of me. Three main factors enter here:

(a) my current needs
(b) the nature of the object
(c) the location of the object

The RWM incorporates (b) and (c). My choice of action depends on (a) and (b), and its execution on (c). This will be reflected in the brain regions involved.

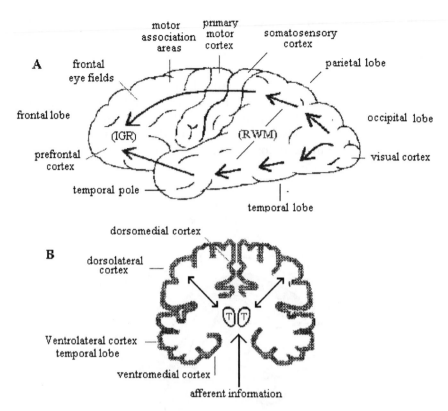

Figure 2.1 (A)   *Dorsal and ventral processing pathways projected on to lateral aspect of the brain.* (B)   *Schematic sketch of coronal section through the cortical hemispheres in a plane cutting through the thalamus* (T).   *Afferent sensory information is relayed by the thalamus to specific cortical regions with reciprocal feedback. All other cortical regions also have such reciprocal connections with thalamic nuclei.*

Representations relating to (b) will involve the occipito-temporo-frontal pathway and the feature recognizing processes known to be a speciality of the inferior temporal lobe. Those relating to (c) involve the occipito-parieto-frontal network and the special capacities of the parietal lobe.

As regards (a), the fact that the glass of water is relevant to my current needs is decided in the **prefrontal** cortex. This is now widely accepted as the top level at which the significance of objects is evaluated in the light of the subject's current needs, and at which actions are planned accordingly [9.7]. Prospective actions are here weighed according *to expectancies of need satisfaction* which they elicit. Hence the importance of the two named pathways projecting to the frontal regions. The needs in question will be expressed here by projections from the limbic system, already mentioned in the last chapter as a family of brain structures jointly representing a subject's motivational and emotional state. The most basic needs find expression in one of its members, the **hypothalamus** (Figure 2.2). It consists of a bunch of nuclei some of which are sensitive to the physiological needs of the organism, such as hunger and thirst, others to deficiencies in vital blood concentrations, i.e. in the hormonal balance, or to sexual and maternal drives. We shall come across additional members at a later stage [9.2]. Some are specifically sensitive to the satisfaction of needs. Thus there are centres in the septal nuclei, the so-called 'pleasure centres', at which stimulation can cause pleasurable sensations. However, this does not mean that pleasurable sensations and feelings of gratification are narrowly localized. They are known to be critically dependent on the **neurotransmitter** dopamine, and dopamine signals have a widespread influence on the limbic system as a whole.

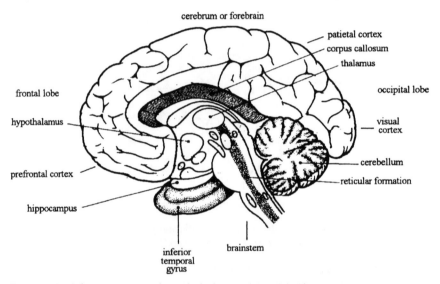

Figure 2.2 *Schematic section through the human brain (1). The section between the brainstem and forebrain is called the* midbrain. *The two cerebral hemispheres are joined by a fibre bundle called the* corpus callosum.

In consequence of the significance which the prefrontal cortex attributes to that glass of water, the priorities that this establishes need to be communicated to the visual, parietal and temporal regions involved in the representation of the *what* and *where*, and in the control of the reaching and grasping movements. Thus the two 'bottom-up' pathways shown in Figure 2.1 need to be supplemented by 'top-down' pathways, in which the impulses flow in the opposite direction and result in the selective enhancement of the relevant neural activities or connections in the posterior networks. This reciprocal flow has been confirmed for the major bundles of fibres involved. One of the most prominent is the *superior occipitofrontal fasciculus*, a vast bundle of fibres that for much of its way runs parallel to the **corpus callosum**. In the bottom-up direction it provides rich projections from the posterior cortical areas to the prefrontal cortex and also picks up further cortical inputs on the way. Its fanlike origins lie in the visual, temporal and parietal areas, and it links these with the prefrontal cortex with specific fibres for impulses travelling in either direction. A second is the *inferior occipitofrontal fasciculus* which originates in the visual areas. It then continues to the frontal pole of the temporal cortex, while picking up from points along the whole length of the inferior temporal lobe. It is extended to the inferior and middle **gyri** of the prefrontal cortex by another bundle, the *uncinate fasciculus*.

The visual cortex and beyond

The right half of the brain deals with the left half of the body, and vice versa. For both eyes the inputs from the right halves of the visual fields are processed in the left cortical hemisphere, and those of the left halves in the right hemisphere (Figure 2.3). In the visual cortex of both hemispheres a number of **topographically** organized and interlinked areas can be distinguished with distinct sensitivities to particular features in the visual inputs (Zeki, 1993). In Figure 2.4 they are labelled as areas V1 to V6, although V5 is also known as MT. V1 forms the first level of cortical responses to the visual inputs. It is called the *primary* visual cortex or *striate* cortex from its striped appearance when stained, while the adjacent areas are called the *parastriate* or *extrastriate* regions.

V1 receives its inputs from the eyes via the **lateral geniculate nucleus (LGN)** of the thalamus (see Figures 2.2 and 2.3). It receives about 85 per cent of all optic nerve fibres from the **retina** and forms the basic cortical level in the detection or 'extraction' of such primitive optical features as blobs, stopped or angled bars, edges, and their orientations. That is to say, it contains groups or columns of neurons whose rate of discharge is specifically linked to the presence of one of those basic features in their receptive fields. V1 is crucial to conscious vision. Loss of this region means blindness.

Prior to this cortical involvement, some processing has already occurred in the retina. The retina of the human eye contains 126 million photo-receptor cells, but only a million fibres pass up the optic nerve. The information they carry is the product of processes in the retinal **ganglia** which *inter alia* increase contrasts where there are changes in the levels of illumination, thus accentuating the edges of objects and the contours of shapes.

Additional levels of discrimination then occur in V2–V6. These are linked by parallel pathways with selective destinations (Zeki, 1993). V2 is especially sensitive to the orientation and motion of detected structures. It also contains cells responsive to disparity in the images produced by the two eyes due to their different location – one of the brain's cues in the perception of depth. V3 appears to be mainly sensitive to dynamic form, while V4 specializes in the perception of colour and V5 (MT) in a general perception of motion. At V6 we have already reached a fairly sophisticated level, for it contains cells that respond to the absolute position of an object

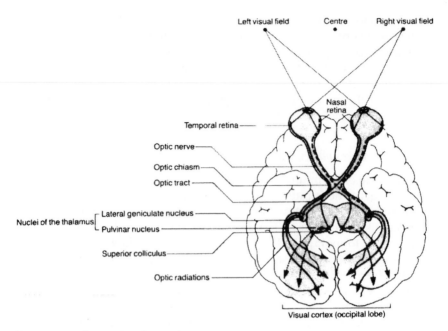

Figure 2.3 *The visual pathways from the eye to the visual cortex, showing also the separate pathway of the ganglion cells to the superior colliculus. Ventral view, without the brainstem or cerebellum (from Churchland & Sejnowski, 1992, by permission of MIT Press)*

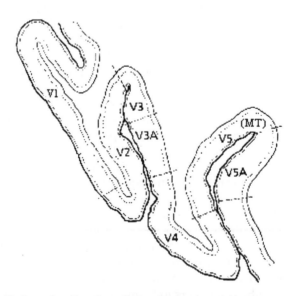

Figure 2.4 *Horizontal section through the visual cortex of the macaque monkey. The subdivisions of areas 3 and 5 are not fully established for the human brain (from Zeki, 1993, with permission from Blackwell Scientific Publications)*

relative to the viewer. V5 and V6 project mainly to adjacent parietal areas, while V1–V4 mainly output to the inferior temporal lobe. Both these facts accord with the two main pathways I have described above. **PET** studies of regional brain activity have shown up the interesting fact that the mere *illusion* of motion, such as that created by certain trick drawings, also activates V5.[1]

Further levels of processing occur at subsequent stages along the afore-mentioned two pathways. All are topographically organized. Felleman and Van Essen (1991) have counted ten levels of visual processing, 14 if you include the retina and LGN. Output from these higher levels of feature discrimination is generally fed back to the regions dealing with the lower levels, possibly to enhance their sensitivity to details that have proved to be relevant at the higher levels. Conceivably, this amounts to a mutual raising of their level of activation which accentuates the feature and its components [2.6].

The level of sophistication of some of these advanced processes is illustrated by neurons in the **medial** temporal area of the monkey that have been found to be selectively responsive to the way in which the scene in front of the eyes expands as the animal moves forwards. Some of these neurons also compensated for the shift in the centre of this expanding pattern that occurs when the eyes move to one side, instead of looking ahead (*Science*, **273**, p. 1544).

As has been said, not all of the RWM enters the IGR, hence conscious-ness. As regards the unconscious portion of the RWM, one of the findings of modern research has been how much of the information delivered by the senses is assimilated, evaluated, and also acted upon, below the level of consciousness. In our everyday life it manifests itself, for example, in the many routine actions we perform semi-automatically. While walking along you do not consciously set one foot before the other – unless you are a fashion model on a catwalk! More specifically, Farah (1997) has listed six fields in which studies of the effects of brain damage have shown visual perception and consciousness to be separated: implicit shape recognition, covert recognition of faces, unconscious perception in cases of visual **neglect** [6.3], implicit reading in pure **alexia**, implicit object recognition and 'blindsight'. Subliminal *recognition* has been demonstrated, for example, in patients with brain lesions that caused them to fail consciously to recognize familiar faces, such as those of family or friends, but who still showed galvanic skin responses to the perception of those faces.

The intensively researched phenomenon of **blindsight** was revealed by laboratory tests in which subjects, blinded in one half of the visual field by damage to the striate cortex, proved to be able with above statistical chance to point correctly at an external source of bright light appearing in the blind hemifield (half-field). They could also discriminate directions of move-ments and the orientation of lines – and even judge whether stimuli in the blind hemifield match or mismatch stimuli in the intact hemifield (Weiskrantz, 1997). One patient could also detect fast-moving objects, and brain scans here showed area V5 still to be active (Zeki, 1993). That this 'seeing unknowingly' is a wholly unconscious process is confirmed by the fact that, typically, blindsight patients will deny seeing what their responses still show to be registered by the brain in some form. For a possible explanation Weiskrantz points to work done on the monkey which suggests that areas V2–V5, as well as V1, receive retinal information via the superior colliculus and pulvinar (see Figure 2.3), two nuclear masses that lie on a secondary pathway from the retina to the visual cortex.

Blindsight does not lie outside the RWM, but belongs to its unconscious portion. An interesting light on this unconscious portion has been shed by observations on a patient whose brain damage destroyed the ability to discriminate *perceptually* between the size of objects. Yet, his grasp still proved to be adjusted correctly to the size of an object when reaching for it (Goodale et al., 1994).

2.3. The brain as an anticipation machine

The definition of states of expectancy

Let me stress again the importance of acquired states of expectancy. Of such things as colour, heat, pressure, smell, we have raw sensations in that we have peripheral receptors that are sensitive to these things. Although the newborn infant attaching itself to the mother's breast displays some primitive discriminatory powers that are 'hard-wired', we have no raw sensations, for example, of the shape of an object, of its distance, its solidity, hardness and other physical properties. We discover properties of this kind in the first instance through exploration and experience. We discover the hardness of an object by pressing on it and what the computer does by pressing the keys. As children we first discover such things at home; as scientists we discover them in the laboratory. Again, we have no raw sensation of spatial relations as such, but discover their nature, e.g. their causal properties and behavioural relevance, through the experienced consequences of our actions – in the first instance through the visual transformation we experience when we move the eyes, head or body. To return to an earlier example, at the lowest level we experience spatial relations in the visual field through the eye movement required to shift fixation from one point of interest to another. Seen from these angles, every action is a question asked of the environment or a check on answers already accepted.

After the demise of behaviourism, psychology no longer had any problems about the notion of expectations. Interest in the role of expectations in human cognition revived principally through the extensive work of Berlyne (1960) on exploratory behaviour, habituation and responses to novelty. The overriding influence of expectancies in the human brain's representational processes also came to be noted. For example, Grossberg (1980) showed that when a given set of cues is followed by expected consequences, all other cues tend to be ignored. Another role of acquired expectancies should also be mentioned, namely the part they play in providing continuity to the RWM, i.e. to our recognition of the present situation as a continuation and modification of the immediately preceding one. The expectancies that are part of the present RWM, and that resulted from what went before, form an important part of the working memory, already mentioned. As Hochberg (1968) has put it: 'A metric of space–time expectancies are the glue that join successive glimpses together into a single perceptual structure.' Even so, the full extent of the role that acquired expectancies play in the brain's world model is still far from being fully appreciated.

It follows that we need a functional definition of states of expectancy. This will be discussed in Section 7.1. For the present, it will suffice just to anticipate the definition at which we shall then arrive.

Definition

By a *state of expectancy*, conscious or unconscious, we shall mean a state of the brain which has two components: It is

- (a) a state of readiness *for the occurrence of a particular event – that is to say, a state which facilitates or advances an appropriate reaction to that event, and*
- (b) a state in which the occurrence of a significantly different event tends to elicit a characteristic reaction of surprise, technically known as an **orienting reaction**. Pavlov called it a 'What is it? reflex'.

The facilitation of an appropriate reaction to the event may take a variety of forms. It could be in the form of associations that speed up its occurrence, as in the phenomenon of 'priming' studied by psychologists, or a direct preparation by the brain for the reaction, such as the expectant stance adopted by a tennis player about to receive a fast serve. A typical orienting reaction would be a switch of attention to the area in which the unexpected event occurred, as when an unexpected movement is perceived in a corner of the visual field.

How states of expectancy are formed and become effective

The acquired states of expectancy we have considered consist of associations formed as the result of experience through the strengthening, growth or multiplication of **synapses** (see Appendix A). This results in some pathways being strengthened, perhaps to the detriment of others, or new ones being formed. Jointly these associations amount to a *structural* representation (as defined) of the property in question – of the elasticity of a rubber band, of the weight of a chair, of the brittleness of a china cup. Such structural representations do not individually become effective until an occasion arises when they become relevant. This may occur at either a conscious or an unconscious level. It occurs at a conscious level, for example, when we review the expected consequences of alternative actions before making a final decision. However the brain may also review at an unconscious level the possible consequences of alternative actions before any particular action is decided upon, where the weights assigned to the alternatives will depend on the extent to which the imagined consequences elicit expectancies of need satisfaction. At the unconscious level these reviews need not be time-consuming serial scanning processes in which one option is considered at a time. There are good reasons to believe that at the unconscious level imaginative representations of alternative possible acts can be excited simultaneously, and that the imagined act offering the most desirable prospects then beats the field on the principle of 'winner takes all' [2.4].

Prediction and the role of the cerebellum

In connection with the predictive powers of the brain I must mention the special role of the **cerebellum** (see Figure 2.2) as one of the brain's main predictors of the consequences of motor commands on the overall posture and movement of the body and its limbs. This speeds up the movement sequences in view of the inevitable delay between the action and the sensory feedback, tiny though it may be. It works together with the posterior parietal cortex and **premotor cortex**. The first is deeply implicated in the **body schema**, our inner body sense [3.1], the second in the formation and storage of motor patterns.

The RWM and consciousness

According to the present theory only those portions of the RWM that enter the IGR are conscious. Two important distinctions here need to be made and clearly perceived if confusion is to be avoided:

1. the distinction between the conscious and unconscious components of the RWM; and
2. the distinction between the *attended* and *unattended* fields of the IGR (cf. Figure 1.1, p. 16).

I shall refer to the latter as the *central* and *peripheral* fields of the IGR, or as *foreground* and *background* consciousness.

Two kinds of selective processes are associated with these distinctions and easily confused. They are selection for *attention* and selection for *consciousness*. The sense in which 'attention' is here to be understood will be explained in Section 6.2.

To clarify the notions of foreground and background consciousness, let me take as a concrete example the work that is occupying me at this moment on my computer.

My original decision to get on with this computer work was a conscious decision, hence based on the IGR according to our assumptions. Since I took a lot into account before making this decision, it involved a very substantial portion of the IGR. In contrast, the actual actions I am performing at the moment take only a tiny portion of the IGR into account, just that tiny portion of the RWM that relates to the computer. As I focus on the computer only a tiny section of my room lies within my visual field, and even less is attended to. But the rest of the IGR still exists as an operational entity. My sharply focused attention has not extinguished it, as would be the case if I were to doze off and fall asleep. It will tell me, for example, where to find a glass of water when I feel thirsty or new copier paper when my printer runs out. At this very moment, in fact, it happens to tell me that I can ignore the knocking noise I hear, because it is caused by workmen on the floor below, and is not a knock on my door. We can see a clear distinction here between a central or attended field of the IGR and a peripheral or unattended field, namely the rest of it. It is my distinction between *foreground* and *background* consciousness.

Some people might use the term 'subconscious' for what I have here called the 'background' consciousness. But I prefer to reserve this term for states or processes that are strictly unconscious but parallel conscious ones, such as unconscious desires.

To return to the RWM, how is the rest of the room represented in my brain while I am attending to the computer? The answer seems inescapable that in the first instance it is represented by expectancies about what I would perceive if I were to look up and glance around me. Next in order might come expectancies about what I would perceive and encounter if I were to get up, move around and perhaps handle or use any of the objects in the room. Until I do any of these things, these expectancies remain irrelevant and ineffective, but that does not eliminate them from the RWM. They are still part of it. In the words of J.J. Gibson (1979, p. 206): 'A man is aware of what is behind his head', or Koffka (as cited by Gibson): 'behavioural space does not confront me but encloses me'.

2.4. Imaginative representations

The role of imaginative representations in the RWM

So the powers of the imagination have a large part to play in the RWM. I have mentioned imagined acts and their imagined consequences, for example. Both belong to the category I call imaginative representations. Above we have come to appreciate their importance especially in connection with acquired what-leads-to-what expectancies. They can occur at unconscious as well as conscious levels and transfer between them. The latter has been confirmed in the laboratory by demonstrations that with practice a mental image used in a matching task may fade from consciousness, but returns again when the task is made more difficult (Pani,

1982). The same applies to internal representations of possible motor acts, also called *motor images*, and to another important category, that of internal representations of a desired state of affairs. All our consciously guided activities are typically governed by a conscious representation of the desired result or 'goal'. This acts as reference frame in the planning of the required motor sequences and in the determination of feedback loops. Similar reference frames will be operative at an unconscious level in those many operations which we perform routinely in a semi-automatic fashion, from moving the fingers over the computer keyboard to driving a car. Many animal activities, too, have been shown to be governed by such reference frames (Gallistel, 1989), though it remains an open question to what extent a distinction can here be drawn between conscious and unconscious frames of reference [5.10].

States of readiness acting as imaginative representations

Of the observations I shall make later about the nature of imaginative representations, one may be of interest now as it directly relates to the definition of states of expectancy cited above: I shall suggest in Section 8.1 that to imagine an object, event or situation is for the brain to enter a state of readiness to perceive an object, event or situation of that type, without, however, expecting it actually to happen. You will recall here that states of readiness also figure as the first of the two components in the definition given above of a state of expectancy. But there is also a difference. In that case, the state of readiness was the direct result of past experience, whereas when we imagine a unicorn and, according to the theory, the brain here enters a state of readiness to perceive one without expecting that perception, only the components of that new composition (horse, horn) are based on past experience (see also Section 7.1).

The imaginative representations of acts

I have mentioned how imaginative representations occur regularly in one of the most important categories of imaginative exercises, namely when choices have to be made and action decisions are preceded by a survey of alternative possibilities, each weighed according to the expected consequences – the final decision being reached by some kind of 'winner takes all' process. And such imaginative exercises can occur at unconscious as well as conscious levels.

The imaginative representation of motor acts can, in theory, take one of three forms, although it is not suggested that the brain is confined to just one of them:

1. an internal representation of the goal of the act – possibly in the form of a state of readiness for the achievement of the goal. In this connection it is worth noting that in the parietal cortex the production of movement

has been found to be encoded not in terms of muscles but in terms of *goals* (Perrett et al., 1990).

2. an imaginative internal representation or 'motor image' of the organized sequence of movements that need to be called up for the execution of the act. A sequence of muscle commands may here be construed before the movement sequence runs its course. Such motor images have been extensively studied both at conscious and unconscious levels, notably by Jeannerod (1997).

3. a state of readiness to act in a particular way without this being followed up by execution of the act. There is ample evidence that most acts are to some extent preceded by motor preparations (Libet, 1993), and in theory these could serve as imaginative representations of the act itself. Scalp electrodes can record preparations of action in the form of so-called 'readiness potentials'. In subjects making self-paced movements, readiness potentials have been recorded which could precede the actual movement by as much as 1,050 milliseconds. According to Libet and his group, it depends on whether the movement is mentally prepared. In a spontaneous act, the preparatory period may have only half this span (Libet et al., 1982).

As regards the development of act–outcome expectancies, the following hypothetical sequence of associations is worth considering. Through repetition there will come a point at which the brain begins to anticipate the outcome of the action while the action is in progress and so has a chance to prepare itself accordingly. The next stage will be one at which the outcome is already anticipated by the very initiation of the act. This can be readily explained in terms of reactions that become **conditioned** to the preparatory brain processes that precede the execution of the act. Finally, the very representation of the act in any one of the three imaginative forms listed above comes to elicit imaginative representations of the expected outcome. Which of these will occur in practice may differ from case to case.

Parallel reviewing of act–outcome expectancies

When the brain reviews the anticipated consequences of alternative actions before any particular action is decided upon, the weight assigned to the alternatives will depend on the extent to which the imagined consequences promise to satisfy the organism's current needs or desires, either directly or indirectly. There are two important points to be made in this connection. The first is that a review of the anticipated consequences of alternative actions is generally needed only in novel situations. In familiar situations, the right choices will already have become established. The second concerns the fact that such reviews may occur at either a conscious or an unconscious level, and *at the unconscious level they need not be time-consuming serial scanning processes*. When options are reviewed at the conscious level, this tends to be a sequential process in which the different possible actions and their expected consequences are considered in turn (Shall I agree to this proposal or reject it, or postpone my decision?). But the speed with which acquired act–outcome expectancies can influence choices at the subliminal or 'intuitive' level, suggests that imaginative representations of alternative possible acts are here excited simultaneously, and that the imagined act offering the most desirable prospects beats the field on the principle of 'winner takes all'. In consequence of the associations that compose the RWM, each activated action image would activate representation of the expected consequences, critically including the expected degree of need satisfaction. And there would be positive feedback from the latter to the respective action image, thus raising it to a level of dominance. We know that such feedback exists in the conscious surveys of possible actions. So why not here? Unfortunately, the precise nature of the neural connections it requires in either case is still far from clear, and, so far as I know, studies of how much simultaneously excited motor images may interfere with one another have only recently been set in train (Stoet, 1998).

When novel situations pose a difficult problem, the internal review of possible actions and their expected consequences acquires a special importance and may also then become a lengthy one. In his classic studies of insightful behaviour in the apes, Köhler (1925) suspended a banana from the ceiling above the reach of the animal, but boxes were provided which the animal could move under it and pile up if necessary. Köhler noted then how suddenly the solution would come to the animal without any overt trial-and-error behaviour – hence as a true case of insight – but also how this was invariably preceded by a period of 'pondering' which suggested that the animal was performing an extensive *internal* trial-and-error search.

Sleepwalking

Sleepwalking is never to be dismissed lightly. The amazing things sleepwalkers can do may involve risks to life and limbs. There is not much harm done if the sleepwalker makes a cup of tea, but sufferers have also attempted to climb out of a window, or leave home through the front door and take a spin in the family car. For persons prone to such night-time excursions (some 2 per cent of the population) the windows and doors of the bedroom should be locked at night, but with keys left in places that a fully conscious brain can find in case of a fire. One patient in a Leeds hospital recently walked all the way home, even crossing the city's ring road. According to case studies conducted by Peter Fenwick at the Institute of Psychiatry in London, sleepwalkers can not only drive cars but also ride motorbikes or horses and even attempt to mend fridges. Sleepwalkers can also be extremely aggressive. This accords poorly with the comedy picture of a zombie-like creature striding across the stage with staring eyes and outstretched arms. Fenwick believes that the condition can occur both at the point of transition from the dreamless sleep to the dreaming 'rapid eye movement' or **REM sleep**, and as a way of acting out dreams.

How then does sleepwalking appear in our model? Sleep is a cyclic phase in which the organism suspends its interactions with the surrounding world and, along with this, also the RWM. Now it seems to me that in sleepwalking we have a case in which both a RWM and the power of imaginative representations are reconstituted, but without the reconstitution of the IGR that would normally occur simultaneously when we wake up from normal sleep. And with the reconstitution of the RWM also comes the operational availability of all the semi-automatic action patterns that are part of our learnt skills and well-practised routines.

Hallucinations

I have illustrated the large part that imaginative representations play in the RWM, at both the conscious and the unconscious level. In terms of our model, hallucinations occur when imaginative representations fallaciously intrude into the RWM section of the IGR and thus become illusory perceptions. This could conceivably be the result of excessive activity in regions connected with the hallucinated modality – along the ventral processing pathway in the case of visual hallucinations. Indeed, **fMRI** studies of patients with the so-called Charles Bonnet syndrome have shown hallucinations of colour, faces and textures to correlate with heightened activity in the ventral extrastriate visual cortex, and that this increased activity persists between hallucinations (Ffytche et al., 1998). Hallucinations have also been produced by electrical stimulation of the inferior temporal lobe – which is unsurprising in view of these observations.

On the face of it, hallucinations would be expected to occur most readily where there is inadequate sensory feedback (including failed perceptual expectancies) to oppose the illusion – for example when the patient hears voices – or when the contextual sensory feedback breaks down, as appears to occur during extended periods of sensory deprivation, or under stress, especially when it is already weak, as when a shipwrecked sailor sees a phantom ship on the horizon.

2.5. More about entry into consciousness

To recapitulate: according to the first of the four main propositions defining our basic model of the primary consciousness, the brain forms an extensive internal representation of the current state of the organism which includes representations of the total situation facing the organism, both as regards the *outer* and the *inner* world [1.4]. This was called the Integrated Global Representation or IGR. Given that the brain is organized to respond to the current needs of the organism, it is in this way able to respond to those needs in the light of the current total situation. However, according to the second proposition entry into the IGR is subject to limitations in cortical capacity or access. According to the third proposition the primary consciousness *is* the IGR, and entry into consciousness thus means entry into the IGR. 'Voluntary' or 'willed' actions were defined as actions resting on conscious decisions, hence actions determined by the IGR.

That entry into consciousness is a far from straightforward process has been vividly shown by the work of Benjamin Libet and his colleagues in San Francisco, and by what this revealed about the time factors involved in human responses to simple stimuli and in the genesis of simple voluntary acts (for a summary see Libet, 1993). The investigated stimuli were applied either to the skin or to the thalamus. Among the most notable findings were the following:

- For skin stimuli of above threshold intensity, a minimum duration of up to 500 milliseconds (ms) is required to produce awareness, although for exceptionally strong stimuli this could be reduced to 100 ms.[2] When the skin was pricked, scalp electrodes showed an immediate response in the somatosensory cortex in the areas receptive to touch. At that point in time the subjects were not conscious of the stimulus. However, over the next 500 ms the activity spread to other areas and only after that interval of spreading activity did the subjects report a sensation. The Oxford pharmacologist Susan Greenfield has called the source of the spreading activity – here the somatosensory cortex – the *epicentre* of the commotion, and has compared it with the ripples that spread outwards when a stone is thrown in a pond (Greenfield, 1998). In the light of this, one cannot help feeling that entry into consciousness is not so much a selective process as a *breakthrough*.
- The stimulus is timed by the brain subjectively. That is to say, its positioning in the brain's model of the world is *retroactively* referred to the earliest time of arrival at the cortex. It would seem, then, that the processes which govern the construction of the brain's world-model have built-in compensations for the delays occurring in the intervening processes.
- The content of the experience can be altered by extraneous influences during the 500 ms. For example, the sensation produced by a single stimulus to the skin can be retroactively enhanced by a stimulus train applied to the somatosensory cortex.
- Very brief stimuli to the thalamus can have repercussions at an unconscious level without reaching awareness.

The subjective timing, mentioned above, adds powerfully to the evidence that in the RWM we are dealing with an *interpretation* by the brain of its sensory inputs in the interest of an effective representation of the here and now. Other observations make the same point. While the eyes move, for instance, there is no blurring of vision, because the brain simply suspends vision throughout that brief interval. Yet, we experience no break. Again, when you strike a tennis ball, you will experience the sight, sound, feeling and motor act as simultaneous events despite the different transmission times of these stimuli.

The fact that we are not conscious of a stimulus applied to the skin until a considerable amount of activity has spread outwards from the somato-sensory cortex raises the question of what brain regions we must expect to be involved here. This is of obvious interest in connection with the question of the seat of consciousness in the brain. According to the present theory, awareness of the stimulus implies that it has become part of the conscious portion of the RWM, the portion that has become part of the IGR. The RWM covers both the what and the where. The *what* is represented by the responses in the somatosensory cortex, whereas for a representation of the *where* the stimulus has to become part of the body schema, a part of the RWM that involves the parietal cortex [3.1]. In so far as the consciously experienced pinprick can become the subject of controlled attention and action planning, we shall see that the prefrontal cortex is implicated and possibly also the anterior cingulate cortex [4.2]. These are just the main cortical regions, each of which will be acting in conjunction with subcortical structures, notably the associated nuclei of the thalamus. There is clearly enough here to account for the observed time delay between the application of a stimulus and awareness of it. In addition to all this, the brain's top-level evaluation of the significance of the event and the subject's emotional reactions to it will activate yet more structures, notably under influence of the limbic system. So much then for the 'ripples that spread across the pond', to use Greenfield's phrase. They seem to leave few major brain regions entirely untouched.

2.6. The question of the underlying neural connections

Ultimately, of course, brain research will discover the concrete neural processes that discharge the representational functions we have discussed. But that day still lies in the distant future. The best we can do in this direction is to achieve conceptual clarity about the functional structure of the primary consciousness and draw what conclusions we can about the brain's implementation of these functions. This includes conclusions about the brain regions involved in some of the named functions, with suggestions even for the IGR and, therefore, the seat of consciousness. Most of that will be left to Chapter 9. At this point I just want to note some very general considerations about the neural connections required for a subject to become aware of an applied stimulus.

Let me begin with the metaphor I used in Section 1.5 after I had defined the meaning of functional representation. I said then that the activity of a set N of neurons acts as a functional representation of an object X if the brain 'looks at' the activity of N when having to produce responses that are correctly related to the object X. How is this metaphor to be translated into neural terms? I have to resort here to the notion of the *receptive fields* of neurons. If you are not already familiar with this notion, then please turn to Appendix A. In either case, note the distinction I draw there between the *potential* receptive field of a neuron and the *dominant* one. Let us go back to the example illustrated in Figure 1.2 (p. 20). Let $n(A)$ denote the set of neurons whose output constitutes the action decision that has to be correctly related to the object O, and $nR(O)$ the set of neurons forming the representation R(O). Then $n(A)$ 'looking at' $nR(O)$ implies that the output of the set $nR(O)$ of neurons forms part of the *dominant* sphere of the receptive fields of the $n(A)$ neurons. But since the brain cannot just conjure up new neural connections to suit a passing situation, this implies that the output of the $nR(O)$ set of neurons must already have been part of the *potential* receptive fields of the $n(A)$ neurons. And the possible feedback loops shown in the figure presuppose that they are among the potential receptive fields of the $nR(O)$ set and $n(A)$ set respectively.

These considerations, therefore, stipulate a minimal range of neural connections that must already exist – as an *enablement*, so to speak – before the set $nR(O)$ of neurons can effectively come to function as a representation of object O in connection with the action A.

We can apply this argument to the case study discussed in the last section, that of a stimulus applied to the skin and the regional activities that then spread outwards from the somatosensory cortex, eventually to arrive at the IGR network of neurons, notably in the prefrontal cortex. It implies something important about the neural pathways that must already have been in existence. For it implies that *no stimulus can enter the IGR, hence consciousness, unless the neural activities representing the stimulus are already included in the potential receptive fields of the relevant IGR network of neurons* (which here includes the prefrontal sections of that network). This gives us a slightly more specific view of the capacity or access limitations that govern entry into consciousness, for it shows the upper limit set to conscious awareness by the existing totality of neural connections.

The binding problem

The binding problem is the problem of how the features of an object that are extracted in different parts of the brain can yet result in a unified perception. In some cases it has been observed that a tightly bound set of neurons engaged in a common function fire in synchrony, for example the alerted 'place cells' in the **hippocampus** [6.5]. It has also been found that groups of cells in the visual cortex responsive to the same optical feature, such as a bar presented in a specific orientation, will fire in synchrony, even if their receptive fields do not overlap (Zeki, 1993). Some authors see in this synchrony a possible answer to the binding problem. Francis Crick (1994) even suggests that entry into consciousness may be a question of entering into a state of synchronous firing. However, it has not yet been established whether this synchrony is sufficiently widespread, and it also raises the key question of whether the synchrony of discharges observed in a set of neurons is an *effect* or a *cause* of a stimulus activating that set as a functional unit, for example as a representation of some feature of a perceived scene.

I have mentioned how the visual inputs are processed at the cortical level in a succession of higher levels of feature extraction, and that these higher-level regions generally feed back to the lower levels [2.2]. Since the structure of a complex feature will be represented by the components and relations made explicit at the lower levels, it is plausible to assume that this feedback raises the level of activity of the lower-level groups of neurons concerned, so that the whole now forms a high-activity assembly that represents this complex feature both functionally and structurally. This is supported by the observation that in a figure-from-ground separation, the neurons representing the figure show a higher level of activity than those representing the ground. Given sufficiently close connections, such higher levels of activity could, therefore, be a *cause* of synchronous firing. This notion of binding was, I believe, first advocated by Gerald Edelman (1992). It takes the form of what he calls 'reentrant connections'. By this he means feedback from an area conducting a higher level of stimulus processing to one conducting a lower level. This could result in a combined output from them to other parts of the brain with the required degree of integration.

If we take the opposite view and assume the synchrony to be the actual binding factor, we run into severe problems. For example, through what mechanisms is a particular set of neurons selected for synchrony? And through what mechanisms can behavioural responses become attached to the activity of a population of neurons that is distinguished only by its synchronous firing? Another difficulty for the synchrony theory is the fact that binding occurs at different levels. There is the binding that links the contour elements of a figure, the binding that causes neurons responding to a figure to be more active than those responding to the figure's ground, the binding that links the various nonoptical properties of an object, the binding that joins the neural networks of the RWM into a functional unit, and, still further up, the binding that joins the neural networks of the IGR into a single functional unit. Would they not all need distinguishable synchronous frequencies? Unfortunately, too, the present brain imaging techniques cannot enlighten us about areas of synchronous neural activity. My own (and purely intuitive) guess is that the synchrony is a by-product of close connections between a set of activated neurons and may, in a positive feedback way, also enhance even further the already existing high level of activity.

Two features processed in different regions might conceivably be bound together if there is a third region into which they both project and where integration might occur. Semir Zeki has examined this in a couple of specific cases, but where he found such a convergent region, he also found that the two sets of inputs maintained their own territories in this region and there was a bare minimum of overlap (Zeki, 1993, p. 304). Zeki also suggests that the binding of an object's features may occur only after the separate features have reached consciousness – in our terms, at the level of the IGR.

Others believe that attention can exercise a binding function by way of tagging neural assemblies undergoing activity enhancement, e.g. Roelfsema (1998). Later we shall come to another suggestion, namely that the optical features of a perceived object are bound together by expectancies about their common motion either when the object moves or when the retinal image moves in consequence of eye movements [6.4]. I shall also then cite work which suggests that infants are already sensitive to this effect at an early age. In addition, the optical features of an object may be bound together by way of object-centred internal representations of the spatial relations between them [7.2]. In point of fact, I see no reason why just one of these various possibilities should be the only right answer. They could all work hand in hand, although I remain sceptical about synchrony as the actual binding factor.

Notes

1 For an illustration, see Plate 21 in Zeki (1993).
2 For details of the relevant time delays, see Section 4.7.

3

AWARENESS OF THE SELF AS AN ENTITY AND OF ONE'S THOUGHTS AND FEELINGS

3.1. Introducing self-reference and self-awareness

The 'self'

One assertion on which one can probably count on a large measure of agreement, despite all other differences of opinion, is that *a sense of self is fundamental to consciousness*. This will be the first topic of this chapter, and so I begin with what I have loosely described as awareness of the self as an entity. It is one of the three main domains of awareness which, I claim, a scientific theory of consciousness needs to cover. Awareness of oneself as a distinct and autonomous agent, responsible for one's actions, plays a vital role in our everyday life.

In our model, 'awareness' when conceived as a faculty of the brain is synonymous with 'consciousness' conceived as a faculty of the brain, and this is identified with the IGR. In contrast, the meaning of 'awareness of X' depends on the context. It can mean either that X is covered by the IGR, as in 'awareness of the surrounding world' or that X is a component of the IGR that is being attended to, as in 'I was aware of a strange noise'. In the case of self-awareness we shall be dealing mainly with the former.

I have used the substantive phrase 'the self' reluctantly and only because it may help to convey a broad idea of the domain of awareness I have in mind. It is a fuzzy notion and would certainly need a lot of clarification if it is to be safely used. In the literature you may see it defined *inter alia* as 'one's own individuality', as 'the object of introspection' and as 'the subject of successive states of consciousness'. These are just a few examples. The *Journal of Consciousness Studies* has recently devoted four volumes to 'The self'.[1] This revealed an astonishing variety of notions. The majority of the contributors were philosophers, among them Peter Strawson of Oxford University, well known for his many publications on this subject. In one of these he has listed no fewer than eight different ways in which 'the self' may be conceived (Strawson, 1997):

1.   a *thing*, in some robust sense;
2.   a *mental* thing, in some sense;
3. and 4.   a *single* thing, that is single both *synchronically* considered and *diachronically* considered;
5.   *ontologically distinct* from all other things;
6.   *a subject of experience*, a conscious feeler and thinker;
7.   an *agent*;
8.   a thing that has a certain character or *personality*.

One can see the range of philosophical arguments invited by this list – arguments about the validity of these concepts, and about the origin, function, embodiment or ontological status of these different 'things'. In view of this, Eric Olson, of Cambridge University, has argued that the very notion of 'the self' should be removed from the philosophers' concerns, there being no agreed use of the term 'self' and no characteristic features or even paradigm case of 'selves'. Thus 'the term only leads to troubles otherwise avoidable' (Olson, 1998, p. 645). What interested me most about this paper was that the author himself is a philosopher. With the exception of the school of 'logical positivism' of the Vienna Circle, it has been rare in the history of philosophy for an author to recommend that an item should be scratched from the faculty's menu.

Self-reference and self-awareness

None of this affects the predicate 'self' as it occurs in such biological concepts as 'self-reproduction', 'self-organization', 'self-maintenance' and 'self-regulation'. In these cases, 'self' refers to the biological organism or parts thereof. And that is also the primary sense in which I shall use the term in what follows. An example is my notion of *self-reference* as defined in Section 1.4. Since the IGR is a representation of the current state of the organism, all stimuli and representations that become part of it also become part of this function. This is what I have called their self-reference. Since Proposition 3 identifies the primary consciousness with the IGR, it establishes self-reference as an integral part of every conscious experience, at least at the level of the primary consciousness.[2] This establishes the organism as a whole as the 'entity' in my description of one facet of consciousness as 'an awareness of the self as an entity', although this may be supplemented by higher levels of representation, as I shall explain.

One advantage of having a definite theory of consciousness is that one can give definite meanings to what in common currency may be somewhat fuzzy notions related to consciousness. For example, 'self-reference', 'self-awareness' and 'self-consciousness' are often used indifferently for the same phenomenon. I tend to avoid 'self-consciousness' since this is often used for the embarrassment felt when one is noticed by others, as a girl may feel awkward when entering a party in a startling new dress.

I shall reserve 'self-reference' for the fact that, according to the present theory, the contents of the IGR have the functional status in the brain of an internal representation of the current state of the organism. I shall also describe this as *implicit self-awareness*, to be contrasted with *explicit self-awareness*, of which I envisage three main levels:

- The *basic experiential* or *'apprehensive'* level. By this I mean how the above-mentioned self-reference manifests itself experientially and in the qualia of conscious experience. It is best summarized in the words of William James already quoted [1.4]: 'Whatever I consciously experience is experienced in a special way as belonging to myself.' It applies to mental as well as to physical experiences – for example, to thoughts and memory recall. As Rosenfield (1992) has pointed out: every recollection refers not only to the remembered event, person or object, but also to the person who is remembering. It also accords with J. J. Gibson's remark that awareness of the world and awareness of self seem to be concurrent (Gibson, 1979).
- The *conceptual/autobiographical* level. For example, when the self-reference experienced in the sensation of a toothache or in the perception of a red spot issues in explicit self-reports like 'I have a toothache' and 'I see a red spot'.
- The *conceptual/contemplative* level. This occurs when introspectively I engage in *thoughts* about what kind of object or person I am. This can obviously take on many forms and may issue in positive or negative feelings of value as well. By 'introspection' I here mean a selective attention that focuses on the experiential component of self-awareness mentioned above.

One variant of such contemplative self-concepts may be described as the *sense of identity*. Typically, this is the product of a search for features or qualities that can be called uniquely one's own. Some may seek to find this in their past life or heritage, while others may look at their present doings, aims and ambitions. Self-assessment of a kind may also enter at this stage, raised by the question, 'What *sort* of a person am I?' Baars (1988) speaks here of 'self-monitoring': the practice of monitoring one's performance against some standard. That standard may or may not be a moral one. A related notion is that of *self-esteem* or *self-regard* – a positive review of one's general assets as a person. Another question, too, can enter what I have called the conceptual/contemplative self-awareness, namely the question of how one is seen by others. It is a concern with one's 'public persona', as distinct from the private thoughts and feelings one might reveal to a close friend.

The importance of the body sense: the body schema

Since the self-reference implied in the IGR relates to the physical body, the core of perceptual self-awareness resides at the representational level in the body schema, the brain's internal representation of the body, its posture, movements and surface. It is part of the RWM and its conscious components belong to the portion of the RWM that is included in the IGR.

Two categories of input are relevant to the body schema: the **interoceptive** – receptors in muscles, joints, tendons and the **vestibular** organ (the 'balancing' organ situated in the ear) – and the **exteroceptive** (tactile and visual). That these two sources of information are normally fully integrated – or 'calibrated', if you like – is evident from the simple observation that from the internal 'feel' of the position of your arm when the eyes are closed you can predict where your arm will be seen when they are opened again. However, the interoceptive inputs are the dominant ones. If the afferent nerves from an arm are severed, the arm is experienced by the subject as a foreign object, even though it is *seen* as part of the body. If the eyes of a subject are fitted with inverting prisms that show the world upside down, the feet will still be felt to be at the bottom and the head on top. Later in this section I suggest that this dominance of the interoceptive inputs is due to the body schema having an innate structural foundation, that has evolved in consequence of the invariance of the body's internal organization from one generation to the next, as against the variability of the surrounding world. The fact that the body schema deals with *spatial* relations explains why it figures in our model as part of the brain's internal representation of the *external* world, hence as part of the RWM.

The parietal lobe is closely implicated in the representation of spatial relations, especially of nearby space. And it seems that the body schema and the representation of spatial relations inside the space that can be reached by the arms and hands form an integrated functional unit. Cells in the parietal cortex of the monkey have been found to fire if a morsel of food was within the monkey's reach, even if the animal did not reach for it. If the morsel was outside its reach, they remained silent (Mountcastle et al., 1975). At the human level a telling demonstration of this functional unit has been given by Karl Pribram at Radford University. He called it the 'egocentric body space'. In these experiments he fitted the eyes of a student with prisms that inverted the world. He then found that if he placed his own hand within reach of the student, the student would see it the right way up, but as soon as he moved it outside that reach the student saw it upside down! (Pribram, 1999).

In view of what I have mentioned before about the importance of motor information in visual perception, it is interesting to note that motor activities also play a key role in the integration of the interoceptive and exteroceptive body information – a fact first reported by Head (1920). In due course the full extent of this integration also became apparent (Schilder, 1935). It forms the vital link between personal and extrapersonal space. As we now know, the required calibration begins soon after birth as the infant waves its arms about and learns to relate what it sees to what it senses internally (Van der Meer et al., 1950).

According to Piaget (1954), the self and the surrounding world are still a single entity in the earliest stages of childhood. This ceases to apply to nearby space as the infant begins to learn the consequences of its actions in trying to touch or grasp objects within its reach or begins to crawl around. Through these actions it also appears to learn the perception of the distance that separates objects from its own body, i.e. the perception of three-dimensional depth, without passing through an intermediate phase in which its actions are guided just by the two dimensions of the visual field (Rader & Stern, 1982). However, it is still a matter of dispute how much of what emerges at these early stages is produced innately (Legerstee, 1998).

The need to correlate and integrate interoceptive and exteroceptive body information may possibly hold the key to the pathological phenomenon known as *depersonalization*: the state when the patient feels he is merely an outside observer of his body. It is known to occur in a variety of psychiatric conditions, including schizophrenia, epilepsy, brain tumours, drug abuse and severe migraine. It seems to me that we have here a dissociation between the part of the body schema derived from the external senses and the part derived from the inner body senses, caused by a failure of the latter to enter the IGR.

This *cognitive* depersonalization needs to be distinguished from the *emotional* type in which the patient's emotional attachments and responses to other people are severely blunted. The patient may still claim to love his wife but lack the emotional concomitants. Whereas the cognitive deficit would seem to be attributable to dysfunction in the RWM/IGR complex, this emotional deficit points to a dysfunction in the limbic system, possibly in the **amygdala**, subcortical structures known to be closely associated with emotional responses of a social kind.

Damasio (1994) draws attention to the large number of both cortical and subcortical structures to which the ongoing representation of the current body states is distributed. These include the **somatosensory** and parietal cortices, parts of the limbic system, the hippocampus and the **brainstem**. In this connection, it is interesting to contrast his notion of self-awareness with the one that I have presented above. In partial agreement with the present analysis, he sees the body image as one of the main contributors to our awareness of 'the self'. However, he takes the importance of the body image much further, viewing the body as what he calls 'a theater for the emotions'. This is expressed in a theory of feelings that centres on the body and postulates that the brain's internal representations of events or situations are tagged according to their emotional significance by what he calls 'somatic markers'. In our model, by contrast, they are 'tagged' by expectancies of need satisfaction.

Phantom limbs

One of the curiosities of the body schema is the phantom limb. After the amputation of a limb the brain still appears to retain a representation of it in the body schema, including the possibility of experiencing movement and localized sensations in that 'virtual' limb. Oddly enough, it can also occur in up to 20 per cent of people born with a missing limb. Such congenital amputees can describe the missing limb's size, shape, position and movement. A complete break in the spinal cord can also produce a phantom *body*.

To explain these phenomena in terms of our model, we have to look again at the body schema as part of the RWM. Now, the RWM is an internal representation of the external world, and its body schema, too, maps the body as part of that external world, i.e. as a physical object. However, it occupies a unique position here. For the external world into which we are born may differ radically from one generation to the next and also from case to case within the same generation. We are innately equipped with learning capacities that enable us to adapt to these differences and so come to form an appropriate RWM in the light of our sensory experiences of the surrounding world and its properties. In contrast, the body with which we are normally born has essentially remained the same across the genera-tions: the same number of parts and extremities in the same arrangement, with the same degrees of freedom, etc. The body schema does not need to have the same plasticity and fluidity as the rest of the RWM. It is therefore plausible to assume that this body schema has a structural foundation that is 'hard-wired' in the sense of consisting of a distributed neural network that is genetically determined. This conclusion accords with the 'innate neuromatrix for the body-self' postulated by Melzack (1990).

In consequence of this hard-wired structure, the body schema does not shrink if a limb is lost at either an early or a later stage, and it retains the full dimensionality of that limb. Nor, apparently, are its connections with the somatosensory cortex lost. This proves critical, because an amputation tends to be followed by a reorganization of the somatosensory cortex. The topography of this cortex first came to be known in the 1950s through the pioneering work of Wilder Penfield, the famous Canadian neurosurgeon. After removal of the relevant section of the skull he stimulated the underlying cortex with microelectrodes. From the sensations reported by the subject he inferred to which part of the body the stimulated spot was receptive. Two salient facts came to light. First, the cortical areas allocated to different parts of the body were roughly proportional to the sensitivities of these parts. Thus the hands and the face occupied the largest areas. Second, the areas were completely jumbled up. For example, the face might be next to the hand and the genitals next to the feet.

After amputation the de-afferented and disused receptive areas of the somatosensory cortex tend to be invaded and annexed by some neighbour-ing area, thus becoming sensitive to stimuli from a different source. But this does not appear to make these areas lose their original functional role in the body schema, and owing to the jumbled-up locations this can give rise to bizarre effects. Borsook and colleagues describe a case in which stimuli applied to the face were felt by the patient not only as what they were, but also as precisely located and modality-specific sensations in a severed upper limb (Borsook et al., 1998). Similar cases have been reported by other researchers.

Although I have talked throughout mainly about the cortex, we must not forget the subcortical structures involved in all this, especially the thalamus. Phantom sensations can also be generated by microstimulation of the relevant thalamic regions (Davis et al., 1998).

3.2. Problems avoided by this account of self-reference

In connection with self-awareness I had to mention the different ways in which we may see or judge ourselves. Nevertheless, from the biological standpoint the key property of the primary consciousness is the implied self-reference. This follows from the proposition that brain events become conscious events only by virtue of being part of the IGR, and that the IGR is a comprehensive internal representation of the current state of the organism. As I have pointed out, this reference to the physical organism also accords with the sense in which the word 'self' commonly occurs in the biological sciences in such phrases as 'self-reproduction', 'self-regulation' and 'self-maintenance'.

It is worth noting how my account of self-reference, and of the different kinds of self-awareness derived from it, avoids some of the problems that the question of self-awareness creates for theories in which self-reference is not seen as an integral part of conscious experience. We have a typical example in those theories that view the brain as a computer and seek to capture all aspects of the brain's main functions in the language of information processing and computation. To describe self-awareness the theories I have in mind had to assume that in some sense the brain loops back on to itself or even that it models itself. As a telling illustration of the point I am making, consider the theory of self-consciousness presented by Philip Johnson-Laird in his still well-known book, *Mental Models* (Johnson-Laird, 1983). This forms only a small part of the book, much of which has been of special interest to me because of his demonstrations of how often our everyday reasoning is conducted not by way of an application of the rules of logic to articulated propositions, but by *picturing* situations and their consequences or incompatibilities. That the suspect could not have committed a murder in Islington at 9 p.m. on Friday if at that time he was watching a film in Piccadilly is established in the mind just by the impossibility of picturing him doing both.

Let me return to Johnson-Laird's explanation of self-consciousness. According to his account, the contents of consciousness consist of 'the current values of parameters governing the high-level values of the operating system'. This leads him to view self-awareness as the brain modelling itself. Thus he falls back on the analogy of a (hypothetical) self-describing Turing machine and comes to see self-awareness as a case of models being embedded inside models along the following lines: 'At stage

0, the program can construct a model of a proposition p; at stage 1, it can construct a model of itself as a program operating at stage 0; and, in general, at any stage it can construct a model of itself operating at the previous stage' (p. 472). Hence he concludes that self-awareness 'arises from both the recursive ability to embed mental models within mental models and the mind's possession of a high-level model of the capabilities of its own operating system' (p. 477). I think this illustrates well to what length you may be driven if you limit your conceptual framework to the computational one. I shall give another example in the next chapter [4.11]. Even the basic computer notion of 'operating system' seems to me very nebulous when applied to the brain.

Our model also avoids a problem with which you can be saddled if your account of self-awareness implies that awareness of the self changes the self of which it is aware. For this may land you in an infinite regress of the kind 'I am aware that I am aware that I am aware', which has at times been hotly debated. It raises the spectre of a hall of mirrors. One suggested way out has been to interpret this 'regress' as 'a pattern of events ordered on a time based sequence' (Rose, 1973, p. 23). In other words, each awareness in this sequence refers to an instant just after that to which the previous awareness refers.

In our model this particular problem does not arise, because, according to our Propositions 1 and 3, self-reference is an integral part of conscious experience: it is built into all the contents of consciousness. It manifests itself as an uninterrupted awareness that my thoughts are *my* thoughts and my feelings are *my* feelings – just as my arms are experienced as *my* arms in the sense I have explained. This awareness is not of the nature of a perception of something, as that term is commonly understood. In Gilbert Ryle's words, experiences are not *perceived*, they are *had* (Ryle, 1949), *and the having of something is not changed by being had*. From this point of view 'introspection' is really a misnomer. In introspection you are not peeping inside. You are *attending* to features of your conscious experience, not *perceiving* them. Metaphorically speaking, the self that directs the spotlight of our attention can never be caught in its own beam. The philosopher David Hume has given a subtle reason why 'the self' is never perceived: one can never catch oneself *without* a perception. William James said that his own search for the 'I' revealed only feelings of tension chiefly in the mouth and the throat.

3.3. Self-awareness and attention

It has been claimed that attention can be so tightly focused that we become unaware of all but the intense stimuli of the work that is holding our attention – even of ourselves as concentrating agents (Kinsbourne, 1988). Here I must refer you back to Chapter 2, where I pointed out that such narrowly focused attention merely singles out a small field of the IGR as the most relevant to the task on which one is engaged, and that this does not imply an extinction of the rest of the IGR in the sense in which the whole of the IGR is extinguished in deep sleep or a coma [2.3]. Indeed, the intentional pursuit of this task as such rests on a full internal representation of the total situation, hence on the full IGR. It follows that it is wrong to assume that sharply focused attention on an object or task implies a total loss of self-awareness – of *explicit* self-awareness, yes, but not *implicit* self-awareness, as these terms were defined above. As you will recall, the contents of the IGR, hence of consciousness, have self-reference because the IGR is an internal representation of the current state of the organism, and implicit self-awareness was defined as the way in which this self-reference manifests itself as part of the qualia of conscious experience. However hard I am concentrating as I write this, the fingers that are moving over my computer's keyboard are still experienced as *my* fingers, categorically distinct from foreign objects such as the keys they are hitting.

A full loss of self-awareness would mean the body dropping out of consciousness in the same sense in which in the phenomenon of neglect the awareness of a whole side of the body can be lost through lesions in the parietal lobe of the cerebral cortex, as I shall describe in Section 6.3. There are *two* selective processes at work. One selects components from the RWM for entry into the IGR, hence into consciousness; the other selects parts of the IGR as the currently attended field. It follows from what has been said about entry into consciousness [2.5] that the first of these is not a straight-forward attentional process. My tightly focused concentration on the computer affects only the second of these processes. The unattended part of the IGR is still part of the content of the primary consciousness, though it has receded temporarily into the background, into what I have called the peripheral or background consciousness.

3.4. Awareness of one's thoughts and feelings

Since we are dealing only with the primary, subverbal levels of consciousness, the only thoughts the theory needs to cover are imaginative representations in the many different forms in which they occur at the conscious level – as when I contemplate possible actions and their anticipated consequences, remember a holiday adventure, dream of a yachting trip or engage in one of the many ways of everyday reasoning that Johnson-Laird has shown to be so frequently conducted in terms of mental images. The growth of IT and computer graphics has also produced a general shift towards the presentations of arguments in a visual form and is bound to be reflected in our inclinations to *visualize* logical sequences of events rather than applying the formal rules of logic. As regards the *awareness* of one's thoughts, according to our model this is implied in the self-reference attached to all imaginative representations that are included in the IGR.

Regarding the brain processes underlying imaginative representations, I have already mentioned the view, finally to be argued in Chapter 8, that to imagine an object or event is for the brain to enter a state of readiness to perceive that object or event without, however, expecting this perception to occur. In other words, the state of perceptual readiness here assumes a function different from the one it has in normal perceptual processes.

As regards awareness of one's *feelings*, this has been accounted for in Proposition 4 of the present theory [1.4] through its treatment of the qualia, of the 'what it is like' to have this or that experience. The proposition identified the qualia with the conscious components of the total effect, or total 'impact', an experience has on the organism, in other words with the components that are embraced by the IGR. This is a sufficiently broad description to cover most of what we commonly mean by feelings, such as feelings of attraction, repulsion, sympathy, joy or sorrow. *Emotions* can also be mentioned in this context, as a class of feelings generally accompanied by a state of arousal and a need to seek expression in word, gesture or deed. I shall return to the question of the qualia again in the next chapter [4.5].

Notes

1 4(5–6), 1997; 5(2), 1998; 5(5–6), 1998 and 6, 1999.

2 I can see no reason why higher levels, such as verbalized thoughts, should be an exception.

4

A CLOSER LOOK AT THE FOUR
MAIN PROPOSITIONS

4.1. The primary consciousness

The first step in my search for the biological unity of consciousness was the decision to understand consciousness in a sense in which it could be a property also of creatures lacking a language faculty, such as the prelinguistic infant, the deaf-mute and nonhuman animals. I called this the primary consciousness. In creatures possessing language this subverbal level of awareness still needs to be understood first, since it is likely to be the basis on which their more sophisticated faculties rest. It also establishes consciousness in terms that enable it to have an evolutionary history that stretches back in time beyond the emergence of language. Moreover, to answer the most fundamental questions about what consciousness is, what it does, why it evolved and how it arises in the brain, it suffices to understand the nature of the primary consciousness. In Chapter 1 I listed the three main facets of consciousness which a scientific theory needs to cover as *awareness of the surrounding world, of the self as an entity*, and *of one's thoughts and feelings*. Four key propositions then outlined a model of the primary consciousness that satisfies these conditions and also covers both the first-person and third-person perspective. In this chapter we shall return to these four propositions for further comment.

This notion of primary consciousness should not be confused with a notion introduced under the same name by Gerald Edelman (1992). This covers just the RWM and imaginative representations. All else, such as the qualia and self-awareness, are categorized as higher orders of consciousness. On the other hand, Edelman shares this book's view that any scientific theory of consciousness needs to appeal to biology, that the mind cannot be understood in the absence of biology. Thus he addresses the question of how consciousness emerges during evolution and development. And here he suggests that consciousness is the product of integrated assemblies of neurons that develop in accordance with selective principles similar to those envisaged in the Darwinian theory of evolution.

My 'primary consciousness' differs also from the notion of 'core consciousness', introduced by Antonio Damasio (1998), another follower of a neurobiological approach. Broadly speaking, his notion is restricted to what in the present model is described as the conscious portion of the RWM. For what this omits, see Figure 1.1 (p. 16).

4.2. The IGR

Proposition 1

> *The brain forms an extensive internal representation of the current state of the organism which includes representations of the total situation facing the organism both in the* outer *and the* inner *world.*

This extensive internal representation of the current state of the organism thus brings together as an integral whole the main elements which the organism needs to take into account in the choice of appropriate actions. I therefore called it the Integrated Global Representation or IGR. The relevant elements relating to the inner world are here assumed to include not only physiological stimuli like hunger, thirst or pain, but also current mental events, foremost events belonging to the category I have called *imaginative representations*. For representations relating to the outer world, the IGR draws on the RWM. Proposition 3 identified the primary consciousness with the IGR.

Our IGR may remind some readers of Bernard Baars' 'Global Workspace' (Baars, 1988). But this is again a different concept. Baars is mainly concerned with the distribution of information throughout the brain so that it could become available to all its specialist functions and enable due integration to take place. And his 'Global Workspace' is conceived as a central information exchange that would make this possible. In my model the integration occurs at various levels, the highest level occurring in the IGR.

As regards our assumption that the IGR is a representation of the current state of the organism, we find ourselves in substantial agreement with Damasio (1994). Given that the mind arises from the activity of neural circuits, he suggests that those circuits were shaped in evolution by functional requisites of the organism. Hence normal mind will happen only if those circuits contain basic representations of the organism. This brings me to the question of the body schema.

Pain and its location

Sometimes people who like to stir up a bit of philosophical argument will ask where the pain resides when you stub your toe. Does it reside in the toe, where you feel it, or in the brain where all those excited neurons fire? The body schema plays a vital part in the answer.

The location of stimuli applied to the body comes to be represented in the RWM through their projection into the body schema [3.1]. Our

conscious body sense, including awareness of the stubbed toe, is the part
of the body schema that enters consciousness by being included in the IGR.

Evidence of this schema as a real entity in the brain's conscious world
model comes from the phenomenon of neglect, an effect of certain brain
lesions which can cause whole sections of the body to vanish from the
patient's consciousness [6.3]. Certain lesions in the right parietal lobe, for
example, can cause a severe neglect pertaining to the left upper extremities.
It is a real gap in the brain's conscious world model. In the case of a
disowned left hand, for instance, the neglect continues even if that hand is
moved to the right side of the body. The patient cannot even be persuaded
of the existence of that hand by arguments drawing on the fact that the
hand is on a continuum through the forearm and upper arm with the rest
of the body (Bisiach & Geminiani, 1991). He can see the hand but can make
no sense of what he sees. The authors rightly suggest that it cannot be a
gap in *perception*, but must be one in *representation*.

Put in simple functional terms, pain is designed to signal that there
is something wrong somewhere on or in the body and that it is of sufficient
importance to be taken into account in the organism's evaluation of
the total situation. Hence the signal's inclusion in the IGR. In fact, pain
is an immensely complex subject, never yet fully understood in all its
ramifications. You can have injury without feeling pain and pain when
there is no injury. Distressingly, too, amputees can have agonizing pain
in a phantom of the missing limb. Pain is both a sensation and an
emotion. Being a subjective conscious experience it comes under our
Proposition 4, according to which the quality of our subjective experience
(the 'qualia') is formed by those components of the total effect an
experience has on the organism which are included in the IGR. It is the
complexity of the total effect of a traumatic stimulus that accounts for the
many ramifications of the pain phenomenon and the difficulties that face
the investigators.

When the traumatic stimulus is applied to the body surface, the common
response will have two phases: a fast 'reflex' reaction, like quickly
withdrawing a finger that has touched a hot surface, and a less urgent
adaptive set of reactions designed to deal with the nature of the injury, both
by way of motor responses (e.g. moving in ways that relieve the injured
limb) and internal adjustments, including learning changes to prevent it
happening again.

In accordance with this division, two sets of contingently 'nociceptive'
(harm-reporting) fibres are found to innervate the skin: the fast A-delta
fibres and the much slower C fibres. Both are responsive to light pressure,
heavy pressure, heat and chemicals; the former also to cooling and the latter
also to warmth (Melzack & Wall, 1996). Both sets of fibres enter the spinal
cord where a great deal of processing occurs straight away, including an
activation of reflexes, of which the knee-jerk reflex is a familiar example.
In accordance with its claim to priority, the input of the A fibres here
overrides that of the C fibres.

The result of this processing is passed up the spinal cord via 'transmission cells' to reach the brainstem, **midbrain** and somatosensory cortex, spreading out in a profusion of networks that seem to involve a seemingly disproportionate portion of the whole brain. This is perhaps not surprising in view of the emotional and motivational dimensions of the pain experience and the involvement of the highest brain centres in the organism's overall reactions to the traumatic stimulus or injury. Thus right from the spinal cord upwards, the flow of excitation is 'gated' by descending impulses from the higher brain centres which may either suppress or accentuate it. We can see in this top-down control an informed evaluation of the relative importance of the nociceptive impulses in the light of past experience and the current total situation. That importance clearly depends on a great many individual factors, such as childhood experiences, cultural as well as genetic influences and the subject's current motivational state. In the course of highly motivated actions, as in an athletic competition, pain may hardly be felt. Nor may it be felt in the state of shock that follows a serious injury. The sometimes remarkable absence of pain after a serious injury might also be an expression of the top-level brain processes having taken charge of the situation, so that pain-induced arousal would serve no further purpose.

Owing to all this intermediate processing, the specificity of the afferent impulses at the periphery is not matched by a corresponding specificity of the psychological experience. Pain sensations can be of a great variety. Pains can be pricking, cutting, numbing, throbbing, pounding, etc. And this is not just related to the original afferent impulses but additionally appears to be due to the complexity of the total impact a specific traumatic stimulus can make on the organism. For some inexplicable reason, the pain threshold may also differ according to the time of day.

Since the prefrontal cortex and cingulate cortex are deeply implicated in the brain's top-level evaluation of the current situation, it is not surprising that pain-sensitive cells are found in these regions. Neurons have been found in the anterior cingulate that respond to pain stimuli, with different neurons responding to different kinds of pain. However, stimulation of neurons in this region does not suffice to produce a sensation of pain.

In accordance with their top-level role, the 'downward' outputs from the prefrontal regions are instrumental in the control of pain-produced arousal via the thalamus. In a drastic surgical operation known as leucotomy or frontal lobotomy, first performed in Portugal in 1935 to relieve severe neuroses, the connections are severed between the thalamus and the prefrontal cortex. The patient can now still feel the pain, but is much less troubled by it. Over a number of years this procedure was frequently used to deal with such neuroses, especially in the USA. But owing to its negative side effects on the emotive and motivational life of the patient, it was abandoned when new developments in the use of drugs and behaviour therapy proved effective without such negative consequences.

A distinction needs to be drawn between *superficial* pain, like that of the stubbed toe, and *deep* or *visceral* pain. In the latter case the projection is much less precise, and may also be at variance with the true location of the source, an occurrence technically known as 'referred pain'. Not infrequently, for example, a heart condition is felt as a pain in the upper arm. The faulty reference is always in one direction: from deep to superficial tissues. The phenomenon has been explained by some authors as due to the proximity of the rather sparse **visceral** fibres to the massive fibres from skin and musculature, so that nerve impulses from the one pathway may accidentally pass to the other. However, Melzack and Wall (1996) attribute it to patterns of sensory innervation established early in embryonic life. Since no reflex reaction is required in visceral pains, only C fibres form the primary afferents.

Phantom limb pain is another case of confused location and one that can cause a great deal of distress. Here, an amputee experiences pain in the severed limb, often closely localized. Over 70 per cent of amputees may be affected by it, some soon after an amputation, others only weeks, months or even years later. Amputees have identified exercise, objects approaching the stump, cold weather and 'feeling nervous' as main triggers (Wilkins et al., 1998). But certain stimuli to healthy parts of the body may in some cases also prove to be triggers, such as a pinprick to a healthy limb. Unfortunately, the responsible trigger mechanisms still remain a mystery. Since pain in the phantom limb frequently occurs at the same site as it occurred in the diseased limb before amputation, some memory mechanism may also be involved. The general case of sensations in phantom limbs was discussed in Section 3.1.

4.3. Protecting the cortex from overload

Proposition 2

The IGR is subject to capacity and/or access limitations.

Hence not all of the total situation facing the organism will enter the IGR, as regards both the outer and the inner world, nor all of the total impact current events make on the organism.

One well-known way in which the cortex is protected from overload has already been mentioned. It relates to its motor-executive functions, when subcortical structures take charge of standard routines in the execution of the consciously decided action plans. PET scans of local brain activity, for example, have shown a diminished activity in the involved frontal and parietal areas of the cerebral cortex when a task defined by arbitrary rules becomes a familiar one (Deiber et al., 1997). Since many of the steps that go into the execution of the subgoals of an action plan will be of a routine nature for which the overall context is irrelevant, they can be left to a semi-automatic motor organization and thus relieve the higher centres. Thus, in learning to type the actions are initially performed in a deliberate step-by-step fashion, each search for the right key being performed with the full engagement of the subject's attention. With practice, however, the actions will in due course become coherent self-pacing movements. The fingers now flit over the keyboard.

The limitation of cortical capacity can also show itself through competition and interference, for example when cortical areas already serving some particular purpose are grabbed to serve a new purpose. Dual-task experiments, in which the subject is asked to do two tasks at the same time, have typically shown that the more automatic and unconscious a task becomes, the less it will interfere with the other task, and the less it will degrade as a result of the competition (Baars, 1988). In a typical experiment, the subject may be asked to point as quickly as possible to a light signal, which is then made to appear just as the subject is starting a sentence.

Competition and divided attention may also form an important restriction on concurrent stimulus processing within individual modalities (Duncan, 1998). In a classic experiment Donald Broadbent fed two different sequences of three numbers simultaneously to the subject's ears (Broadbent, 1952). The subject would then report first one and then the other – switching between the ears, as it were. The author explained this in terms of attention being controlled by a 'filter' that prevents overloading some central, 'perceptual', channel of information flow. A similar alternation has since been observed when the two eyes are presented with different visual inputs in the same part of the visual field.

4.4. Self-reference holds the key

Proposition 3

The first identity statement:

The primary consciousness is the IGR

Let me pull together some features of the IGR that justify this assumption.

- The IGR has a built-in dimension of self-reference, the basis of self-awareness, as I have explained in Chapter 3, and there is a considerable consensus (found also in the dictionary definitions of consciousness) that self-awareness is a crucial ingredient of consciousness. It brings to mind what Immanuel Kant described in his *Critique of Pure Reason* (1781) as the first principle of our thinking, namely that the variety of conscious experiences are united in the unity of self-consciousness. According to our model, that unity resides in the unity of the physical organism whose current state the IGR represents.
- The ability to report a stimulus is commonly taken as proof that a subject is conscious of the stimulus. And to report a stimulus the subject must have an internal representation of the fact that the experience is part of the current state of the organism.

- By virtue of what the IGR embraces, decisions based on the IGR are the most comprehensively informed decisions, and it is therefore of obvious benefit that these decisions should figure at the top of the brain's internal command structures. That top level is commonly taken to be the *conscious* level, resulting in what we call our *voluntary* or *willed* actions.[1]
- In view of this benefit, the identification of the primary consciousness with the IGR offers at least a partial explanation of the evolution of consciousness prior to the emergence of language in the evolution of life.
- As I shall explain later in this chapter, the theory also permits an interpretation in causal and functional terms of the main divisions of mental events, and it can resolve the apparent contradiction between the concept of a *free will* and the causal determinism assumed for the neural processes of the brain. Finally, along the lines of our fourth proposition, it can explain the subjectivity of conscious experience and the qualia.

4.5. The qualia: are they really the 'hard' problem?

Proposition 4

The second identity statement:

> *The subjective or qualitative aspects of conscious experience, the qualia, consist of those components of the overall effect an event has on the organism which are included in the IGR, and, according to Proposition 3, thus become part of our conscious experiences.*

It is of obvious value to the organism if its top-level of decision making, hence the IGR, has information about the overall effect an event has on the organism. Thus the proposition explains why conscious experiences have this strongly qualitative character and why we have such subjective experience in the first place. Sometimes it is called the 'raw feel' of an experience. The proposition also offers a simple answer to a question that has provoked more controversy than almost any other: the question of how a scientific explanation of consciousness can account for the subjective character of all conscious experience. The main features of that subjective character are its uniqueness, privacy and intrinsicness, and I have explained how our model of the primary consciousness accounts for all of these.

The debate was triggered by Thomas Nagel's seminal essay 'What is it like to be a bat?' (Nagel, 1974). He argued that it is absurd for *us* to try and imagine what it is like to be a bat. The real question is what it is like *for the bat* to be a bat. Hence the subjective character of experience is essentially connected with a single point of view – what we have called the first-person perspective. This, he argued, makes an objective physical theory of the subjective character of mental phenomena an impossibility, because it seems inevitable that such a theory will abandon that single point of view. It is an important point for him because he identifies consciousness itself with the subjective character of experience. He argues that this subjective character is not analysable in terms of any explanatory system of functional states, since these could be ascribed to robots and automata that behaved like people even though they experienced nothing.

According to our model of consciousness, this is a fallacy. Jointly our four main propositions cover both cognition and feelings in terms of a single comprehensive functional state of the brain, namely the IGR. And *if* (a very big *if!*) a robot had this comprehensive functional state, had this IGR and hence the qualia, then it *would* experience things.

A common mistake is to demand that a completely detailed physical account of the brain processes underlying subjective experience should actually *convey* what it is like for us to see red, taste the milk, feel a pain, etc. It is a fallacious view because science is not in the business of conveying anything, be it sensations or feelings. That belongs to the work of poets, novelists and painters. All that a physical account of the brain needs to explain is how the qualia come to have their distinctive properties, namely their wholly private, wholly individual and wholly intrinsic character.

By identifying the raw feel of an experience with the conscious components of the overall effect which the experience has on the individual, our model meets these conditions. For the intrinsicness, privacy and uniqueness of the qualia just follow from the fact that this overall effect will always be represented *to some extent* in the IGR, and will invariably be a subtle product of the subject's current motivational state and personal history, untraceable in its origins and ramifications. In short: despite the fact that our model of the primary consciousness is a physicalist one, it is able to account fully for the qualia, and challenges the view that the subjectivity of conscious experience precludes a neurophysiological account of consciousness.

In recent times, Nagel's position has been supported notably by the philosopher David Chalmers. He has dubbed the problem of the qualia the 'hard' problem of consciousness, by which he means any problem that questions the possibility of a scientific answer (Chalmers, 1995, 1996). Chalmers claims that the problem of the qualia cannot be solved by the normal methods of the cognitive sciences, although he also states that he vaguely senses there might be a way out. In our model, Proposition 4 shows the way out.

As one 'way out', Benjamin Libet (1994) has postulated the existence of a 'conscious mental field'. He sees this as a hypothetical field, associated with the cortex, which has to be accepted as a fundamental phenomenon not explicable in physical terms. He also claims that this theory is in principle testable. It would, he says, require isolating a slice of cortex *in situ* from all neural connections to the rest of the brain, leaving only the blood supply. Electrical or chemical stimulation of this slice should then produce a conscious experience. However, as he turns to the practical difficulties of achieving such an isolation, he has to conclude with regret that it is beyond the techniques available today. He still hopes that it may become possible some time in the future so that his theory could be proven. I, too, would be interested, because on my analysis the experiment is bound to give a negative result.

Daniel Dennett (1991) escapes the problem by denying subjective states of awareness altogether. Indeed, the literature on this particularly awkward question arouses his ire and contempt. He sees this literature as 'a tormented snarl of increasingly convoluted and bizarre thought experiments, jargon, in-jokes, allusions to putative refutations, "received" results that should be returned to sender, and a bounty of other sidetrackers and time-wasters'. According to Dennett it merely *seems* to us that there are such things as the qualia, but this is just a mistaken judgement on our part about what is really happening. Indeed, according to Dennett, the only sensible course is to walk away from the question and not waste time reviewing it.

Sometimes Chalmers' view is supported in the rather more fanciful form of a philosopher's thought experiment. The argument runs something like this: if one had complete knowledge of the current physical state of a person's brain, down to every atom, molecule and neuron, could any scientific theory predict what the current experiences felt like to that person? And the speaker, of course, will expect a negative answer. But I deny him that satisfaction. Because one needs to be aware of precisely what is meant by asking 'what it is like' to have this or that experience, or what an experience 'feels like'. The meaning of these questions is determined by the kind of answer they can expect and, as indicated by the word 'like', these questions can expect only one kind of answer, namely a *comparison* with other experiences: 'It tasted like sea water', 'It felt like a pinprick' or, more indirectly: 'It brought tears to my eyes.' Seen in this light, it seems to me clear that from a strictly theoretical point of view, it would *in principle* be possible to infer those comparisons from that complete knowledge of the current physical state of a person's brain, here assumed for the sake of the argument, because one would *in principle* be able to detect the features shared by the two experiences.

4.6. An interpretation of the main divisions of mental events

As I have said before, one advantage of having a definite theory of consciousness is that one can give definite meanings to what in common currency may be somewhat fuzzy notions related to consciousness. In this section I shall apply this to the main categories of conscious mental events which we commonly distinguish by such names as perceptions, sensations, feelings, desires, intentions and so forth. I want to show how these categories can be given definitive interpretations in terms of the IGR and its functional composition – remembering that according to our model *brain events become conscious events only to the extent to which they are included in the IGR*. Thus:

Perceptions. Perceptions are commonly understood as our conscious apprehension through the sense organs of objects in the outside world. In our model they are interpreted as the conscious components of the contribution that the sense organs are currently making to the RWM.

Sensations. The notion of 'sensation' needs to be distinguished from that of 'perception'. You *perceive* a red rose, but its redness comes to you as a *sensation*. The latter notion has had a chequered history – largely in the hands of philosophers. Bertrand Russell, for example, saw in 'sense data' a category of mental phenomena incapable of further division and therefore to be accepted as primitives in a philosophy of mind. In contemporary psychology the notion is most commonly taken to denote the mental correlates of the excitation of the senses by a stimulus. In our model we can take this to mean those components of such excitations that enter consciousness through projection into the IGR.

Feelings. If 'feelings' are taken to mean *what it is like* to have this or that experience, then our account of them has already been covered by the fourth main proposition. This identified the qualia with the conscious components of the total impact an experience makes on the organism, i.e. the components that are embraced by the IGR. As I have said before, this description is broad enough to cover most kinds of feelings, including those of love, joy or sorrow.

Emotions. We can regard emotions as special kinds of feeling which, as the word already says, include an element that *moves* you and thus implies some urge for action. Often a mere outward expression of the emotion will provide the desired relief.

Mental images. According to our model, these are imaginative representations, not necessarily in the visual modality, that are rendered conscious through becoming part of the IGR (see Chapter 8).

Thoughts. Since this book deals only with the primary consciousness, hence only nonverbal levels of representation, the only *thoughts* our model covers consist of the play of imaginative representations at this nonverbal level, as when we try to figure out how to fit a carpet into a room, visualize the possible consequences of an action or picture a scene described in a novel – to cite just some of the many possible examples [3.4].

Desires. These may be interpreted as a subcategory of thoughts, namely imagined situations that elicit expectancies (either conscious or unconscious) of need satisfaction or other pleasurable sensations, including the cessation of a noxious sensation, such as the pangs of hunger.

Intentions. An intention to achieve this or that result may be interpreted as a *desire* (understood in the sense given above) that has taken control of one's actions as a conscious goal-image.

Voluntary acts.   Voluntary or 'willed' acts are technically understood as acts determined by conscious decisions. I prefer the expression 'willed' acts, because 'voluntary' acts can also be understood as acts not forced on you by someone holding a gun to your head. We can define 'willed' acts as *acts determined by intentions* (understood in the sense given above) – the implication being that they are determined by conscious decisions and, according to our model, therefore, by decisions based on the IGR.

The will or volition.   Historically, the notion of the will as a dynamic force has attracted an attention that went beyond psychologists studying human motivation. In the philosophy of Schopenhauer it even became a global or cosmic driving force. Most psychologists will probably agree that the notion of the will or volition is best seen as a feature of our *conscious* life. In accordance with the present theory and the interpretations given above, we could therefore describe the will or volition as *a person's commitment to a consciously conceived goal*.

4.7. The freedom of the will (1)

On the basis of these interpretations, the notion of a 'free will' can also be given a precise meaning and fitted into the theory. I define the freedom of the will as *the unimpeded ability of volitions, as defined above, to control our actions*, or, as Willard V. Quine has put it, the 'freedom to do as we will' (Quine, 1960). Reasons why this may not satisfy everybody will be considered when we return to the subject in Section 5.2.

Quine rightly argues that the freedom of the will means that we are free to *do as we will*, unless someone holds us back or there are other impediments. In other words, our actions count as free in so far as our will is a cause of them. Certainly the will has its causes in turn; no one could wish otherwise. If we thought wills could not be caused, we would not try to train our children; we would not try to win votes; we would not try to sell things or to deter criminals.

I shall return to this interpretation in the next chapter. It effectively disposes of the belief, shared by many scientists (including Einstein), that in view of the causal determinism in the underlying brain processes, the notion of a free will is an illusion. According to the above interpretation of a 'free will', the question of the determinism or indeterminism of the underlying brain processes is an irrelevance.

Ever since the discovery of quantum indeterminacy in the 1920s, philosophers and theologians have looked to it as a release from the shackles of determinism and as an answer to dilemmas concerning man's freedom of will and God's power over the Universe. It has not died down in the 70 years that have passed since. In modern times, for example, the Oxford mathematician Roger Penrose invokes it in his treatment of the freedom of the will (Penrose, 1989, 1994). But it should have died down.

The ultra-microscopic quantum indeterminacy is ironed out statistically in the macro-processes involved in the brain processes with which we have here been concerned (even though it has been argued that the so-called **microtubules** inside nerve cells could make an exception). Moreover, quantum indeterminacy would merely substitute randomness for determinacy, and it is hard to see how that can fit any notion of a free will – or any inspiring notion of God, for that matter.

The notion of a free will I have introduced does not, for example, conflict with the discovery that conscious decisions may be preceded by a slow negative wave in the cortex, recordable with scalp electrodes and known as a 'readiness potential'. According to Kornhuber and Deecke (1965), the discoverers of this effect, it could precede a self-paced movement by as much as 800 ms. This work was followed up notably by Libet in the study of simple voluntary acts. In experiments in which the subject was asked to flick a wrist at any arbitrary moment, Libet arrived at the time relationships depicted in Figure 4.1. The case of pre-planned acts is also shown. Of special interest is the point in time when the subject was aware of the wish to move, namely 200 ms before the muscle activation.

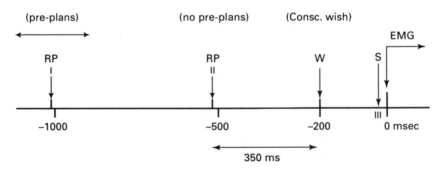

Figure 4.1 *Diagram of a sequence of events, cerebral and subjective, that precede a self-initiated voluntary act. Relative to 0 time, detected in the electromyogram (EMG) of the suddenly activated muscle, the readiness potential (RP) (an indicator of related cerebral neuronal activities) begins first, at about –1050 ms when some pre-planning is reported (RP I) or about –550 ms with spontaneous acts lacking immediate pre-planning (RP II). Subjective awareness of the wish to move (W) appears at about –200 ms, some 350 ms after onset even of RP II but well before the act (EMG). Subjective timings reported for awareness of the randomly delivered S (skin) stimulus average about –50 ms relative to actual delivery time (from Libet, 1993, with permission from John Wiley & Sons)*

According to Libet, these results show that so called 'voluntary' acts are not caused by conscious wishes to move. They are caused by prior, causally determined and unconscious cortical processes. Real freedom, he claims, exists only inside the 200 ms time interval between the conscious wish and the act, during which the act could then still be vetoed. In contrast, according to the interpretation of the nature of desires, intentions, volition and the freedom of the will I have given above, the flick of the wrist, when it comes, constitutes the *unimpeded execution of an intention* – hence a freely willed act according to our definitions. So this does not conflict with the existence of any cortical activities leading up to that act in a deterministic fashion.

4.8. The nature of functional descriptions

Since we have throughout been using functional definitions, I must not omit to mention that the biological notion of the function of an organ or process may itself need clarifying. Specifically, I have to take issue here with John Searle (1990), when he asserts that the functional description of a biological organ or process, such as the role of the heart in the circulation of the blood, is 'simply one of the causal levels described in terms of our interests' and that 'where functional explanations are concerned the only *facts* are brute, blind physical facts and the only norms are in us and exist only from our own point of view' (p. 592). Searle sees no difference in the facts asserted by *the heart pumps the blood*, and *the function of the heart is to pump the blood*. This is a grievous mistake. If you are told that the function of the spark plugs in your car engine is to ignite the fuel mixture, you are told not only their causal effects but also that they owe their structure and very presence in the engine to their capacity to have these causal effects. This is a statement in which the causal level of the action is fused with the causal level of this component's origin or development. It has nothing to do with the speaker's interests. The spark plugs have other causal effects as well: their action causes a noise. But no one would say that the production of that noise was a *function* of the spark plugs. As Andy Clark (1990) expressed it in his peer commentary:

> It is surely true that the heart has the function it has quite independently of my attaching normative importance to that function (pumping blood). For that physical structure would not exist were it not for the ability to perform that function – it has been selected (by non-conscious Mother Nature) *because* of its functional role. (p. 601)

4.9. Do functional explanations here pose a special problem?

The idea of defining mental processes in functional terms, notably defended by Jerry Fodor (1975), has been a provocative one for philosophers, who have dubbed it *functionalism*. It has been attacked notably on the grounds that any functional account of a mental process permits that process to be implemented by alternative kinds of hardware, for example by silicon chips. This is quite true, but hardly a valid objection to the theory. 'If you allow contraptions made of silicon chips to achieve consciousness,'

I have heard it said, 'then you must be wide of the mark!' How little one may in fact be off the mark was recently illustrated when light-sensitive microchips were developed that could be implanted in the eye to partly replace a dysfunctional retina by creating electrical impulses that could travel up the optic nerve. Conversely, researchers at the Max Planck Institute for Biochemistry in Munich have grown a brain cell of a rat on a silicon chip so that its outputs can be fed to a computer. The basic solution was to let the membrane potential of a nerve cell act as the 'gate' potential of a transistor.

It is quite true, therefore, that *in theory* the IGR could be modelled on silicon chips. But if you look again at all that has been said about the IGR and the RWM and what the latter includes by way of multiple levels of what-leads-to-what expectancies, it clearly becomes a question of the degree to which this would be achievable in practice. I shall return to this point in a moment. It also then becomes a question of where the line should be drawn when attributing consciousness to a system without making a mockery of the word.

Functionalism has also been attacked on the grounds that (a) it cannot cope with the qualia, and (b) it leaves the relation of function to structure unexplained (Searle, 1992). Our Proposition 4 refutes the first objection, as has been explained in Section 4.5. And Part II of this book will show how well our model can relate function to structure.

4.10. The directiveness of organic activities

Mention has frequently been made in these chapters of activities of one kind or another having to be 'appropriately' or 'correctly' related to the circumstances in which they take place. These phrases relate to a widespread characteristic of organic activities, namely their *goal-directedness* or *directiveness*. We are touching here on a feature that is often called the *teleological* character of the activities of living organisms, namely the fact that their activities and processes, internal as well as external, typically appear to be goal-directed in the sense of being conducive to some biologically significant outcome, often vital to their survival. The significance and implications of this feature occupied the mind of Aristotle, and over long periods of time it has fired arguments among theologians and philosophers as well as biologists. Some theologians, for example, claimed that this was the strongest evidence for *design* in the natural world, and design, they mistakenly claimed, presupposes a designer.

Right up to the Second World War and the growth of cybernetics that followed it, two radically opposed schools of thought competed with each other: the 'mechanists' and the 'vitalists'. The former claimed that there was no such objective property as goal-directedness in organic activities. All talk about such directiveness, they said, was merely anthropomorphism, a case of us mentally projecting into these organisms the rational nature of our own activities. At the opposite pole the vitalists claimed that it was indeed an objective property; moreover a property that could not be accounted for in normal physical or chemical terms. Hence one had to assume the existence in living organisms of some special forward-looking forces, for which they had invented such names as *élan vital* (Bergson) and *entelechy* (Driesch).

Soon after I became interested as a systems theorist in the brain and its activities I undertook a formal analysis of this feature. I concluded that the different kinds of 'goal-directedness' shown by the activities of living organisms were objective properties that had a formal unity. They all consisted of a specific type of correlation between an action or process and the circumstances in which it was produced. This correlation could be accurately defined in mathematical terms and I called it *directive correlation*. For a summary, see Sommerhoff (1974).

This analysis did not produce new explanations but it cleared up the muddled thinking that the whole topic had tended to produce. It showed that both those schools of thought were wrong. Contrary to what the mechanists believed, this directiveness *is* indeed an objective property, and, contrary to the vitalist view, it *is* indeed compatible with the ordinary laws of physics and chemistry. Meanwhile, these basic facts had already been demonstrated in practical terms by the extensive development in the Second World War of feedback-controlled devices and the early guidance systems. It is important therefore to note that when I use such phrases as 'appropriately related' or 'correctly related' responses, these relationships can be translated into a mathematically definable type of correlation, should the need for greater clarity arise.

4.11. Computer simulations and computational approaches

One can understand the notion of a computational approach to the brain both as a perspective and as a method of inquiry. The perspective in question is the assumption that the brain can profitably be regarded as a computer. I shall leave my rejection of this assumption to the end of this chapter. Here I am concerned with the method of inquiry, by which I understand the practice of (1) testing hypotheses by simulating them on a computer, and (2) generating new hypotheses by way of translating tasks which the brain has to perform into computational algorithms. Both have proved powerful and the first especially is widely used. In this section I want to look at their relevance to the model of consciousness we have developed so far.

Testing hypotheses

It has become part of modern practice to regard computer simulations as an important way of testing hypotheses and exploring their implications.

Indeed, I have had one correspondent claim that he could not be convinced by any hypothesis, including one about the nature of consciousness, until he saw a computer simulation of it or a model in the form of an artificial neural network (see Appendix A). That is a mistake. However desirable it may be to test hypotheses by computer simulations, it is short-sighted to shut out those that do not lend themselves to this approach, or for which it is exceedingly difficult. Before a computer simulation can test a hypothesis it needs to be formalized. That is to say, the hypothesis needs to be formulated in terms of purely symbolic expressions, including the formal relationships asserted for them. For example, a hypothesis that attributes certain learning changes in the brain to modifications in the strengths of a known set of n synapses, might be formalized as the transformation of an n-dimensional vector, whose components consist of numerical weights attached to the synapses concerned. You will meet other examples in the approach of David Marr, which I shall outline below. An alternative way of testing hypotheses relating to brain functions is to model this function in artificial neural networks.

Now, if we look at the four key propositions on which our model of the primary consciousness rests, only the first, Proposition 1, would demand a computer simulation, since the second, Proposition 2, merely relates to capacity limitations, while Propositions 3 and 4 merely assert identities. But if you look at what the IGR comprises by way of complex representations relating to the inner as well as the outer world, it hardly seems feasible to formalize all of this in the manner required by a computer simulation without running the risk of gross distortions that would deprive us of any real benefit. And the difficulty of modelling the whole IGR in artificial neural networks seems equally insuperable. Just modelling the RWM in terms of acquired what-leads-to-what expectancies, and to a degree that is sufficiently realistic to act as a test of our hypotheses, would seem to lie beyond the realm of practical possibilities. We are not dealing here with just a few acts and their expected consequences, but with an enormous range of possible acts forming a complex hierarchy. At the lowest level of this hierarchy we have such simple acts as eye movements and what they tell us about spatial relations in the visual scene. At the level above we have movements of head and body, and what their effects on the visual inputs tell us about spatial relations in the real 3D world. Higher up – and in this direction there is virtually no limit – we have representations of the properties of objects in terms of the experienced consequences of manipulating them in one way or another.

This is not a happy conclusion from the standpoint of those who are dreaming of – or even insisting on – computational simulations of all the brain's cognitive functions – which would in our model include the RWM and IGR. But if a deeper insight into the nature of consciousness is our goal, these facts can be no excuse for ignoring or even rejecting the hypotheses on which this book's explanation of consciousness rests.

Creating hypotheses: the computational approach of David Marr

The computational method of creating hypotheses, as I have said, can be a valuable tool. But we must remain aware of its limitations. Its first step is to find a formal definition of the particular task that some brain mechanism is assumed to perform. This is followed by a search for computational algorithms that could solve the task, and finally by a search for constellations of neurons whose activity might conform to those algorithms. This procedure was pioneered in the theory of vision published by Marr in 1982. Briefly, the tasks to which Marr applied this approach concerned the detection by the brain of specific features in the visual inputs, such as blobs, edges, angles and orientations. And he suggested particular constellations of neurons in the brain's visual pathways as possible 'feature detectors' of this kind.

According to Marr (1982), the business of the visual system is to make explicit the information contained implicitly in the optical inputs, and the problem is to find algorithms that will do so. The image on the retina records merely the different intensity values at each point. Edges, boundaries, contours, surfaces and shapes are *implicit* in this image. These features are made *explicit* if there are neurons or constellations of neurons that respond selectively to the features in question. As a first step, Marr here looked for constellations that would make the intensity changes themselves explicit by responding selectively to them.[2]

He then repeats this approach for more sophisticated 'primitives', such as discontinuities, blobs, edges, terminations, segments and boundaries. Jointly these 'descriptions' formed what he called the 'primal sketch' of a perceived scene. By adding descriptions of surface orientation, depth and discontinuities, he arrives at his '2½D sketch'. This is not fully 3D because it still relates only to the image on the retina and changes every time you move your eyes. And depth is given only half a dimension because, as distinct from left and right, its spatial nature is not represented. It is what is sometimes called a 'flat-form' view of the objects of the external world. Moreover, that flat-form view will differ according to the angle at which an object is seen. To arrive at the 3D representation of an object, Marr asserts, you need a reference frame that is aligned on the object and representations of its parts relative to the object as a whole. Take a chair, for example. To recognize this as a distinctive piece of furniture, you need to have already stored in memory the set of general features that qualify an object as a chair. When you look at a chair the brain will automatically pass from the resulting 2½-D sketch to a 3D representation by aligning this reference frame on the object and then matching the result to the stored memory.

Marr's type of theory should not be ignored. Ours is a top-down approach to sensory perception, whereas Marr's is a bottom-up approach. And, as a matter of principle, neither should ignore the other. There is no denying that constellations of neurons are in principle capable of carrying out certain mathematical computations. Striking examples of hard-wired neural connections of this kind have been found in a number of primitive animals whose neural connections and activities can be more readily explored. Neurons in the brain of the leech, for example, appear to be able to calculate certain trigonometric functions as an aid in locating the origin of external stimuli.

However, the question of algorithms is not the main issue here. A major weakness of Marr's feature detectors is that they do not map the structure of the represented features. By definition, therefore, they are merely *symbolic* representations of the features concerned. This raises the problem of the *meaning* of those symbols and how that meaning is represented in the brain – for example the physical nature of spatial relationships, such as their causal properties and behavioural relevance. Typical examples would be the causal properties that determine what eye movements will be needed to change fixation from one object in the visual field to another, and what movement my arm has to make when I am reaching for an object perceived nearby. Marr's collection of feature detectors reflects nothing of this kind.

Some, Douglas Hofstadter among them, argue that the meaning of symbolic representations can be represented by 'meta-symbols' and 'meta-meta-symbols', and so on (Hofstadter, 1989). Meaning thus comes to be based on hierarchical structures and relationships between symbols representing features at various levels. This, surely, does not solve the problem of meaning I have outlined above, the meaning that is based on behavioural relevance. In this and Marr's system the whole dynamism of sensory perception is lost. There is no room in either system for perceptual representations based on active exploration and hence on movement – such as occurs, for example, in the exploration of shapes through tracking their contours with the eyes, or through registering the eye movements required to jump from salient subfeature to salient subfeature. The adaptiveness of our visual system is also lost. As I shall illustrate in Chapter 7, when the optical system is changed – for example by having prisms fitted to the eyes that invert the image – the brain will eventually adapt, but only by evaluating the now changed visual experiences that result from moving eyes, head or body.

In short, when the brain interprets the visual inputs in the light of past experience and other prior knowledge, including its interpretation of the information derived from the experienced consequences of moving eyes, head or body, it does much more than just process static snapshots of the world as Marr assumed. We shall look at more details of this in Chapter 7.

Feature detectors were not a new concept. As early as 1962 Hubel and Wiesel had caused a sensation when they demonstrated in the visual cortex of the cat the existence of cell groups that showed a maximal response to basic features in optical displays, such as orientated line segments, stopped bars, angles and movement. This was soon followed by similar observations in the monkey and formed the beginning of a field of empirical research that has ever since continued to expand.[3] Unfortunately, these observations did not quite fit Marr's theory. Indeed, he had to concede that only a few neurophysiological correlates had so far been found for his selection of primitives. However, that is beside the point, because the real 'feature detectors' discovered by Hubel and Wiesel are also no more than symbolic representations of the features concerned. They, too, do not map the structure of the features they represent, let alone the causal nature of the spatial relationships involved.

The computational school of thought

Since Marr's publication, his approach has become a powerful movement – leading in some circles even to the dogmatic rejection of all alternative approaches (Boden, 1988). Its main effect has been to trigger a massive search for computational algorithms that could serve some cognitive function, now widely known as computational neuroscience. Much of this work illustrates the contrast between the computational approach and the functional one we have followed. It often shows the same weakness as Marr's approach, for example in treating vision as an analysis of snapshots so that the vital role of motor information in the processes of visual perception is lost, as is the fact that the key problems solved by the brain in cognition and consciousness are *representational*, not algorithmic and computational. Nor are these approaches inherently able to deal with subjective experience and the qualia, or the difference between conscious and unconscious brain events. And to the extent to which they fail to deal with the dynamics of the brain's interactions with the world, they tend to squeeze out the very consideration of functional relationships. In this respect, I concur with John Searle (1992) when he condemns the computational models of the mind as being 'profoundly anti-biological' (p. 190). None of this, of course, detracts from the value of these approaches as exercises in AI.

There has always been a tendency to interpret the brain in terms of the latest technologies. Descartes saw the brain – like the body itself – as a hydraulically operating machine. In the twentieth century it was at one time compared with a telephone exchange; then it became a cybernetic machine; then memory came to be compared with the distributed record of images in a hologram, and now the brain is seen as a computer. No such analogies will work. The brain is a singular product of a phylogenetic and ontogenetic evolution that has concentrated on its power to interpret sensory data in the interest of reliable representations of the situations facing the organism at any point in time. For similar reasons it is a mistake to cling to the distinction between computer software and hardware when dealing with the brain. The patterns of the billions of neural excitations that flood through the brain at every moment, often in parallel processes, bear no fruitful resemblance to the system of instructions that form the backbone of computer software.

The chief danger of the computational approach is that one ties oneself to a purely computational lexicon of basic concepts, and in the matter of the brain's cognitive functions this fails to offer an adequate choice of concepts to capture the essence of such important functions as consciousness. Let me take as an example Steven Pinker's widely read book, *How the Mind Works* (1997). The title intrigued me because I do not believe that one can explain how the mind works without explaining consciousness. Although the author, a psycholinguist at MIT, believes that the problem of consciousness may for ever elude science, he does seem to realize its importance and so he has a shot at seeing how far he can get. And this attempt is a good illustration of the severe problems encountered by anyone whose toolkit is limited to computational concepts.

Pinker's first problem is what to understand by consciousness. He refers us here to what he takes to be the common meaning of the word, namely 'to be alive, awake and aware' (p. 134). But this is falling into a trap I have mentioned before. Since *awake* and *aware* imply consciousness, his statement is a tautology. And, of course, in sleep we are still alive. Second, the author has to confess that this approach has nothing to say about sentience, i.e. about subjective experience and the qualia. In other words, the approach fails on what many people regard as the very heart of the problem of consciousness. Accordingly, he also misses out on what we have defined as self-reference (Chapter 3), and he can see self-awareness only from a third-person standpoint as what I have called self-concepts. He describes it as 'an entry about oneself alongside one's database about other people' (p. 134). Third, since all mental events are depicted by him as symbol systems engaged in the processing of the information stored in data banks, all he is able to say about beliefs is that they are '*information, incarnated as configuration of symbols*' (p. 25, his emphasis). He has nothing to say about the all-important brain functions that deal with the *meaning* of the symbols the brain may be processing. Fourth, although he has interesting things to say about specialized modules that solve well-defined tasks like shape-from-shading, he does not explain how the outputs of the modules are integrated to yield unified and conscious visual perceptions – an important issue in view of cases, such as sleepwalking, where their outputs are fully effective in the absence of consciousness, and also in view of the fact that what we normally mean by *seeing* is the *conscious* perception of things.

The division between conscious and unconscious processes in the brain is described by Pinker as a division between 'two pools' in the 'mass of information processing in the nervous system' (p. 135). The conscious one includes the products of vision and the contents of short-term memory. It can be accessed by the system's underlying verbal reports, rational thought and decision making. The unconscious 'pool' is given a description in similar terms and this is followed by some discussion of their mutual relationships. There is not much to be gainsaid here, but it remains a barren description, because it tells us nothing about the functional basis of this division. As in all computational approaches, the functional properties and architecture of these vital brain processes lie beyond the adopted universe of discourse.

Human memory functions, too, are unlike those of computers and are beyond the grasp of purely computational concepts. Note, in particular, that when we talk about memory recall in the human case we mean more than just access to stored experiences: we mean re-entry of those experiences into the contents of consciousness. Stored experiences can also enter *unconscious* processes. And we do not call that memory recall.

The notion of information processing that is the bedrock of computational approaches can be a useful one in all sorts of contexts. But to acquire real explanatory power 'information' needs to be defined accurately, as it is, for example, in the definition used in modern information theory. There it is expressed in formulae that parallel the entropy formulae of thermodynamics, although that would be of little use in the discussion of the brain's functional architecture. Instead, Pinker defines information as 'a correlation between two things that is produced by a lawful process' (p. 65). Although information clearly *implies* this, it is a bit risky to offer it as a definition. There are untold instances of such correlations in the physical world in which it would be questionable to call it information. The rotation of the two wheels while I am riding my bicycle, for example, satisfies his definition. Note also that this definition says nothing about the direction of information flow: it would be as legitimate to say that the visual information flows *down* the optic nerve as to say that it flows *up* that nerve.

However, I humbly have to confess here that I can offer no satisfactory alternative. My main difficulty is that the information processing which occurs, for example, in visual perception, is not the kind of serial process that comes to mind when one meets the phrase. Unlike the processing of cheese, it does not proceed in a linear sequence of operations. It is widely dispersed throughout the brain in both sequential and parallel stages. And at each of these stages there are likely to be reciprocal connections back to the regions from which that stage was supplied. In addition we have the integrating functions performed by subcortical structures, notably the thalamus. It seems to me that at each such dispersed division of labour, complicated by feedback, the meaning of 'information' becomes less and less clear.

The mistaken perception of brain functions as purely formal processes can also have repercussions in the public mind. In a symposium edited by Blakemore and Greenfield (1987) Searle cites from the *New York Times* a statement attributed to Freeman Dyson to the effect that since we now know that mental processes such as consciousness are purely formal processes, there is an evolutionary advantage to having such processes go on in silicon chips and wires, because that kind of stuff is better able to survive in a universe that is cooling off than organisms such as us made out of messy biological machinery!

Notes

1 'Top-level', of course, is not here to be understood in an anatomical sense. Although the cerebral cortex is bound to be heavily involved in the representations which the IGR encompasses, it should never be thought of as operating in isolation of the subcortical structures.

2 For readers interested in the mathematical side, this is a good illustration. Marr argues that a graph of an intensity change along some given axis would show a ramp at that particular point. The first derivative of this graph would show a positive or negative spike and the second derivative a positive spike followed by a negative one (or vice versa), hence a *zero-crossing*. Marr then suggests that a certain class of specially connected neurons in the retina act as filters producing second derivatives and these in turn would produce neurons driven by zero-crossings. Their output would thus make explicit the intensity change at the respective location.

3 For a detailed account, see Zeki (1993).

5

QUESTIONS AND ANSWERS

5.1. Some fundamental questions that now have an answer

Let me pause for a moment and review some of the fundamental questions that are answered by our four main propositions, now that we have seen how they cover the three main facets of consciousness – awareness of the surrounding world, of the self as an entity, and of one's thoughts and feelings – and how they cover them not only as objective brain functions, but also as subjective experience. I shall put the questions in the form in which I have met them at one occasion or another.

- What does consciousness *do*? In particular, why do we have this *inner* life of awareness and qualia, inaccessible to anyone else, but of such importance to each one of us? What does it add that makes living organisms more effective in getting on with their life? If it adds nothing, why should it have evolved? Are our subjective experiences of sights, colours, sounds and taste just subjective epiphenomena with no real significance in the 'objective world'?

   These questions were answered by identifying the primary consciousness with the IGR (our Proposition 3) and the qualia with those components of the total effect an event has on the organism that are embraced by the IGR, hence enter consciousness (our Proposition 4). The IGR renders the organism more effective because it embraces representations of the total situation facing the organism both externally and internally. Incorporating the qualia clearly adds to the latter and thus to the range of factors the brain can take into account in the production of appropriate responses.

- Might not consciousness be just a redundant by-product of evolution?

   NO. The biological usefulness of the IGR makes it more than a redundant by-product of evolution.

- Could not every so-called conscious function of the brain be carried out just as well without consciousness? In other words, could not the same neural events have occurred just as they do, and influence our behaviour just as they do, without anyone ever having consciousness? Might not *experience*, therefore, be just something *additional* to the brain's performance of particular functions?

NO. Since, according to our model, the IGR *is* consciousness, the same neural events could not have occurred without consciousness being established.

• If consciousness has a role, this must affect behaviour. What are its effects?

The effects comprise all actions commonly described as 'willed' or 'voluntary' actions, because these are by definition actions based on conscious decisions. According to our model they are thus actions determined by the IGR. I have explained that I prefer 'willed' to 'voluntary' because conscious decisions made while a gun is being pointed at one's head are sometimes described as involuntary.

• What general conditions must a brain event satisfy to become a conscious experience?

It must become part of the IGR.

• Conversely, what is it about a state of the brain that makes it a mental event?

If you follow the recommended practice of restricting 'mental' to *conscious* events, then my answer is that they are states of the brain which are embraced by the IGR. If, on the other hand, you use 'mental' in a wider sense so that subliminal events can be called mental if they have a decisive influence over conscious mental events, such as Freud's 'unconscious wishes', then this notion should be strictly confined to events that satisfy one or other of the categories I have listed in Section 4.6, bar their inclusion in the IGR. Otherwise there is no limit to the brain events that could be called mental, and the term becomes virtually meaningless.

• Do functional explanations create special problems?

NO. See Section 4.9.

• Has a split-brain patient a split consciousness?

NO. Because consciousness *is* the IGR, and the IGR represents the current state of the organism. It has a unity that resides in the unity of that organism. This unity is not affected by any distortions, gaps or contradictions that a split brain may cause in the representations that are part of the IGR [5.5].

- Do animals have consciousness? And, if so, how could this be shown?

  In our model they have consciousness if they have an IGR that comprises the three categories of representations that we have accepted as the three main facets of consciousness. And this can be a matter of degree. The biggest problem is to demonstrate self-awareness as defined in Chapter 3. We shall look at this in Section 5.10.

- Could we eventually develop computers that have consciousness?

  In principle, the conditions computers would have to satisfy to be credited with consciousness are the same as for animals, but the problems faced in bringing this about are unique (see Sections 4.11 and 5.11).

- Is consciousness truly serial?

  The common answer is that it certainly seems to be serial. We experience one thing after another and talk of a 'stream of consciousness'. It is serial in our model by definition, since the IGR, hence the primary consciousness, functions as a representation of the *now*. It is the psychological *present*. This does not rule out particular contents of the IGR having continuity and thoughts extending over finite periods of time. Nor is it affected by the fact that some of the constituent processes may take time – from 50 to 250 ms according to Blumenthal (1977). Remember in this connection the subjective timing discussed earlier [2.5].

- How free is our will?

  The freedom of our will is just the freedom to do as we will, that is to say, the unimpeded capacity to perform actions that are determined by states of the brain that I have defined as *volitions* [4.7]. These, in turn, were defined as a person's commitment to an *intention*, the latter being based on states of the brain defined as *desires*.

- How can the bits of hardware that make up our brain have emotions?

  The emotions are a particular category of feelings, and feelings are a particular category of components of the IGR [4.6]. They are had by the *person* whose IGR it is. They are not had by the brain's hardware.

- Since reality is represented in our brains solely in terms of the model it has formed of it, can we ever know what physical reality is *really* like?

  The question is meaningless, because an answer to the question of what physical reality is *really* like could only be another model of that reality.

- Lastly, is brain research actually justified in the assumption that every mental event, including the 'raw feel' of conscious experience, is also a brain event that patient research could eventually identify as arising from particular neural networks and their activities? If so, in what brain processes does consciousness reside and where are they located in the brain?

An answer to the two parts of this question is given in Sections 5.12 and 9.8 respectively.

The question of physical reality was also raised by a correspondent who clearly belonged to the school of philosophical idealism. He objected that in discussing the brain's internal representations of external objects, I was taking the objects for granted. But, he wrote, are not the objects themselves the creation of the conscious mind? I replied that the objects themselves are not the creation of our minds; only our internal representations of the external realities are such creations. The realities themselves are the things that determine the consequences of our actions, and they are not of the brain's creation. In my reply I also asked whether he would raise the same issue if he saw a biological paper discussing the cognitive maps that animals can form of their surroundings. And if not then, why raise them when I discuss the same kind of thing in humans? I have met similar philosophical idealism in a paper by Seager (1995), who claims that consciousness is an absolutely fundamental feature of the world.

The nature of emotions has been a matter of dispute throughout the history of psychology, but most disputes have centred on the source of the emotions. Arguments have turned on such questions as the relative role of visceral arousal and cognition in the genesis of emotions; and whether crying should be considered part of the emotional experience of grieving. Our model of consciousness favours the view that emotions arise from significant discrepancies between the experienced state of the world and the subject's expectations of that state. These may be either positive (happy surprises giving joy), or negative (bitter disappointments causing sorrow). In either case they cause a state of arousal that tends to initiate both a reorientation to the world and relief through outward expressions of surprise, joy or sorrow. The qualitative dimensions of experienced emotions, of course, are covered by our treatment of the qualia.

In all of this we have to keep in mind the distinction between the first-person and third-person perspective. After eight years in which a young victim of the Hillsborough stadium disaster had remained in a coma, the boy again regained consciousness. As one newspaper reported: 'he was once again aware of his environment and could communicate with his parents'. What he was eventually able to communicate or still tried to communicate, possibly in reply to his parents' anxious questions, was not reported – no doubt how he felt, possibly things he wanted to know, where he was, or some struggling recollections. It could have been anything that makes up the riches of our experienced inner life. From the third-person perspective of the nurses and parents, his brain recovered a set of objective operating powers that manifested themselves in the boy's gradually returning responses and display of awareness. For the boy, it was a return to life.

5.2. The freedom of the will (2)

In the last chapter I gave a brief account of my position on the question of the freedom of the will [4.7]. Let me now expand this, beginning with the words in which I stated the problem in an earlier publication (Sommerhoff, 1990, p. 224).

> On the one hand, the brain is a physical entity composed of atoms, molecules, etc. And from the standpoint of science it must be assumed that all processes and events that happen within the brain are governed by the laws of physics and biochemistry. Hence, whatever our behaviour may turn out to be, we must assume that it is the product of activities in the brain that have run their course in strict conformity to these laws.
>
> On the other hand, in everyday life we also take our behaviour to be governed by our mind; and we generally tend to think of this entity as a *free* agent. We feel that our intentional activities are the result of freely made choices, that we can act as we please. Hence one may feel driven to ask: *how is it that our brains, which are made of atoms and molecules obeying the laws of nature, yet support thinking, which seems not to be governed by those laws?* Many people regard this problem as central to the problem posed by the human mind.
>
> No doubt this apparent antithesis between the notion of causal determinism and the notion of a free will has contributed significantly to the feeling that sensations, thoughts, fantasies, memories, volitions, etc., are in some sense non-physical attributes of the people to whose mental life they belong.

In Section 4.7, and as repeated above, I have given the notion of a 'free will' a definite meaning which relates it clearly to my account of the nature of consciousness: the freedom of the will means the unimpeded ability to act in accordance with our volitions, i.e. in accordance with our commitment to a consciously conceived goal. I am aware that there will be readers whom this does not satisfy and who feel that it fails to resolve the apparent antithesis between freedom of the will and physical determinism. It still leaves the will predetermined by physical causes. Now, no one is likely to claim that the will is uncaused. As John Stuart Mill has pointed out, the notion of free will is impossible if it supposes volitions to originate without a cause. In psychological terms, the will to act in some particular way is generally caused by antecedent mental events of one kind or another: thoughts, feelings, etc. The objection arises from the claim that these antecedent mental events have neural correlates whose activities are governed by the laws of physics and biochemistry. But this is irrelevant. The point is that these determinist neural activities contingently produce the states of the brain we have defined as *volitions* and cause the unimpeded production of actions determined by these volitions. And it is the latter that we really mean by the freedom of the will.

This answer to the question of the free will is given from a third-person standpoint. However, it is also worth looking a little closer at the first-person standpoint, at our introspectively derived sense that we are free in our thoughts and actions. Typically, when you ponder a decision, you will contemplate the various alternative actions that are open to you, and weigh their consequences before making up your mind. And all along you will feel that you could have turned your thoughts to different aspects of the matter and finally have chosen otherwise. This is the freedom of your thoughts and choices as it will appear to you introspectively. But, in what is this inner sense of freedom really rooted? Surely only in your awareness of yourself as the author of those thoughts and as the agent of those actions. In other words, we are dealing here merely with yet another manifestation of the self-reference discussed in Chapter 3, in this case with the fact that 'whatever I consciously experience is experienced in a special way as belonging to myself' – to repeat William James' way of putting it. This feature of conscious experience is fully covered by our model [3.1].

5.3. Molyneux's question: when sight is restored to the blind

In the late seventeenth century, William Molyneux wrote to the philosopher John Locke wondering whether a man born blind who had learnt by touch to distinguish between a cube and a sphere made of the same metal, would be able to identify by sight alone those two objects if his sight were suddenly restored. In his *Essays concerning Human Understanding* (1690) Locke answered in the negative. Ever since, the question has exercised the minds of both philosophers and scientists from time to time.[1]

The first empirical investigation was conducted in 1728 by William Cheselden, an ophthalmic surgeon who gave sight to a boy of 13 or 14 by removing highly opaque cataracts. The boy was not asked to distinguish by sight a cube from a sphere, but a dog from a cat – on which test he failed. Since eyes can take a long time to settle down after a cataract, clearer evidence comes from cases in which sight is restored by corneal grafts and a good retinal image then becomes instantly available. A case of this nature, a man of 52 who underwent this operation, is reported by Gregory and Wallace (1963). It is summarized in Gregory (1987). I shall return to it in a moment.

What should our analysis lead us to expect in the case of that boy? Now, there is strong evidence to suggest that perception and recall of a shape or figure are coded in terms of the movements required to follow its contours or jump from one salient subfeature to another. I shall return to this point in Chapter 7. In a blind person's exploration of a shape by touch, or **haptic** exploration, as it is called, the defining features of that shape will come to be represented in the RWM in terms of what the hand or fingers encountered in the course of what movements. One might, therefore, expect that, on regaining sight, it would not be too difficult for the brain to learn to transfer from exploratory movements by the hand or fingers to the movement of the eyes when they are exploring the contours of a shape. And this could work well when distinguishing a cube from a sphere. However, blind persons do not normally distinguish a dog from a cat by a haptic exploration of their shape. There are better features to go by, such as the feel of their snout or fur and litheness of their body. It is not surprising, therefore, that the boy failed on the dog and the cat.

That such a transfer from haptic exploration to optical exploration actually occurs is shown by the patient reported by Gregory. He could instantly recognize by sight the hands on his pocket watch, having had years of experience feeling them. Again, he had learnt to recognize upper-case letters inscribed in solid wooden plates, which make street names, brass plates and the like easier to identify. Hence he had no difficulty recognizing such upper-case letters by sight. The eye movements that occurred in tracing their shape were easy to collate with the corresponding haptic movements. In contrast, it took him months to learn the recognition of lower-case letters. On the same grounds, it was only to be expected that both the boy and the man were initially at a total loss as to how to make sense of paintings and portraits – there being no haptic movement at all available for transfer. Similarly, the man proved to have difficulties with shadows. Walking down steps on a sunny day he could step on a shadow and fall. Mirrors, of course, were just miraculous machines for him, and they always remained so.

In cases where no ready transfer is possible and the patient can only be told what things are, the sight of those things will enter the brain rather in the manner of symbols for the object concerned – symbols whose meaning he just has to learn. No wonder the boy who owed his sight to Cheseldon's operation complained that at first he learnt to know and then again forgot a thousand things a day.

Sometimes a transfer has to be triggered. In a case I heard reported in a broadcast, a blind man had taught himself to play the piano. After an operation restored his sight, he had to touch the piano before these skills were restored to him.

Vision, as I have said, is the conscious fraction of the contribution the eyes currently make to the brain's internal representation of the sur-rounding world. I have also pointed out the importance of movement in these processes – a topic to which I shall return in Chapter 7. Unfortunately, neither fact is always sufficiently appreciated. This causes plausible lines of explanation to be ignored in approaches not only to Molyneux's question but also to the general question of the brain's internal representations of spatial relations.

5.4. Dreaming

Seen in a biological perspective, sleep is a cyclic phase in the life of the organism during which its dynamic interactions with the surrounding world are temporarily suspended in the interest of internal adjustments and restorative processes of one kind or another, including the production of new proteins. During sleep the brain passes periodically from the so-called 'slow wave' sleep to the 'rapid eye movement' sleep or 'REM'. It is during this phase of rapid eye movements that dreams occur. It is also a phase marked by a consolidation of learning and memory. During both phases there is an interaction between the hippocampus, medial thalamus and the cerebral cortex. During the slow-wave sleep the hippocampus seems to be doing all the talking while during the REM the cortex talks back. As the London psychiatrist Peter Fenwick once put it in a lecture: you can imagine the cortex saying in reply to a fact reported by the hippocampus: 'this reminds me of . . .'. Sleep is not a mere recuperation of the brain, like stretching your legs after a hard day's work. It is a very active and complex phase, and the effects of sleep deprivation on intellectual performance and concentration are well known.

The hippocampus is deeply implicated in the formation of long-term memory, and it seems that memory here comes to be reinforced by the play of associations and information flowing back and forth. Studies in rats have shown that the REM period is extended when sleep follows a period of learning new territories. The hippocampus of rats also contains cells sensitive to 'place', that is to say, to the rat's location in a familiar environment [6.5]. When rats sleep, these cells can be shown to be firing again. But it is idle to speculate whether or what the rat is dreaming here.

Dreams can be extremely vivid and that forces me to address the question of whether in the so-called *lucid* dreams the dreamer can be said to be conscious. Since the RWM is useless during the period when the organism's dynamic interactions with the surrounding world are temporarily suspended, we would expect the RWM to be fully suspended, including both its conscious and unconscious components. However, at the unconscious level a kind of body schema still seems to remain operative and occasionally also much larger chunks of the unconscious RWM, as shown in sleepwalking [2.4]. Whereas we have clearly distinguished this from a state of consciousness, in some dreams the dreamers are aware that they are dreaming and may, up to a point, even feel that they are in charge of the script. It is tempting to think of this as fully fledged self-awareness and to that extent one might be tempted to call this consciousness. Now, it seems to me that whether we should or should not call this consciousness is ultimately a matter of convention. However, I would oppose a convention that includes lucid dreams in its notion of consciousness. It seems to me undesirable to speak of consciousness when there is no full awareness of the surrounding world, because it glosses over the crucial biological importance of the difference between sleep (when awareness of the surrounding world is suspended) and wakefulness (when it is again restored). Both in practice and from a biological standpoint, this is one of the most important contrasts that occurs in our daily life. Our views can get very confused if we adopt a language convention that glosses over this fact.

5.5. The split brain and the unity of consciousness

Among the many lessons learnt about the brain from the effect of lesions of various kinds, some of the most interesting have come from cases in which the corpus callosum was cut – that bundle of 800 million nerve fibres that link corresponding points in the two cortical hemispheres, supplemented by a small fibre tract called the anterior commissure. Since the mid-1940s the operation has been performed on a number of human patients in severe cases of epilepsy in the hope of stopping the explosive neural discharges reverberating between the hemispheres. As in frontal leucotomy, this drastic intervention has been superseded by improved methods of medication. Since the overt effects of the operation on the subject's behaviour and reasoning powers appeared to be minimal, systematic investigation of the effects had to await the methodical approaches pioneered by Roger Sperry and his colleagues at the California Institute of Technology (Sperry, 1987). The topic is of interest in this chapter because of the question of whether this 'split brain' also means a split consciousness.

Each hemisphere receives information from, and controls, the opposite side of the body. Thus the right half of the field of vision of *both* eyes is processed by the left hemisphere and the left half by the right hemisphere. After the operation, both hemispheres still retain reciprocal relationships via the lower brain regions, but this lower level can only partly compensate for the losses sustained.

That awareness is no longer whole was demonstrated by tests in which the two hemispheres were separately engaged. For example, when human subjects were asked to identify an out-of-sight object by touch with, say, the right hand, they could not then match it to the same kind of object when explored out of sight by the left hand. Similarly, when a picture was flashed into the right half of the visual field, the patients could not afterwards compare it with pictures flashed into the left visual field. Patients could not write down with the right hand what had been presented to them to the left of their eyes' point of fixation. A monkey could learn one response to an object presented to the right half of the visual field, alongside a conflicting response to the same object when presented to the left half.

A notable discovery was the inability of the right hemisphere to express itself in speech. It could comprehend speech to the extent of understanding an instruction to retrieve by hand a common object whose name was projected to the right cortex only. But it could not put words to an experience or perform more than the simplest calculations. When stimuli were given to the left cortex, the patients could readily describe the experience. But when they were given to the right cortex, the request to describe them frequently met with no response at all, or merely with some confabulation. Since those experiments were done, modern brain imaging has suggested that the left hemisphere deals with word production and grammar, while the right is engaged in intonation and emphasis. The right hemisphere also seems to have a superior sense of space, a broader view of objects or figures, hence a better capacity to explore complex objects by hand or eye. In addition it showed a superior recognition of emotions (hence, perhaps, its greater engagement in intonation and emphasis). However, none of these divisions have ever proved to be entirely clear-cut. The ways in which the two hemispheres supplement each other are not always transparent.

The division of the brain also has more penetrating effects. Gazzaniga and co-workers have shown that the two separate hemispheres could apply incompatible criteria to the evaluation of a situation and show different preferences (Gazzaniga & LeDoux,1978). In the control of motor behaviour they could follow disparate programmes. One patient could even add two numbers on the right while at the same time subtracting two numbers on the left. However, the two hemispheres could also be made to co-operate. This was shown in an experiment in which the subject had to drive a plotting pen around a course, with the left hand controlling motion in one direction and the right hand in the other.

What is one to make of all this in relation to the effect on the unity of the subject's consciousness? It is here that controversies begin. Some authors have used such phrases as the patient being 'split into two selves', having a 'divided mind', a 'double consciousness' or 'two wills'. Others have talked about the right hemisphere 'lacking consciousness', or about the left hemisphere being human, but the right one no more than an automaton.

In our model, the primary consciousness is identified with the IGR and the IGR consists of an internal representation of the current state of the organism. Hence the primary consciousness has a functional unity which resides in the unity of the organism whose current state it represents. Although the IGR may suffer all sorts of defects and its representations in the left hemisphere may be at odds with those in the right hemisphere, they still function as representations of the current state of the whole organism. And that organism has remained a single physical entity. Moreover, the unity of the organism remains fully represented by the body schema, and the body schema of split-brain patients is not affected by the split-brain operation. It is duplicated in the hemispheres, and the corresponding sensory and motor functions are also cross-integrated at subcortical levels [2.1]. Body co-ordination, too, remains unimpaired. On these grounds, therefore, I would deny that the split-brain operation destroys the unity of consciousness. It is also worth noting that throughout all this experimentation no sign was found of the recognition by one 'half' of the brain of the other 'half' as a separate person.

5.6. The thought experiment of a spectrum inversion

A favourite thought experiment of philosophers opposed to a functionalist theory of the mind–brain relation, is that of a hypothetical spectrum inversion. It was first suggested by Locke. Suppose, they say, that a section of the population had a red/green inversion in the sense that through some anomaly they had the connections from their red and green retinal detectors inverted in the brain. The red detectors now fed the neural pathways normally fed by the green detectors and vice versa. No doubt these people would learn to use the words 'red' and 'green' in the same way as the rest of us: 'green' for grass and 'red' for blood. And they would learn the same behavioural discriminations as well: stopping at red traffic lights and passing through the green ones. Yet, the argument runs, the experiences they call 'seeing red' or 'seeing green' would be quite different from those that the rest of us have. This is then taken as proof that any account of experiences merely in terms of causal and functional relations leaves out the qualia, the subjective quality or 'raw feel' of an experience.

This is a fallacy. The fourth of the four main propositions that defined our model of the primary consciousness explicitly covers the qualia. It interprets them as the conscious components of the total effect an experience has on the organism, i.e. the components that enter the IGR. And this account of the qualia also shows that it is quite meaningless to talk about the subjective quality or 'raw feel' of some experience being the same in two different individuals or even in the same individual at two different points in time. As I have explained, even for the single individual there is, strictly speaking, no such thing as experiencing equal qualia at different points in time. All one can say is that a particular sensation was to him or her *like* a pinprick both at time t_1 and t_2. Similarly, one cannot strictly speaking say of two different individuals that they had identical sensations, identical qualia. All one can say is that for individual A the colour of the rose was *like* that of blood only much more agreeable, and so it was for individual B. Or that the toothache felt by C was as agonizing as a similar experience appeared to be for D. And I must remind you here of the warning I gave in Chapter 4 that one has to be aware of precisely what is meant by asking 'what it is like' to have this or that experience, or what an experience 'feels like'. The meaning of these questions is determined by the kind of answer they can expect and, as indicated by the word 'like', these questions can expect only one kind of answer, namely a *comparison* with other experiences. And these comparisons are not affected by that hypothetical inversion of the retina's neural connections.

5.7. Zombies

I have never warmed to thought experiments as one of the philosopher's favourite tools. It is, of course, always interesting to examine logical possibilities, especially when they can be accommodated within the laws of nature. However, the hidden premises or preconceptions on which they often rest can deprive them of their force – as the notion of spectrum inversion has illustrated.

Zombies are another example of such thought experiments (but see Dennett, 1997). The zombies envisaged here have little in common with the living dead of Haitian voodoo lore and horror movies, who, at the bidding of voodoo priests, shuffle around with expressionless eyes like some remotely controlled robot in human guise. The philosophers' zombies are like humans in all respects except that they are assumed to lack sentience, in other words, subjective experience and the qualia. In effect, we are asked to imagine a world just like ours except that the humans who are part of it have mental states that lack any introspective and qualitative dimension. According to our interpretation of the qualia in Proposition 4, this means lacking an IGR altogether. According to this proposition, the qualia are the conscious components of the total effect an experience has on the organism, that is to say, those components that enter the IGR. And it is obvious from our definition of the IGR that there will always be *some* such components.

This thought experiment tends to be part of the general war waged about the nature of the mind, and cited in support of the view that consciousness is inessential. Given any functional description of human cognition, the argument runs, it would still make sense to imagine beings that satisfy all the functions involved but still lack consciousness. Indeed, since they satisfy all these cognitive functions, they would be indistinguishable from normal humans and might even pass the Turing test with flying colours. I have already disposed of this argument [5.1]: an adequate functional description of human cognition would have to include the IGR and would, therefore, imply consciousness.

What, then, would humanoid creatures be like that lacked an IGR? They could still have an extensive RWM and the capacity to form imaginary representations. They could be driven by hunger, thirst or other physiological stimuli; and they could have an internal representation of the goals of their actions. They could learn to make adaptive responses through trial and error and the effects of rewards or punishment. They would feel no pain but could still acquire aversive reactions if they burnt their fingers. They could have a language and they might even learn to manipulate symbols, calculate, and draw logical inferences. But they would lack the higher levels of integration of emotion, thought and action that happen at the level of the IGR. They would lack self-awareness and introspection, hence also the ability to identify with the thoughts and feelings of others. They might even develop a psychology. However, this would be an exclusively *behaviourist* one. Self-reports could only be reports about themselves as seen from a third-person standpoint. Altogether, their private and social life would be a poor advertisement for the view that consciousness is inessential.

5.8. Reductionism

When the properties of a complex system are explained as consisting of the properties of its components and their mutual relationships or interactions, the explanation is commonly called a reductionist one. The physical and chemical sciences have been most successful in implementing this, for example explaining the heat of gases in terms of mean molecular kinetic energy, the strength of solids in terms of their crystalline structure and molecular forces, or the nature of chemical reactions in terms of the electron configuration of atoms. None of this would be worth mentioning, were it not for the fact that the term is sometimes used in a pejorative sense, implying that the explanation in question has destroyed essentials. It springs from the seemingly irresistible temptation to turn reductionist explanations into 'nothing but' statements, such as 'chairs are *nothing but* collections of atoms and molecules', or 'mental events are *nothing but* the activities of neurons'. In fact, since the phrase 'nothing but' implies that the reductionist explanation concerned substitutes a *lesser* thing for the thing it explains, the activity of the 'nothing but' brigade has made 'reductionism' almost a term of abuse – especially when aimed at any materialist theory of the mind. 'Can all our wonderful thoughts be just a firing of neurons?' they exclaim. They overlook that a full explanation of mental events in terms of the activities of neurons would not just talk about these activities as such, but also about the structure of the multiple connections between them, about the functional assemblies of neurons that are formed in this way, and about the functional architecture of the whole system in which they play a part.

Both brain research and our model view mental events as more than just a firing of neurons. They view them as complex system properties produced by the connections and interactions of those neurons and the functional architecture of the result. It might conceivably be suggested that *even that* might still make it a lesser thing, for example if the possible variety of neural patterns of activity and their interrelations failed to match the possible variety of the contents of our conscious experiences. Yet, there is not a shred of an argument to suggest that the variety of possible activity patterns in the brain's 100 billion neurons, with up to 100,000 synapses per neuron, is likely to fail in this respect – to fail in what Wittgenstein has called a matter of 'adequate logical multiplicity'.

5.9. Do human foetuses have consciousness?

Does the human foetus have consciousness? If not, at what postnatal stage does it arise? The first question can arouse strong emotions, especially in the abortion debate, while the second tends to leave people lost for a rational answer. This is largely due to a tendency to think of consciousness as an all-or-nothing property. A creature either has it or it does not. But this is a fallacy. As our model makes quite clear, consciousness is an *extensive* property: a matter of degree. That is to say, the IGR can in principle be more or less comprehensive. The representations it contains can differ from case to case in the scope and detail of what they cover in their domain. Take the awareness of the surrounding world, for example. For the foetus, the surrounding world is the womb plus the external noises that may penetrate it. In the last three months of pregnancy the foetus is able to recognize the mother's voice and also the father's. Organized responses to touch can be demonstrated after seven weeks of pregnancy. If the notion of pain is understood to be a *conscious* sensation, then, according to our model, sensations of pain arise at that stage in the development of the IGR at which it embraces the somatic or visceral stimuli concerned. Below this level, though, noxious stimuli are not without effect. They are known to harm the progressive development of the nervous system.

In contrast to other primates, the human brain undergoes its strongest development after birth, when the previously formed neural connections expand at a remarkable rate. By the time the infant has mastered the properties of its closest environment, after two years or so, the volume of its brain will be three times what it was at birth. This postnatal growth is of unique adaptive value, for it proceeds under pressure of the infant's sensory experiences, hence subject to the constraints imposed by the environment. If during those initial postnatal phases one eye is inoperative, for example, the cortical brain regions that would normally be allocated to it are invaded by those serving the other eye.

One could conceive of even a very rudimentary foetal RWM at only about 26 weeks after the beginning of gestation. For until then the state of the foetus is more like REM sleep. What about a rudimentary IGR, hence primary consciousness and feelings? I have mentioned the view that the basic structure of the body schema is laid down innately [3.1]. It is conceivable, therefore, that in the later months of gestation an internal representation of the current state of the organism builds up as the nucleus of an IGR, to which a rudimentary RWM then also comes to be added, plus some of the effects produced by the kind of simple stimuli to which the foetus can respond at the stage in question. This would amount to rudiments of what our model defines as subjective experience and the qualia.

5.10. Do animals have consciousness?

My main concern in this book is not what things can be conscious, but what consciousness is. Even so, the question of animal consciousness follows naturally. There is no problem about the RWM. Autonomous and intelligent living beings need a model of the world and how it works, including a model of their place in that world, and there are many ways of finding out to what extent the different orders of life do have such an internal model. The problem comes with the IGR. Do they also have an IGR? In view of the scope we have assigned to the IGR and the evident usefulness of having such an extensive and integrated internal representation, there is an obvious presumption in favour of an affirmative answer. But it still requires proof, and there lies the difficulty.

Now, as I said before. it is all a matter of degree. According to our model, consciousness is an *extensive* property. The IGR can in principle be more or less comprehensive, as can the RWM. A cognitive map of the surrounding world may be richly detailed, as in the adult human case, or merely a map of the spatial relations between a few salient landmarks, as it appears to be in the honey-bee. Rather than asking *whether* animals have consciousness, we should therefore ask *to what extent* different species may have consciousness, what 'skeins' of consciousness they may possess.

Unfortunately, in the case of animals there is a major barrier to determining even this. Although experiments can be designed to ascertain the presence (and roughly also the scope) of a RWM and even imaginary representations, the problem comes with self-reference and self-awareness. In humans we have the evidence of self-reports and a manifest ability to understand the mind and feelings of others. All of which we lack in the case of nonhuman animals – with the possible exception of chimps and other higher primates that have shown a certain capacity for empathy and understanding the mind of their fellows, for example in their frequently observed attempts to deceive their rivals about the place where they have found or hidden some food. On the whole, though, I cannot say more than that the biological usefulness our analysis attributes to the IGR creates at least a presumption in favour of this comprehensive representation existing also in animals *in some measure*. We would also have to take into account that their cortical capacity limitations may be considerably greater than in the human case [9.7]. Granted then that there is a presumption in favour of an IGR existing in some measure in other species, it is in my opinion best to leave it at that, rather than trying to define a minimal level at which the line should be drawn in order to achieve uniformity in the attribution of consciousness. It could only be an arbitrary line.

However, the question also has an emotional dimension that could bias our beliefs. Our personal attitudes towards the animal world tend to hinge on the extent to which we can see purposes in their actions and emotions in their behaviour, as any dog owner knows. Identifying with these purposes or emotions can produce feelings of empathy for the creatures concerned and feelings of kinship. The fact that animals share with us the general struggle of life can add to this sense of kinship, as can the fact that they have *evolved* and as such are as irreplaceable both as individuals and as a species. I am not saying that this sense of kinship is felt noticeably in each of us individually. But I believe it to be a ground for the development of cultural attitudes in which animals are respected beyond their contingent utility as domesticated beasts or pets. And much of this respect, as well as the love we can feel as individuals, hinges on the belief that they have consciousness and feelings.

5.11. Could computers or robots have consciousness?

'What does a computer do?', asks Gardner (1996, p. 65). 'It twiddles symbols – symbols that are meaningless until we attach meanings to them.' It twiddles them in blind obedience to syntactical rules provided by the software. This does not preclude the possibility of acquiring capacities in certain fields that exceed even those of their designers or any other human being, bar a genius. IBM's chess-playing computer Deeper Blue is an example. But the brain does more than twiddle symbols. The key factors here are the *meanings* of any symbolic representations it may incorporate, and those meanings have their roots in the experiences incurred by the organism as it interacts with the surrounding world, driven by its needs. Now, robots, either real or simulated on a computer, can be given such experiences up to a point in either a real or a 'virtual' environment. Even humanoid *needs* could be simulated in their software in the form of programmed preferences. But that still leaves them only at the level of the zombies I have discussed above – far short of an IGR with its built-in self-reference, hence consciousness. In fact, it is difficult to see how self-reference and self-awareness could here be simulated in a meaningful way. We saw in Section 3.2 some of the difficulties encountered by theoretical systems assumed to loop back on to themselves. There is also something else software cannot achieve. This is to copy the way in which the needs of living organisms spring from their intrinsic nature as self-maintaining, self-regulating and self-reproducing systems. Even at this basic level biology cannot be imitated.

Believers in what is known as 'strong AI', such as Minsky (1986), have contended that all brain functions, including consciousness, can be formalized by being reduced to algorithms, and might thus be replicated in computers. I have already mentioned the immense difficulties that stand here in the way of a realistic simulation even of the RWM [4.11], especially the problem of casting into an algorithmic form the crucial role of the acquired act–outcome expectancies that compose it. These form multilevel hierarchies – with act–outcome expectancies relating to just eye movements at the lowest level, expectancies relating to the experienced consequences of moving the head, body or limbs at higher levels, and those relating to complex action sequences at the very top of the hierarchy. Designers could, of course, supply the what-leads-to-what expectancies as a ready-made data base in the robot's software, to be consulted by the computer or robot as and when the situation requires it. However, that would remove one of the brain's most important capacities, namely its ability to cope with novel situations.

Igor Aleksander and his team at Imperial College, London have designed computer programs that create a virtual world and a simulated creature with the ability to recognize and categorize objects according to programmed criteria – such as recognizing yellow bananas or red apples. Moreover, their simulations can create imaginary representations of objects, e.g. the image of a blue banana. The Magnus computer demonstrated by his team can also explore that virtual world and learn from the effect which its actions have in that world according to that world's pre-programmed characteristics. Strictly within limits it can scan a range of possible actions and weight them according to the expected outcomes. And it can simulate needs, e.g. 'hunger', in the form of a state that it can enter and will then show a selective preference for certain categories of objects, like apples and bananas – the state to end when any such object has been 'grasped'.

All of this, however, amounts to no more than an ability to create the rudiments of a RWM. It remains far removed from an IGR with its built-in self-reference and the components we identified with the qualia – far short of the simulation of feelings, self-awareness and true introspection. The mere ability to recognize redness or blueness falls far short of our human awareness of some of the total impact made by seeing a red apple or yellow banana – far short of 'what it is like' to perceive these objects. Having failed to simulate an IGR as defined in our model, the program also lacks the distinction between conscious and unconscious internal events and between voluntary and involuntary movements.

The main hope for robotics lies in the artificial neural networks (see Appendix A) and the learning abilities that are being achieved here in ever more sophisticated applications, especially in the recognition of shapes and even structural relations hidden to our eyes in their inputs. Teams in advanced telecommunications research in Kyoto, Japan, are working on a system that will contain no fewer than 40 million artificial neurons, compared with the few hundred of today's well-tried systems. This is actual hardware, using a special type of computer chip called a field-programmable gate array. It is a significant number when compared with the 12 million neurons in the brain of the honey-bee, but more than 1,000 times less than the number of neurons in the human brain.

In the unlikely event of the IGR problem being solved in some future robot, the interesting question arises of our moral attitudes to such an artefact. Would we accord it human rights, for example? I believe that even if a robot were created that satisfied our criteria for consciousness, we would still be disinclined to receive it into the noble community of conscious beings. We would never accept it as our kin even as we accept animals as in some sense our kin. We would never extend to that robot all the obligations such kinship entails. We would respect even the most advanced type of such a robot only as the ingenious creation of one or more of us, but would not transfer that respect to the artefact itself. We would not accord it any rights. All the grounds I have listed for respect towards animals would be missing. We are unlikely ever to view the destruction of any robot, no matter how advanced a type, as murder, or condemn the ruthless exploitation of it as slavery. Inasmuch as the advanced robots' behaviour might be made to simulate at times a joyful, sad, fearful or other emotional behaviour, we might even empathize with them up to a point – rather as children empathized with the at one time fashionable tamagotchis. But cynics would be quick to disparage this as childish behaviour and remind us that robots are only machines. And if through some accident of design some of these robots turned out to be hostile to us in their actions, we would have no compunction about destroying them, other than regret at having to destroy a fine piece of machinery. The bits and pieces would be given no solemn funeral, but sold as spares or scrap. In short, we would value robots even of the highest calibre only as triumphs of human design and according to their usefulness – perhaps on account of what their design has provided by way of superior physical strength, low vulnerability in dangerous situations, useful learning capacities, or superior calculating powers. And I agree with Kevin Warwick at Reading University and others who regard the problem of creating conscious robots as a bit of a red herring.

5.12. Looking across to the philosophies of mind

One cannot very well advance a scientific theory of consciousness without a sideways glance at the philosophies of mind. Traditionally, their main concern has been with the logical possibilities that exist in the relation between mind and brain: for example the possibility of the mind being a single nonmaterial and wholly distinct substance acting on the brain, perhaps at some select point. Descartes, after Plato the most famous exponent of this *dualism*, believed there to be such a point. He took this to be the pineal gland, because he saw it as the uppermost unitary structure in the brain below the two hemispheres. In his classic *The Concept of Mind*, my one-time tutor, Gilbert Ryle, described the invisible entity that is here supposed to inhabit the brain as 'the Ghost in the machine' and exposed it as a confusion of logical categories (Ryle, 1949). Nevertheless, dualism has still some supporters, even among scientists. They find it hard to accept the assumption that mental events can be identified with systems of neuronal activities. Consciousness, in particular, must be more than this, they feel. 'How else', asks the biologist Sheena Meredith, 'can we explain choice, sensation or volition?' (Meredith, 1991). Somehow, they feel, it leaves out the reality of our mental life. I hope my account of consciousness will have shown that it does not.

Or might consciousness perhaps be a mere by-product of the brain, influenced by it, but unable to influence it in return? This view is known as *epiphenomenalism*. In one version of this, consciousness is described as a mere spectator in the brain (Carpenter, 1996). I find this view hard to explain except on the assumption that its supporters are exclusively wedded to the first-person perspective. Otherwise it makes no sense. For if consciousness is a mere spectator, it can have no effect on behaviour and the behaviour of a conscious person should be indistinguishable from that of an unconscious one.

Then there are other schools of thought, such as *parallelism*, according to which mind and brain are two universes of events running in parallel, and the *double aspect theory* which claims that mind compares to brain as does perceiving a cloud from the inside and perceiving it from the outside. The first, it seems to me, confuses universes of *discourse* with universes of *events*, and the second is just a pretty metaphor for the distinction between the first-person and third-person perspectives. Rather more topical is another metaphor one meets only too often, even though it does not bear close inspection: that mind compares to brain as computer software to computer hardware. The comparison of brains with computers is one that has to be approached with the greatest caution. Analogies between the instruction-giving software of purely *symbol-manipulating* systems like computers and the representational functions of *adaptive dynamic* systems like the brain exist only at dangerously superficial levels.

However, the majority of scientists engaged in brain research take little interest in the issues that occupy the philosophers of mind. They simply work on the materialist or 'physicalist' assumption that all mental events, including the contents of consciousness, are also brain events which diligent research may eventually be able to identify and explain – that there is no room in the brain for any outside agency to influence neural firings in an orderly way. For them it is simply a working assumption which no evidence has so far forced them to abandon. It is also backed by the argument that if there were any intervention in the brain by anything non-physical, the brain would no longer obey the laws of physics and chemistry. Philosophers call it the *Central State Identity Theory* or simply the *Identity Theory*. They distinguish between 'token' and 'type' identity theories, and are divided on the issue. According to the former, if two individual mental events differ, so will their neural substrates. According to the latter, merely distinct categories of neural events correspond to distinct categories of mental events. The common assumption in the neurosciences clearly belongs to the former.

Thus there will be some philosophers who find it hard to accept our Proposition 3, the proposition that identifies the primary consciousness with the IGR. But here they have to give way, for, unlike scientists, philosophers are not in the business of finding and testing explanatory hypotheses. From our biological standpoint this proposition is a hypothesis that is recommended because it successfully explains the phenomena under consideration and is supported by the empirical evidence.

They could, of course, question from a logical standpoint the legitimacy of what the scientists are here asserting. And here the opponents of the

Identity Theory sometimes fall back on 'Leibniz's Law': the argument that if two entities are identical, then all their properties must be identical. Clearly, the perception of a green object is not represented in the brain by neurons turning green! The argument overlooks the fact that what we call the 'properties' of entities are just ways of categorizing them according to one or other set of criteria. And the criteria we apply depend on the criteria we *can* apply, which, in turn, depends on our mode of access to the entities concerned. Access to distant galaxies with infrared telescopes will lead to different categorizations than access via ultraviolet telescopes. In our case there is a radical difference between the categories of mental events that we can distinguish introspectively, and the categories of neural events that neuroscientists can distinguish according to their findings. Introspectively, we can distinguish different categories of mental events, such as sensations, perceptions, thoughts, desires, imaginings and memory recall, to name just a few. This gives us one set of categorizations and concepts. Neuroscientists, in turn, have a different range of possible categorizations available from the observed behaviour of neurons and their mutual relationships, their spatial distributions and associated pathways. This gives them another set of concepts. Yet, both sets relate to the same states of the brain, differing only in our mode of access to them. The two different sets of concepts do not reflect a duality of *ontologies*. So there is nothing in all this to challenge the identity hypothesis.

Opponents of the Identity Theory have also argued that the concept of 'correlation' denotes a particular relationship between two sets of *distinct* entities. They claim that the common talk about searching for the 'neural correlates' of mental events implies that mental events and neural activities are ontologically distinct entities. This, too, is a fallacy. One can also search for a correlation between descriptions of the same realities but made from two different standpoints – in our case from the first-person and third-person standpoint – just as one can correlate the view of a landscape recorded by a satellite with that seen from the ground.

Until his recent death, the eminent neurophysiologist Sir John Eccles was perhaps the best known scientific exponent of the dualist stance – backed by the philosopher Karl Popper (Eccles & Popper, 1977). His objections to the Identity Theory were again different. The physical world, including the brain, is what Popper called a *closed* world: physical events can only be influenced by other physical events. So, Eccles asked, how can the physical *neural* events be influenced by *mental* events, such as the intention to act in this or that way? There is a simple answer to this: they are influenced by the neural events with which mental states are to be identified – whatever these may prove to be. Eccles also found it hard to conceive how so heterogeneous a structure as the human brain could produce something that had the unity of consciousness – a topic we pursued in Section 5.5. Hence he saw the mind as an entity separate from the brain, though exchanging information with it and acting on the brain

– not at the pineal gland, as Descartes supposed, but at the locations in the frontal cortex where action plans are composed.

Note

1 For the responses of Descartes and Berkeley (both negative), as well as for the case studies I cite, see Gregory (1987), pp. 94–6.

PART II

THE FABRIC OF THE UNDERLYING BRAIN PROCESSES

6

THE RWM

6.1. Evidence in support of the concept

To recapitulate: it is of evident benefit to an organism if the brain can use the information and past experience available to it to form a coherent internal representation of the world that currently confronts the organism, a running internal representation of the external *here* and *now*. I have called this the Running World Model or RWM. It is based on the brain's interpretation of its sensory inputs on the basis of past experience and other prior knowledge. It covers both the *what* and the *where*, is essentially speculative, and depends for its correction on the sensory feedback. Not all of the RWM is included in the IGR, hence not all of it is conscious. Its conscious components constitute what we experience as our *perception* of the outside world. The unconscious components – also known as *implicit cognition* – can nevertheless enter effectively in the execution of motor activity, as I have illustrated with reference to the many routine operations that we do semi-automatically. More examples were given in Section 2.2. Implicit cognition can also enter into the conscious processes of visual perception (Milner & Goodale, 1995), a point to which I shall return in the next chapter.

The threshold to consciousness, however, is not a rigid one. It is subject to competition and interference. Again, the occurrence of an unexpected event in the unconscious realm of the RWM may lift it into consciousness. Thus we may become conscious of the ticking of a clock only when unexpectedly it stops. It is interesting to note in this connection that recent research has shown the unconscious part of the RWM to have greater acuity than the conscious part inasmuch as it is not fooled by the kind of optical illusions that can fool our conscious perception of the world (*New Scientist*, 17 June 1997).

In certain extreme circumstances the RWM can assume control of behaviour in the absence of consciousness, as in sleepwalking [2.4]. Cases are also known in which a patient during an epileptic fit performed elaborate tasks, like making a chocolate drink or even preparing clinical notes, while judged by other criteria to be unconscious.

The empirical evidence overwhelmingly supports the notion of a Running World Model or RWM as I have described it. Here is some, beginning with an earlier example:

When I see a street scene in which one car is half hidden behind another car, my perception is that of one whole car behind another whole car. According to Kellman and Spelke (1983), babies already show this kind of complementation of partly occluded objects at about four months. As Searle (1992) has put it: 'All (normal) seeing is *seeing as*, all (normal) perceiving is *perceiving as*' (original emphasis).

When you wake up in the morning you may be confused for a few moments, but presently you know again where you are, where the bathroom is and how to fill the bath with hot water. Knowledge of where you are and the bathroom's location belongs to a subspecies of internal models of the surrounding world, known as *cognitive maps*, whose existence and scope can be established experimentally, in animals as well as in humans.

You can continue to walk while vision is interrupted by sneezing or by wiping your eyes, or deflected from where you are going by glances at the sky.

Infants of just 6.5 months can successfully reach for an object in the dark, having seen it before the lights were switched off (Goubet & Clifton, 1998). Microelectrode penetrations in the premotor areas of a monkey's cerebral cortex (see area 6, Figure 9.2, p. 139) have shown cells that fire in a sustained manner at the presentation of stationary three-dimensional objects within the animal's near space. They continue to fire when – while the monkey is looking elsewhere and unknown to it – the object is withdrawn (Rizzolatti et al., 1997). All of this points to internal models that enable the system to carry on during temporary absence, distortion or irrelevance of the visual inputs.

As mentioned in Section 2.5, a delay of up to 500 ms can occur between, for example, the application of a stimulus to the skin and conscious awareness of it. But the brain will compensate for this in its representation of the stimulus by *retroactively timing* it to the moment the signal arrived at the cortex. In terms of milliseconds, there can also be a difference in the time in which the 'feature detectors' of the visual cortex respond to specific attributes such as colour and movement (Zeki, 1993). This, too, is compensated in our perception of the world.

In the so-called 'colour phi phenomenon' – when a red and green spot appear one after the other in a brief exposure to the eyes – we have the sensation of a single spot moving from the one location to the other and changing colour along the way. It demonstrates part of the essence of the RWM; namely that it is based on the brain's *preconscious interpretation* of the sensory inputs in the light of past experience, and that is here clearly biased towards the common experience of continuity in the movement of perceived objects.

This 'seeing as' is also illustrated by the phenomena of *completion*: the brain's filling in of the part of a perceived scene or figure that falls on the eye's **blind spot** or on a scotoma, a 'blind' area in the visual cortex. The blind spot is the small circular area, called the *optic disk*, where the retina is interrupted by the bundle of nerve fibre leaving it. Oddly enough, the fibres from the light-sensitive cells run along the front of the retina and not along the back, as one might have expected. When a drawing is viewed with one eye, then any discrete object small enough for its image to fall inside the blind spot will appear to vanish when it moves there. In the case of larger objects, when only a small part may fall on the blind spot, the missing bit will tend to be 'filled in' or 'completed' by the interpretative processes of the brain.

The main point to be kept in mind is that the RWM is an *interpretation* of the brain's sensory inputs, and much of this interpretation is formed below the level of consciousness. We have a good illustration of this in bistable percepts such as the well-known Necker cube: here the brain switches spontaneously between the two ways in which the drawing of a cube may be interpreted in which all edges are shown.

That the brain performs interpretations of visual inputs at an unconscious level is not a new idea. In his discussion of the nature of visual perceptions, von Helmholtz (1867) describes them as unconscious inferences from visual inputs, drawn on the strength of past experiences. In a similar vein, Krechevski (1932) describes internal representations of the outside world as 'hypotheses' formed by the brain. The same metaphor is used by Gregory (1970) in the evaluation of his extensive studies of optical illusions. This does not mean that all responses to visual stimuli are necessarily based on such interpretative processes. The kinds of hues you see when you look at coloured objects are more or less passively determined by the conditions and intensity of the ambient illumination. The distinction I am here making between the raw visual stimuli and their interpretation in the RWM is not very far removed from J.J. Gibson's distinction between the 'perceptual senses' and the 'perceptual system' (Gibson, 1979). In the perceptual senses we are dealing with receptors receiving stimuli passively, whereas in the perceptual system the information is processed in some active sense. As examples I have mentioned the exploration of a shape by tracking its contours with the eyes and the blind man's exploration through touch.

6.2. Selection for attention and for consciousness

The difference between selection for attention and for consciousness is not always clearly perceived, and this can lead to muddled explanations of certain phenomena, such as the phenomenon of *neglect* [6.3].

Attention is a state or 'set' of the brain in which it selectively focuses on specific objects or events to the exclusion of others. It increases the influence exercised by the representations of those objects or events over the brain's ongoing processes, most often by raising the level of activity of the corresponding neural structures, sometimes by inhibiting connections which are themselves inhibitory. Attention may be drawn to those objects or events either wittingly or unwittingly. In the first case it is based on a conscious decision, for example when you consciously decide to hold some external object in view or to respond to some particular sensation. I shall call this *controlled* attention. We have examples of the second case when a sudden flash of light at the periphery of vision or a sudden pain interrupts what you are doing or thinking. I shall call this *captured* attention. Note that controlled attention is a top-down process, whereas captured attention is a bottom-up one.

Now, at any time there are selective processes of one kind or another happening in the brain. Sometimes the 'selection' is forced by capacity limitations, as in selection for consciousness and in Broadbent's experiment when two different sequences of three numbers were fed simultaneously to the subject's ears and were then found to be processed in succession [4.3]. At other times it is not. To avoid confusion here, *I shall henceforth restrict the literal meaning of 'attention' to selective changes of focus occurring at the conscious level (either controlled or captured)*. By the 'attentional set' of the brain shall be understood the *associated* set of priorities established throughout the brain as a whole.

Various investigations have highlighted the role of the higher levels of cognitive processing in controlled attention. Since these higher processes are mainly associated with the frontal and prefrontal cortex, it means not only that these regions must receive inputs from the object-recognizing or event-recognizing regions, but also that they must reciprocally be able to influence those regions in order to establish the required set of priorities in the neural networks concerned. I shall call this the *neural distribution of the current attentional set*.

According to Blakemore (1990) this could be effected in the visual cortex by way of coarse arrays of 'activating' fibres that adjust the excitability of cells so as to establish the required priorities in different parts of the visual field's representation.[1] It may also cause shrinkage in the dominant **receptive fields** of the neurons around the selected stimulus.

Controlled attention will generally be governed by a subject's motivational state as expressed at the neural level by the activities of the limbic system. However, captured attention can also be influenced in this way, as when the eyes of a thirsty person are compulsively drawn to a glass of water.

The differences between selection for consciousness and selection for attention can now be seen more clearly. Selection for consciousness was described in Section 2.5 as the final breakthrough of a stimulus or representation into the IGR by way of a regional activation that spreads outwards from the primary sensory cortices like the ripples that spread from a stone thrown into a pond. Its final destinations are the frontal brain regions that form the top level at which the current situation is evaluated in the light of the subject's current emotional and motivational state. These are *bottom-up* processes and the final product acquires a new functional role (that of the IGR). By contrast, as we have just seen, selection for attention is a process that may be either top-down, as in controlled attention, or bottom-up, as in captured attention, and it produces no change in functional role.

As I walk down a street feeling peckish, I happen to pass a baker's shop. Instantly I am pulled up in my tracks as my eyes are caught by the display of cakes in the shop window. It would clearly be wrong to regard this selection for attention as a selection for consciousness. My attention to those cakes has not caused shrinkage in my *consciousness* of the total situation, merely a sharper division between its focused centre and its unfocused periphery, between what I have called the foreground and background consciousness. It has not banished the rest of the situation from my awareness. Without taking my eyes off the cakes I still remain aware of the fact that I am separated from them by the shop window and that the cakes are not up for grabs but need to be purchased. Since we have here a kind of highlighting of some particular area in my perceptual field, a good metaphor is to think of this common kind of selective attention as a *spotlight* that fastens on particular items in that field – but emphatically not a spotlight on a totally dark stage.

6.3. The missing limbs: the phenomenon of neglect

One of the most interesting phenomena relating to entry into consciousness is the effect of certain brain lesions, known as neglect. They are lesions, mostly in the parietal cortex, that cause parts of the real world simply to vanish from the patient's conscious perceptions. In one of the cases I shall describe below, the patient firmly believes that one of his arms is missing. Although he can see the arm, he cannot make sense of what he sees. Yet in semi-automatic reactions, like steadying himself, the arm still functions normally. It follows that the arm is still fully represented in the RWM, but the representation has failed to be absorbed in the IGR, hence into consciousness.

There is a danger here that the lack of a clear perception of the nature of consciousness may cause these defects, by default as it were, to be attributed to flawed mechanisms of attention when, in fact, they may be due to a flawed breakthrough to the IGR. A review of theories of neglect shows indeed a marked tendency to attribute the observed neglect to deficits in attentional functions (Marshall et al., 1993). Marshall and his colleagues are aware of the dubiousness of some of these explanations, and complain that few current 'explanations' of neglect are anything more than a description of the phenomena phrased in terms that insinuate understanding without actually delivering. They rightly add that, alternatively, neglect could be explained as a failure of access to consciousness.

The brain lesions causing neglect do not leave a grey or black blotch in the patient's perceptions. The objects or spatial fields concerned are simply lost from consciousness. *Subjectively*, they have ceased to exist. In some cases of bilateral lesions in the posterior parietal area, the patients may have potentially a full visual field but can only perceive one object at a time. Alexander Luria, the eminent Russian neurophysiologist, presented one such patient with two versions of the Star of David (Figure 6.1). In one version both triangles were of the same colour, in the other they were of different colours and thus had the character of two distinct objects. In the first case the patient saw the complete star. In the second he saw just one of the two triangles (Luria, 1959). However, Luria has also demonstrated cases in which entry into consciousness was indeed governed by attention. For example, when there were several objects and the patient was instructed to focus on any one of them, he might fail to see even so strong a stimulus as the examiner's finger being thrust suddenly towards his face. Cases have also been known in which a limb had vanished from the patient's consciousness, and when asked to point to the several limbs of a doll, the patient also missed out on that very same limb. It seems that in these cases also the very *concept* of that missing limb was lost from consciousness.

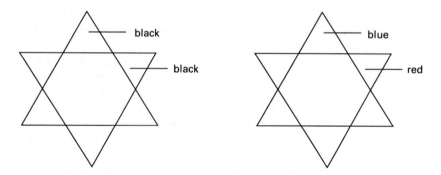

Figure 6.1 *Object-related neglect. When both triangles are black, a star is seen. When they are different colours, only a single triangle is seen (after Luria, 1959)*

In a dramatic case, also reported by Luria, injury of the parietal area in the left hemisphere caused all of the opposite side of the body to be simply lost from the owner's consciousness (Luria, 1959). To the patient it seems that half the body is simply gone. The patient is unaware of its existence, would shave only half his face, and comb only half his hair. In the patient's own words, transcribed by Luria and quoted by Blakemore (1977, p. 82):

> Suddenly I'll come to, look to the right of me, and be horrified to discover that half my body is gone. I'm terrified; I try to figure out what's become of my right arm and leg, the entire right side of my body. I move the fingers of my left hand, feel them, but can't see the fingers of my right hand and somehow I am not even aware that they are there.

Neglect can also affect memory functions. Rosenfield (1992, p. 112) cites a case of the physician Oliver Sacks, in which the patient himself described how his leg had gone missing, both in the present and in the past.

> The leg had vanished, taking its 'place' with it. Thus there seemed no possibility of recovering it – and this irrespective of the pathology involved. Could memory help, where looking forward could not? No! The leg had vanished, taking its 'past' away with it! I could no longer remember having a leg. I could no longer remember how I had ever walked and climbed. I felt inconceivably cut off from the person who had walked and run and climbed just five days before.

Cases of extrapersonal neglect are rather more common than such examples of personal neglect. In some cases of extrapersonal neglect, reviewed by Halligan and Marshall (1993), lesions in the right parietal lobe caused neglect of everything on the left half of things. Patients may fail to remember left-sided details of a familiar scene, fail to eat food placed on the left side of their plate, report objects as missing though they are plainly visible on the left, fill out only the right side of a form, draw only the right side of an object they are asked to depict, etc. In some cases the left–right division was viewer-centred, in others it was object-centred. Neglect of the left half of space may also occur.

Some of these phenomena may be related to the involvement of movement in the processes of visual perception [7.2]. For we must ask why should neglect occur mainly through lesions in the *parietal* cortex? Now, as regards the missing limbs this may be due to the fact that the parietal association areas are deeply implicated in the body schema and stimuli might, therefore, be lost from consciousness by failing to enter this part of the RWM or, more specifically, that portion of the RWM which enters the IGR. However, the parietal areas are also implicated subliminally in the saccadic eye movements that are involved in the representation of spatial relationships in the visual field [7.2]. Loss in these areas could, therefore, result in loss of such spatial perceptions, or their breakthrough into the IGR. Conceivably, too, some cases of this kind of visual neglect might be caused by lesions that restrict the relevant saccadic movements. We have an interesting example of this possibility in the type of neglect, mentioned above, when the patient neglects everything to the left of things. In some of these cases scanning saccades have been noted to be restricted to the rightward movements of the eyes, even though patients had full extra-ocular movements to command, and leftward movements of the eyes were also absent in sleep during the REM phase (Halligan & Marshall, 1993).

In view of the complexity of the process of stimuli breaking through to the IGR, one can see the likelihood of some disruption occurring here, and it seems that the disruption generally occurs in the breakthrough of the RWM into the IGR, rather than in a breakthrough of the stimulus into the RWM. For in some patients stimuli given to the 'neglected' field may nevertheless influence responses to stimuli in the non-neglected field (Halligan & Marshall, 1993). This accords with the fact that those parts of the RWM that fail to enter consciousness may still affect the brain's ongoing processes.

6.4. The extensive range of associations in the RWM

The range of act–outcome expectancies and their associations

Our biological approach has quite naturally focused on an organism's way of acquiring knowledge about the external world through the experienced consequences of its actions. This, in turn, is reflected in the brain's internal representations of the outside world. You could subsume the whole topic under the heading of 'Meaning acquired through movement'. Act–outcome expectancies thus stand high in our list of interests in the RWM.

The young infant discovers the very properties both of space and of the objects it contains through its restless explorations of whatever it can reach with body and limbs. It asks questions of the environment and the answer comes in the experienced results. After von Holst and Mittelstaedt (1950), this principle is also widely known as the *reafference principle*. Activities like searching, exploring, probing, scrutinizing and scanning are specifically designed to produce reafferent sequences of sensory inputs that contain the clues required by the nervous system to achieve the necessary object-reference in the behavioural responses it controls. In a broad sense, of course, the reafference method of knowledge acquisition finds its most sophisticated application in the methods of the experimental sciences. Here the properties of an object are discovered by systematically interfering with it, and then evaluating the observed results in the light of the nature of the interference.

All the features and properties of the outside world that reveal themselves in the specific way in which they affect the outcome of our actions can result in act–outcome expectancies that, in turn, can function as internal representations of the features or properties concerned. This applies to the experienced effects of the simplest movements, as when the features of a shape reveal themselves through the eye movements required in tracking its contours, to the experienced effects of the most complex actions we may use in exploring the external world. Thus the totality of act–outcome expectancies that are part of the RWM forms a complex hierarchy. Much of this affects our thinking as well as our actions. Experimental findings have shown how often humans will reason about objects by exploiting a collection of representations about the behaviour of particular kinds of objects in particular circumstances (Spelke & Van de Walle, 1993).

However, the deep secret of the brain's powers of anticipation lies not just in the formation of act–outcome expectancies from act–outcome experiences as such, but also in the multiple associations that have formed through experience between individual act–outcome expectancies. A child's experience in lifting an object soon comes to elicit expectancies about the effort required to throw that object or to kick it about. And these, in turn, may generalize to objects of a similar appearance. Speaking generally, whenever a particular property of an object manifests itself in different ways, this will in due course come to be reflected in the corresponding associations formed between the respective act–outcome expectancies.

Some other kinds of acquired expectancies as part of the RWM

There are also many things we learn about the world just by noticing things happening, as when we see a china cup falling on a stone floor and breaking on impact. Such passive experiences of sequences of events in the surrounding world may be described as the broader category of *what-leads-to-what-experiences* habituating as *what-leads-to-what expectancies* – the expectancies that if a certain event or sequence of events occurs, then such and such will follow. Like act–outcome expectancies, these, too, can function as internal representations of object properties (the cup's brittleness in this case). Both types can be described jointly as *states of conditional expectancy*.[2]

Expectancies formed on the basis of merely observed events form at an early age. As early as three months, infants may detect regularities, anticipate particular outcomes from particular visual events (Haith, 1993). Recent research has shown that infants of four to eight months can track and anticipate the final orientation of an object following regular invisible transformations (Rochat & Hespos, 1996). They can also detect violations of physical principles, such as spatial continuity and solidity (Baillargeon, 1993). We shall meet other examples in the next chapter [7.1].

Observed motion can also become relevant to infants in a more fundamental sense, namely in relation to the perceived unity of an object. From their studies of object recognition in infants, Spelke and Van de Walle (1993) conclude that the infant perceives a solid object as a spatially connected whole because of the maintenance of its connectedness as it moves. The common motion of its parts leads to the perceived unity of an object, whereas the relative motion of objects leads to the perception of their separateness. Thus the unity as such of an object may come to be represented in the RWM by expectations of the maintenance of its connectedness as it moves. This could be at least a partial answer to the *binding problem*, the problem of how features processed in different parts of the brain can become 'bound' together in the brain to yield an internal representation of the object as a unity [2.6].

All the same, our main interest must remain in the brain's acquired act–outcome expectancies, since act–outcome experiences form the fundamental basis for the acquisition of knowledge about the surrounding world and the acquisition of meanings through subjective experience. An ancient proverb, attributed to Confucius, says: 'I hear and I forget, I see and I remember, I act and I understand.'

To repeat: according to a not uncommon view, the brain forms a model of the outside world from which it then derives expectancies about the outcome of available actions. According to our main assumption, the acquired expectancies *are* the world model, or at least a great part of it. They are elicited by the current sensory inputs as part of the brain's interpretation of those inputs on the basis of past experience. The precise nature of some of these representational functions will be the main topic of the next chapter, with special reference to the representation of spatial relationships.

6.5. Some features of the RWM in animals

It is of more than historical interest that the possibility of acquired expectancies operating as cognitive functions was brought to the attention of animal psychologists through the notion of *cognitive maps*, typical ingredients of the RWM. Tolman (1932, 1948) introduced the notion of *place* learning as distinct from *response* learning, and coined the phrase 'cognitive map' for the particular kind of representation that he took to intervene between stimulus and response. His experiments suggested that rats allowed to explore a maze formed some kind of internal map of the maze that enabled the animal, for example, to make the right kind of detour if a passage was blocked. His experiments also drew attention to the phenomenon of *latent* learning, learning that can occur without obvious reward. It could be shown that rats learn something about the maze just by being allowed to explore it without external reward. Since those days, cognitive maps have remained the main investigated feature of the RWMs of animals.

Tolman added the – at the time, original – idea that these cognitive maps are composed of expectations which the rat acquired during its exploration of the maze – for example, expectations of the consequences of turning left or right at the various choice points of the maze. The idea found little support among the still ruling behaviourists. In their eyes, expectations were unobservable and not, therefore, respectable concepts in the kind of psychology the behaviourists aimed to develop. No attempt was made to define a state of expectancy in objective functional terms, as I shall be doing in the next chapter and have already anticipated in section 2.3.

An elegant demonstration of cognitive maps in rats was furnished by David Olton's radial maze. This maze consists of eight runways that radiate outwards from a central starting point. At the end of each runway is placed a morsel of food that cannot be seen from the starting point. When the rat was entered at successive occasions at the starting point, it showed a clear knowledge of what runways it had already explored at the previous occasions and would, therefore, ignore this time (Olton, 1979).

Another good demonstration of cognitive maps in rats has been furnished by the Morris swimming tank, designed by Richard Morris while at the University of St Andrews. This consists of a pool filled with cloudy water and a submerged platform as exit from the pool. A rat that had been familiarized with the platform could be entered at any point in the pool and would then find its way back to the platform, even though it could not see it, provided only that the animal could see the distinctive landmarks around the pool. It appeared to be using a process of triangulation. The inference that during familiarization it had formed an internal representation of the location of the platform relative to those landmarks was confirmed when a rotation of the landmarks at the time the rat was released was proved to confuse the animal accordingly.

Meanwhile the work of John O'Keefe and his colleagues in University College, London, had shown the hippocampus to be a brain structure heavily involved in the navigational skills of rats (O'Keefe, 1976). It was found to contain cells that keep track of the animal's position relative to a maze, cage or the walls of the room. For each location there was some specific set of such 'place cells' giving a maximal response.

Later work showed that the hippocampus of the rat also contains cells that are selectively responsive to the *direction* in which the animal faces (Taube et al., 1990). As the animal turns this way or that, different cells burst into activity. Even in the dark these cells seem to remember their preferred direction. It is interesting here to note that some of these cells could even anticipate head movements by up to a tenth of a second. Other work showed that our brains, too, are pretty good at keeping track of our bearings. When blindfolded subjects on a swivelling chair were spun and asked to stop when they faced their original direction, the results were surprisingly good. Less surprisingly, recent research made quite a splash when it reported that when London taxi drivers are asked to visualize a particular route in London, their hippocampus shows increased activity (Maguire et al., 1997). This is not to suggest that the place cells and orientation cells hold all the answers. For example, it does not imply that the hippocampus actually carries the functional representation of outer space. It is best thought of as a supporting structure for the surrounding cortical regions [9.2].

Edmund Ross and his colleagues at Oxford added to these complexities when they found in the hippocampus of macaque monkeys, not *place* cells of the kind described above, but cells that responded selectively to locations in external space when fixated by the monkey's eyes (*New Scientist*, January 1999).

The cognitive maps in animals may embody cues in more than one sensory modality. This was noted by Beritoff (1963), who had observed how dogs, when blindfolded in a familiar situation, would still run by the shortest route to the place where they had been accustomed to find the food bowl. Cognitive maps are not confined to the mammalian orders. They are found in birds as well, and even bees appear to form primitive cognitive maps. They can return to a familiar source of nectar when released from an arbitrary point, apparently using a process of triangulation in respect of nearby landmarks of which they have learnt the compass bearings (Gallistel, 1989). In the case of birds, the cognitive maps formed by homing pigeons instantly come to mind. In the present context their power to form expectancies is also noteworthy. Krushinski (1965) showed that if pigeons are first familiarized with a food stimulus that moves at constant speed along a straight line, and if a screen is then interposed behind which the stimulus temporarily disappears, the birds can extrapolate the point at which it will reappear – yet another demonstration of the importance of acquired expectancies.

Animals that have to travel long distances, such as migrating birds, need not only a map but also a compass. Multiple inputs from the stars, visible landmarks, and the direction of the sun (detected even under cloud cover through the light's polarization) are widely used by birds to get a fix on their current position. Some have actually been found to use the Earth's magnetic field as a compass.

As an alternative to cognitive maps, some animals, hamsters for example, learn how to get from their present location to a desired distant one by using dead reckoning, i.e. inertial navigation. To get from the one to the other, they seem to go by the record of their inertial movements.

Notes

1 For a survey and correlation of much of the literature on such enhanced neural activation, see van der Heijden (1992).

2 In addition, of course, we learn about the world through the spoken or written word. However, since the treatment of consciousness here is confined to the primary, nonverbal, consciousness, this contribution to the brain's model of the world need not detain us.

7

ACQUIRED EXPECTANCIES

7.1. A functional definition of states of expectancy

In this chapter I want to take a closer look at the nature of acquired states of expectancy and at their contribution to the RWM, beginning with the functional definition of a state of expectancy already introduced in Section 2.3. This is the third of our key concepts, the other two being the structural and functional concepts of internal representation as defined in Section 1.5. After that I shall turn to the act–outcome expectancies involved in one of the most important constituents of the RWM: the internal representation of spatial relationships, illustrating this with three simple examples.

States of expectancy of an event have two components that need to be separated. First, a state of expectancy of an event implies an anticipation of the event in the sense of a state of readiness for it – by which, in turn, I mean a state that facilitates or advances an appropriate reaction to the event. Thus the expected weight of a chair you are about to lift causes the body to brace itself in anticipation of the effort required.

Second, if the expected event fails to occur – if, despite your effort, the chair will not budge – you will be surprised and take a second look. The occurrence of this unexpected event reveals a gap in the brain's internal model of the current situation and the resulting surprise reaction is likely to initiate a search for the additional information needed to fill that gap, in this case finding the cause of the chair's resistance.

Indeed, what may broadly be described as 'surprise' reactions are the brain's primary reactions to unexpected events – in our example, events that conflict with the RWM's predictions. They are its original responses to everything unfamiliar. To the young infant almost everything comes as a surprise and as a challenge for its attention. In due course, however, as it grows familiar with the type of situation concerned, these surprise reactions come to be replaced by reactions that are more specifically related to the event in question.

These surprise reactions are commonly known as *orienting reactions*. This phrase dates from the work of Pavlov, who described an animal's reactions to unexpected stimuli as 'What-is-it? reflexes' or 'orienting reflexes'. Depending on the circumstances, such orienting reactions cover a broad spectrum. They may range from merely a fleeting shift of attention, such as a passing glance of the eyes, to strong arousal and startle responses. Physiological components of such arousal include changes in pupillary size, breathing, heart rate, electrical skin conductivity and characteristic changes in brain waves.

These remarks have to be qualified inasmuch as the brain's division of events into 'expected' and 'unexpected' generally relates to broad categories within whose limits considerable variety is possible. The picture I have in my mind of the cul-de-sac in which my Cambridge flat is situated includes broad categories of vehicles that may be seen to enter it. The appearance of a fire engine would catch me by surprise.

Some earlier remarks also have to be qualified. I said above that orienting reactions are the brain's original responses to everything unfamiliar, and become inhibited when familiarization replaces them by more specific, and more properly context-related reactions. However, this is a matter of degree. For example, when a novel stimulus is sufficiently strongly attended to leave a memory trace, then even a second encounter may elicit feelings of familiarity. In one set of experiments, 10,000 arbitrarily chosen vivid pictures were shown to subjects for five seconds each. It was then found that even after a delay the majority of these pictures would be recalled by those subjects as having been met before (Standing, 1973). It seems that the mere recording of a sensory perception can diminish the orienting reactions resulting at the next encounter, and that awareness of this reduction may be part of the feelings of familiarity.

To compress the above discussion:

Definition

> By a state of expectancy, *conscious or unconscious, shall be meant a state of the brain that has two components:*
>
> (a) *a state of readiness for the occurrence of a particular event – that is to say, a state which facilitates or advances an appropriate reaction to that event, and*
> (b) *a state in which the occurrence of a significantly different event tends to elicit a characteristic 'surprise' reaction, technically known as an* orienting reaction.

When I ask for a ball to be thrown to me, the hands get ready to grasp it. Electrophysiological studies on muscles in subjects catching a ball showed up anticipatory reactions that began as soon as the ball was released by the thrower (Lacquantini & Maioli, 1989). Of course, a state of expectancy is not the only condition that facilitates neural reactions to an event. A common concept in psychology is that of *priming*. This means that recognition of an object is speeded up through previous exposure to a prompt. For example, presenting the word 'fruit' may prime subsequent responses like 'apple' or 'banana'.

Further notes on states of expectancy

Neural responses to failed expectancies have been observed in a variety of brain structures, foremost the hippocampus. Other examples are cells in the cerebellum that respond to discrepancies between brainstem predictions of a target's motion and the target's actual motion (Carpenter, 1988), and cells in the temporal lobe that detect unexpected, hence behaviourally relevant sensory events (Hietanen & Perrett, 1993).

We need to distinguish between reactions to individual cases of failed expectancies and reactions to events or situations that are altogether *unfamiliar*, i.e. to *novelty*. Reactions to novel events or situations can engage the brain quite extensively. We have an example in the novelty activation caused by the sight of a novel complex picture, as revealed by PET scans. These showed enhanced regional activity in the right hippocampal formation, parahippocampal gyrus, retrospenial cortex, thalamus, sub-callosal area, anterior and inferior cingulate cortex, **putamen** and medial prefrontal cortex (Tulving et al., 1994). Indeed, scalp electrodes have shown that some 300 ms after the occurrence of a significantly novel event a powerful wave of activity sweeps through the whole brain.

Walter (1964) was the first to discover responses to failed expectancies in the electrical potentials that can be recorded with scalp electrodes. In these trials the brain was accustomed to a pair of tones occurring in sequence. When the second tone was then omitted, a contingent negative variation was recorded in the cortical potentials at the time when that tone was due. Here the response was to the unexpected absence of an expected stimulus.

There is one parameter about expectancies that I have not yet mentioned. It is the *confidence factor*: in particular circumstances events are expected with more or less confidence. In functional terms we can equate it with the *relative weight* the expectancy is given in its influence on behaviour in competition with other factors. Since we are mainly concerned with the theoretical role of acquired expectancies in the RWM, rather than their weight in particular applications, I shall have no more to say about this quantitative dimension, important though it must be in detailed simulations.

Attempts to model in neural terms the brain's discrimination between expected and unexpected events have proved difficult. Barlow (1991) and Földiak (1992) have suggested formal models of neural circuits that could become attuned to regularly occurring coincidences or covariations among input-related variables. These circuits, in turn, could be linked to other units in a manner that would produce an output whenever such a 'familiar' covariation fails to occur. Jointly the two systems would thus act as novelty detectors or 'novelty filters' (Kohonen, 1984). But these 'novelty filters' suffer from a common weakness of any bottom-up approach: they detect at a low and merely local level discrepancies from habituated coincidences or covariations of input-related variables, whereas in real situations the experienced novelty of an event depends on the total context, hence on the high-level processes we have identified with the RWM.

More about states of readiness

At the lowest level, anticipatory reactions may consist of no more than an enhanced sensitivity of a particular neural unit to the occurrence of a particular neural input. For example, Wurtz and his colleagues have shown in monkeys that expecting a stimulus S as the result of an action typically produces a preparatory reaction for receiving S, and in the observed cases it took the form of enhanced responses of cells sensitive to S (Wurtz et al., 1982). At higher levels, of course, they may include much more.

Because of the important role which states of readiness play in our model, they need to be clearly perceived as a distinct body of neural connections. First, to the extent to which they are *acquired* states, their composition is governed by the feedback loops of the adaptive processes that brought them into being and may still modify them. For example, when a child learns how to prepare for catching a ball and later improves its skill. Second, in all the examples we have met, they entered the ongoing processes of the brain only *conditionally*: in the preceding example the appropriate reaction would be elicited only when the child sees the ball approaching. The same applies to the act–outcome expectancies, of which the above observations reported by Wurtz are a simple example. However, I must now also prepare you for a significant departure from this conditionality. For in the next chapter I shall hypothesize that the body of neural connections formed as a preparation for an event may also come to enter the ongoing processes of the brain under conditions which radically differ from those under which it was formed, and in combination with other states of readiness. More specifically, as part of the faculty of the imagination, a state of readiness to see a horse may combine with one to see a horn attached to its forehead, without either perception being *expected* and thus enter the ongoing processes of the brain in the role of a mental image of a unicorn. At a superficial level, all this is obvious enough: I can go through the motions of catching a ball even if there isn't one. In general terms, the way a body of connections has been formed in the brain does not predict the way in which it may subsequently come to be drawn into the brain's ongoing processes.

The development of expectancies in infants

The observation of surprise reactions is extensively used in developmental psychology and especially in the study of the development of perception in infants. For example, the more unexpected an event is, the greater is its power to attract the infant's attention. This can be seen in the direction and the duration of the infant's gaze. Such investigations have shown that reality-mapping expectancies manifest themselves at an early age. Infants as young as one month have shown surprise when they have seen a screen being slowly moved in front of a toy, and the toy is not there when the screen is subsequently removed (Bower, 1971). When an object passes behind a screen, infants of three to four months will track its movement with the eyes to the point where it is expected to emerge. At that age, too, an infant will respond with a backward jerk of the head and by raising its hands when the shadow of an object is cast on a translucent screen and its size increased at an accelerating rate, thus giving the impression of an approaching object. Faced with the same display, turtles pull in their heads and monkeys rush to the back of the cage.

Infants only four months old already tend to look significantly longer at an impossible outcome compared with a possible one – for example, if a rigid box appears to be placed behind a rotating screen but fails to stop its motion through some invisible device. Again, if an object in a particular orientation is dropped and the last third of its path is obscured by a screen, infants of four to eight months will anticipate the orientation discovered when the screen is removed. They can also do so if the object at the time was in a state of rotation (Rochat & Hespos, 1996). In 1992, Karyn Wynn, a developmental psychologist at the University of Arizona in Tuscon, showed that if an infant in that age group is shown two toys being placed behind a screen, after which one is secretly removed through a trapdoor, it will look surprised when the screen is removed and it sees only one toy. Was the infant expecting more, or did they have a number concept? To decide this, the experiment was changed. Instead of secretly removing one of the two toys, Wynn added a third one. Again the infant showed surprise. The cases cited above are just a few of the many illustrations one could give of behaviour patterns that invite the concept of expectancy. Broadly speaking, all the infant's knowledge of the external world will be reflected in a corresponding set of expectancies. From a social standpoint the most interesting are the responses the child comes to expect from adults to their means of attracting adults' attention – and which may at times be used quite provocatively (Gobnik et al., 2000). This work revealed the surprising insight into the feelings of others that an infant can have acquired by the age of 18 months or two years. Indeed, by the age of nine months, infants can already tell the difference between expressions of happiness, sadness and anger. The development of this discrimination, in turn, is assisted by an innate attraction to faces and preferences for faces over other objects.

7.2. Internal representation of spatial relationships

My object in this section

The feature detectors of optical primitives, first demonstrated for the visual cortex by Hubel and Wiesel and later modelled by Marr [4.11], do not represent the structure of the features concerned. They are by definition merely *symbolic* representations, and this raises the problem of how the *meaning* of those symbols is represented, in other words, how the causal properties and behavioural relevance of these symbolically represented features are mapped in the brain. I now want to take a closer look at this.

One might try to get around the problem by arguing that, once particular feature detectors are in place, the brain will in due course learn the causal properties and behavioural relevance of what they signal. But this does not tell us how they are mapped, and also puts the cart before the horse. The development of an organism's power to discriminate particular features or properties of the environment is generally driven, directly or indirectly, by the *need* to discriminate them: creatures mainly learn what to discriminate because in one way or another it proves to be relevant in their life. Eskimos can discriminate by sight between 20 or more different kinds of snow. And work by Held and Hein, cited below, has shown that the primitive feature detectors in the visual cortex are not innately present, but innately programmed to develop in response to the experience of structured optical inputs.

The main topic here must be the internal representation of spatial relationships. Actions have to take account of the physical realities of the external world and these include, above all, the intrinsic nature of spatial variables. Somehow this needs to be represented in the brain as part of the RWM. And this representation is more important in the case of spatial variables than other physical variables, such as the weight or hardness of an object, because the latter properties are only *contingently* relevant to our actions, whereas spatial variables are relevant all the time. That, too, needs to be reflected in the functional representations composing the RWM. How, then, are the causal properties of spatial variables represented in the RWM? Presently I shall look at three concrete examples. First, however, let me say a bit about the general importance of movement in the processes of visual perception as part of the way in which the organism extracts information about the surrounding world through the experienced consequences of its actions.

On the importance of movement in vision

The eye is a prehensile and explorative organ and vision is a dynamic process. It is not simply based on passive observations of the world, extracting information from snapshots through suitable 'feature detectors', as assumed by Marr. Visual scenes have to be scanned to become fully composed, and the spatial relationships in the visual field are conveyed to the brain by the eye movements required to shift fixation from one point to another.

In recent times the idea has gained ground that vision is essentially an active process. Looking back on his own extensive work in this field, Jeannerod (1994) has observed that every perception depends on active movement, both micromovement and rapid eye movement. The same point is made by Damasio (1994) and Cotterill (1998).

This applies from the earliest stages of our visual development. According to Kellman and Spelke (1983), infants have from birth a sensitivity to motion-induced information, and, as Kellman (1993) has stressed, the ability to detect that information is fundamental to the development of the perceptual system. Kellman and colleagues had shown some years before that five-month-old infants can already distinguish between their own motion around a stationary object, object motion around them while stationary, and conjoint motion of themselves and the perceived objects (Kellman et al., 1987). Between three and six months of age infants will begin to explore objects with their fingers while also watching them, thus learning to associate these exploratory actions with their consequences in two different sensory modalities – the beginning of forming bimodal act–outcome expectancies. This work has also shown that the development of ocular prehension generally precedes by several months that of prehension with the fingers.

Movement appears to be required in vision too at an even more fundamental level. If a tiny projector is fastened to the eyeball, so that the retina receives a *stationary* image, vision vanishes altogether: the image is replaced by a uniform grey.

There are a number of other well-researched points at which movement information enters the processes of visual perception. For example, one of the cues the brain uses in the perception of depth is the so-called **motion parallax**: when the head moves at an angle to the line of vision the relative distances of objects in the perceived scene are reflected in the relative shifts they undergo in the visual field. Think of how nearby houses fly past against the background of distant ones when you look out of the window of a moving train.

A further example is the so-called 'position constancy': when the eyes move in their sockets, the perceived scene should dance about. It does not do so because the brain anticipates and takes into account the effect of the eye movements in its representation of the current scene. An important point is that the movement of the eye has to be self-induced or 'self-paced'. If the eye movement is forced, for example by pressing the eyeball with the thumb, the scene does dance about. If the eye muscles are paralysed and the subject tries to obey an instruction to move the eyes, the visual scene appears to move in the direction of the intended eye movement (Gyr et al., 1979). In his discussion of the role of movement in sensory perceptions, Cotterill (1998) also notes that Braille readers can distinguish the patterns of dots only through self-induced movements of the fingers over the script. They fail if the 'dots' are moved by an external source.

The movement of an image across the retina can be due to a movement of the object or a movement of the eyes. How does the brain distinguish between them? The brain's main cue here appears to be whether the object shifts its position relative to other objects. This is suggested by the so-called *autokinetic* effect: when a stationary point of light is seen against a completely homogeneous background, then after a short while it appears to be drifting about. You may find that if, when lying in bed, you look at a spot on the ceiling, wondering whether it might be an insect, the spot often seems to move slowly, whether insect or not. The mechanisms of position constancy seem to fail us here. The homogeneous ceiling offers no reference frame and it has also been suggested that the brain has imperfect information about the position of the eyes when they are stationary, as they would be while gazing at that single spot.

Self-paced movements begin to be important in the earliest developmental stages of vision. In 1963 Held and Hein demonstrated that kittens prevented from moving about failed to develop visually guided behaviour. A year later its importance was also demonstrated for perceptual adaptations, that is to say, the brain's gradual adaptations to changes in the optical system. Kohler (1964) examined in humans what happens when the optical conditions are changed, for example when inverting prisms are fitted to the eyes. Systematic studies showed that in due course (which may be a matter of several days) everything will again be seen the right way up. Movement proved to be essential for this process of readjustment. Evidently, the brain here discovered the new relationship between the visual inputs and the real world through the visual consequences of the subject's movements. Again, the movement had to be self-paced, visually cued by the subject. Pushing the subject in a wheelchair did not suffice. It was a vivid demonstration of act–outcome experiences shaping the brain's model of the world and thus how we *see* the world.

While we are on the subject of the importance of movement in vision it is worth mentioning a puzzle that has often exercised the minds of brain researchers. Since all signals travelling in the brain are just electrical charges travelling along nerves, how do we come to experience the same electrical impulses arriving in one part of the cortex as visual, those arriving in another part as auditory, and those arriving in yet another part as tactile? Here, too, I believe that movement plays a large role. In addition to the distinct contribution the different sensory modalities make to the RWM, they are also distinguished by the effect of movements on the sensory inputs concerned. No movement of the eyes will change the noise you hear, but a movement of the head will. No movement of the arms will change what you see, but a movement of the eyes will, and so on.

Now to return to our main topic, I want to give just three concrete examples of act–outcome expectancies capable of functioning as representations of the kind we are here looking for, namely as representations of the intrinsic nature of spatial relationships as regards their causal significance and, therefore, behavioural relevance. My first example looks to the role of the saccades.

First example of how the causal properties of spatial variables can be represented

Unless you suffer from tunnel vision, the eyes will produce an extended optical array, the visual field. Its local points can be singled out by fixation, that is to say, by moving them to the central region of the retina, known as the **fovea** – a vital move since the eye's acuity is greatest at this central region and diminishes towards the periphery. The 126 million light-sensitive cells of the retina are most densely packed in this small central region, and the same applies to the 7 million cells that additionally code for colour, the 'cones' as distinct from the 'rods'. What is reported by one retinal cell at the edge of the field is detailed by a hundred cells at the centre. However, that is not the only reason why the fovea is important. Equally important is its role as a fixed reference point in the brain's internal representations of spatial relations in the visual field. And this is also where the saccades come in.

Ordinarily, the eyes move slowly and smoothly only when they track a slowly moving target, the so-called *pursuit* movements. Generally, they move in rapid flicks, called saccades, designed to fixate a point of interest in the visual field by moving it to the fovea. Since this foveation is the lowest level at which the causal properties and behavioural relevance of spatial relations reveal themselves to the brain, let me say a bit more about the saccades as such, before I come to the main point.

Saccades occur with great speed. They can be accomplished in 20–30 ms and are ballistic movements. That is to say, they cannot be interrupted while on their way. They are initiated and determined in their direction as well as magnitude by bursts of high-frequency firing that makes the eye muscles contract to an extent that depends on the duration of the firing. The burst must, therefore, be controlled by the intended target. When the target is reached, i.e. arrives at the central fovea, the burst is cut off. There is no time for feedback in these proceedings. Saccades are determined by outputs from the cerebral cortex that reach the muscle-control centres in the brainstem via the **substantia nigra** and **superior colliculus** (see Figure 9.1, p. 139). The main contributions from the cortex come from the parietal areas and the frontal eye fields. The first of these we have already met in connection with the representation of spatial relationships. The second belongs to the complex frontal areas that are implicated in the evaluation of stimuli in the light of the organism's current motivation and the initiation of voluntary movements, in this case voluntary movements of the eyes.

Two populations of neurons have been detected in these frontal eye fields. One relates to this evaluation. It responds soon after the presentation of a stimulus and appears to be involved in detecting whether an interesting target is, in fact, present (Carpenter, 1999). The other appears to fire when the brain is about to make a saccade to a particular location in the visual field. These neurons fire in anticipation of the retinal stimulus that will be brought into the dominant sphere of their receptive field by that saccade (Umeno & Goldberg, 1997). This may occur already up to 300 ms before the saccade is executed. We can think of these act–outcome expectancies as oiling the wheels, so to speak. But – and this is a main point – together with neural motor images of specific saccades, the neural activities that predict their outcome clearly amount to a set of act–outcome expectancies that could function as representations of the causal properties and behavioural relevance of spatial relations in the two dimensions of the visual field.

The encoding of retinal topography

The above is also relevant to the question of how the **topography** of the retina is encoded in terms of the neural activities that play a part in all this.

The topography of the respective half of the retina is mapped in the primary visual cortex through the location of the visual inputs that arrive there. But this location is not *encoded* in the discharges of the relevant population of neurons. Their activities are related to the nature of the visual stimuli but contain no information about the location of those stimuli on the retina. So where *is* that topography encoded? The secret may lie in the LIP (**lateral** intraparietal region) of the cortex and its visuomotor neurons, bimodal neurons that are responsive to *both* movements of the eyes and outputs from visual area V1 [2.2]. Moreover, at least a third of these neurons appear to anticipate the result of an eye movement, transiently shifting their dominant receptive field when the movement is about to occur (Colby et al., 1995). Clearly we have here a possible basis for act–outcome expectancies that could act as a representation of the retina's topography, namely in terms of the saccades that would foveate stimuli occurring at different locations on the retina.

Whereas the location of an attended stimulus is here encoded retinotropically, i.e. relative to the fovea of the retina, additional levels of integration in the VIP (ventral intraparietal) area appear to achieve an encoding relative to head position, while yet additional levels of integration in the posterior parietal cortex yield representations of spatial location in the all-important body-centred frame of reference (Anderson et al., 1985; Brotchie et al., 1995).

It is of interest to note in this connection that the selection of objects for fixation, and the provision of the information necessary for motor action, appear to be provided by a single attentional mechanism (Deubel & Schneider, 1996). That is to say, both are included in the priorities assigned by the brain's current attentional set [6.2]. We have seen that in *voluntary* eye movements selection is mediated by the frontal eye fields (area 8 in Figure 9.2, p. 139) as part of the leading role of the frontal cortex in willed actions.

Second example: act–outcome expectancies in 2D shape recognition

Of all the spatial relationships in a visual image, those that constitute the geometric shape of a figure or object are of special importance in view of the part they play in the recognition of different figures or objects. The visual image itself is a two-dimensional array and solid (3D) objects enter it in what is often called the 'flat-form view'. Now, the most plausible way in which the distinctive shape of an object's flat-form view can come to be registered in the brain is in terms of the constraints the shape imposes on eye movements exploring it. This can be either in terms of the movements needed to track its contour, or in terms of those needed to jump from salient point to salient point. However, this only applies to novel shapes. With familiar objects it will no longer be necessary. Through the normal processes of the conditioning that occurs with familiarization, the perceived image of a familiar shape can come to elicit instantly a representation of the geometrical distinctiveness of that shape in the form of *expectancies* relating to the eye movements that *would* occur in tracking its contour or in moving from salient point to salient point.

It has been shown that in recognizing the shape of a figure young infants still have to rely extensively on contour following (Zaporozhets, 1965), whereas adults tend to use such active exploration when meeting a novel shape like an inkblot. But in the latter case the most common action appears to consist of a jumping from salient subfeature to salient subfeature (Noton & Stark, 1971). Wurtz and his colleagues have also shown the importance of fixating salient points in pattern recognition by monkeys (Wurtz et al., 1982).

Observers have remarked that, even when the distinctiveness of a shape is recognized instantly, the brain is still prone to check it actively. Since all perception is of the nature of an *interpretation* of the sensory input, in other words of the nature of an *hypothesis*, it is natural for the brain to check such hypotheses.

As regards the *integration* of spatial position information derived from sequential fixations on different salient points of a shape, Hayhoe and his colleagues have demonstrated that information from previous fixations is preserved in a world-centred representation that is precise enough to support judgements of the geometric shape (Hayhoe et al., 1991).

Third example: act–outcome expectancies in 3D shape recognition

The shape of a solid object is three-dimensional. Recognition of the 3D shape of an object requires in the first instance an integration of the 2D representation directly derived from the visual image with internal representations of viewer-centred depth. The brain has a variety of cues available for the perception of depth, such as **accommodation**, **vergence**, **binocular disparity** and motion parallax. These are supplemented by such indirect cues as perspective (the decrease with distance of the apparent size of objects), surface texture, shadows and occlusions. By suitably combining representations of the apparent size of the object with representations of the distance variable the brain can also achieve *size constancy*: a representation of the true size of an object regardless of the different sizes of its image at different distances.

The details of all this need not concern us here. It shows that there exists a more than adequate range of act–outcome expectancies through which depth can be represented in the RWM: for example expectancies that relate to the motion parallax to be expected when the head is moved at an angle to the line of fixation, or to the changes in apparent size and texture of an object as one advances towards it or retreats. All of these are *egocentric* representations. Returning once again to our old friend the parietal cortex, it is of interest that cells are found in its posterior regions that are selectively responsive to the absolute position in egocentric space of fixated objects (Zeki, 1993). Similar cells in the parietal cortex of monkeys have been found to play a leading role in the control of arm movements when reaching for an object. And, not unlike what happens in the LIP region, there are also cells here that anticipate the movement required to reach the fixated object. This points to the existence of act–outcome expectancies in these regions that clearly reflect the causal significance and behavioural relevance of the distance variable.

In addition to viewer-centred or egocentric representations of spatial relations, the brain can also form representations that have an *object-centred* or *allocentric* frame of reference. The difference is easy to explain in terms of act–outcome expectancies. Let A and B be two objects in external space. Then expectancies about the movements required to move *to* A or *to* B (by eye or body) would be an egocentric representation of that spatial relationship, whereas expectancies relating to the movements required to move *from* A to B (by eye or body), or vice versa, would be an object-centred representation. An example of the latter has been observed in the macaque monkey. In a task in which the animal was required to make eye movements to the left end or right end of a bar, neurons were found in the supplementary eye fields that were selectively responsive to the object-centred direction of these movements (Olsen & Gettner, 1995).

All these spatial representations can occur at either a conscious or an unconscious level. As an advanced example of unconscious egocentric representations of spatial relationships I would cite the demonstration by Rieser and his colleagues that the brain of people walking without vision from one location to another seems automatically to update the RWM as regards the relative direction of other positions (Rieser et al., 1986).

8

IMAGINATIVE REPRESENTATIONS

8.1. Mental images

Imaginative representations, as conceived in our model, appear in many different roles, and they may operate at a conscious or an unconscious level. We meet them as representations of absent, past or future events, or mere fantasies, as when you imagine a unicorn, 'picture' the house you might like to build or 'visualize' a scene described in a book. We meet them, too, as representations of possible acts, the so-called 'motor images', as when we review our options and their anticipated consequences. Again, a great deal of our thinking tends to be conducted in terms of mental images, and, as Johnson-Laird (1983) has shown, even a great deal of our reasoning. Since his work was undertaken, modern information technology has also shown quite generally a steady growth in the use of visual imagery, such as charts and diagrams, not only for presenting complex data at a glance but also for charting arguments, presenting ideas and plotting possible courses of actions or events. It has been noticeable not only in board-rooms and lecture halls, but also in the media and owes a great deal to advances in computer graphics. The younger generation, too, with its extensive experience of videos and computers, is tuned to receive and digest information in a marriage of words and images, especially since visual images have an unrivalled power to show things in context.

To most people it is unquestionable that mental images have pictorial or 'depictive' qualities – not enough to be confused with real pictures, but enough to be called quasi-pictorial. However, not everybody has always agreed with this. Some 20-odd years ago it became the subject of a lengthy dispute between two opposing camps whose main protagonists were the psychologist Stephen Kosslyn and the computer scientist cum psychologist Zenon Pylyshyn. Whereas Kosslyn believed in the quasi-pictorial nature of mental images, and was systematically engaged in establishing this on an experimental basis (Kosslyn, 1978, 1983), Pylyshyn adopted the, to my mind fatal, stance that the brain is not just comparable with a computer in some metaphorical sense, but that it literally *computes*, and that the so-called 'mental images' are just the product of symbolically coded rules and propositions (Pylyshyn, 1973). Some followers of this view even maintained that all contents of consciousness, even feelings, are outputs of essentially linguistic systems and that consciousness is confined to creatures possessing a language faculty (Gazzaniga & LeDoux, 1978).

Kosslyn did not deny that verbal propositions can enter the processes through which mental images are generated. He insisted, however, that the end-product is a special kind of representation with undeniably pictorial qualities. He was backed here by the astonishing discovery that mental images can be rotated and *that this happens in real time*. This discovery came from attempts by scientists to find rigorous methods of studying mental images while avoiding reliance on introspection. They found these in chronometric studies, specifically in studies of measured response times. Thus Roger Shepard and Jaqueline Metzler (1971) asked subjects to discriminate as quickly as possible between two figures in an experiment that required the mental rotation of one of these figures to bring it into congruence with the other before the discrimination could be performed. Their results showed that the time taken to rotate that image is roughly proportional to the angle through which it has to be rotated. Similar results have since been obtained for other transformations. In later work, Shepard (1984) added the demonstration that image rotation and other image transformations were related to the mechanisms involved in the perception of motion. fMRI scans subsequently confirmed that the mental rotation of an image engages cortical areas generally involved in tracking moving objects and encoding spatial relations (Cohen et al., 1996). Comparable results have been obtained in rhesus monkeys (Georgopolous et al., 1989). All of this suggests that mental imagery engages neural systems closely related to those engaged in direct perception.

Kosslyn also demonstrated that mental images can be *scanned*, and that this, too, happens in real time (Kosslyn, 1978). Subjects were asked to memorize a map containing a variety of objects in different locations, such as a rock, a hut, a tree and a lake. They were then asked to mentally recall this map, to imagine a little black spot moving from one object on the map to another, and to press a button as soon as it arrived. Here, too, it was found that the time taken varied with the distance the spot had to travel. Since no eye movement is here required, Kosslyn argued that the result can be interpreted as a transformation of the image, specifically a shifting of different parts of the image to the visual centre. In a modification of this study, he was also able to establish that the subjects were most unlikely to have used verbal propositions in the performance of this task. When similar studies were extended to three-dimensional scenes, they showed that the scanning time varied with the three-dimensional distances – a result that may puzzle those who think of mental images a bit too literally as *pictures*.

Although Anderson (1978) had persuasively argued that in the absence of decisive physiological data it will not be possible to decide whether an internal representation is pictorial or propositional, in the end the imagists proved more convincing. *Inter alia* they were supported here by the evidence that mental images engage neural systems that are routinely involved in visual perception.

Young children are known to have a very vivid mental imagery. However, mental images often depend on descriptive concepts, and distortions can result where such concepts are still defective. This came to light as early as the studies by Piaget and Inhelder (1956) of drawings made by young children. A typical example was the task of drawing from memory a tilted test-tube that had been partly filled with a coloured liquid. Typically they would then draw the surface of the liquid parallel to the bottom of the test-tube instead of horizontal. Again, young children often draw from memory a mirror image of some simple figure they have just been shown. This has been explained as a failure of application in the transmission of the descriptive concepts 'is to the left of' and 'is to the right of'.

How, then, are mental images actually realized in the brain? On the strength of the concepts developed in the last chapters, the answer I propose is given by the following proposition:

> To imagine an object of a certain type is for the brain to be in a state of readiness to perceive an object of that type without expecting the perception.

From a biological point of view this seems a natural way in which the power to create representations of absent or hypothetical objects or events could have evolved from brain states occurring in the perception of actual objects or events. It needs to be expressly noted, of course, that a state of *readiness* in the brain to perceive something is not the same as a state of *expectancy*. It consists of only the first of the two components listed in my definition of a state of expectancy [7.1]. The evolutionary development may, therefore, be seen as one in which that first component became established in a new functional role.

States of readiness to perceive an object must indeed be common occurrences in the brain. To take a simple example: whenever your eyes move away from a perceived object, then, as part of your working memory, you will be ready for what you will see if they move back. And if the object has a movement of its own, this will be reflected in the comparison of the expected with the actual perceived location.

The view that *to imagine is to be ready to perceive* was, I believe, first expressed by Ulric Neisser, and in these clear words:

> To imagine something that you know to be unreal, it is only necessary to detach your visual readiness from your general notions of what will really happen and embed them in a schema of a different sort. When you have an image of a unicorn at your elbow – while quite certain that unicorns are purely mythical – you are making ready to pick up the visual information that a unicorn will provide, despite being fully aware that your preparations are in vain. (1976, p.132)

Neisser also postulated that visual explorations are directed by 'antici-patory schemata' which are 'plans for perceptual action as well as readiness for particular kinds of optical structure'. Though the words are different, the view is the same as I have presented.

The close link between visual images and the neural substrates of visual perceptions (Farah et al., 1988) is supported by some of the most notable features of the visual imagination. For example, we can imagine objects we have never experienced before, such as unicorns and dragons, but the components of such images are always drawn from actual visual experi-ences. The new compositions also obey the general features of spatial perceptions, such as the metric of spatial relations. Moreover, visual images are subject to the general constraints and limitations of seeing, such as the fact that seeing is always tied to a standpoint. Thus we can only imagine what we could see at a glance. It has also been found that the eccentricity of the visual field and the degree of optical resolution are similar for mental images and actual visual percepts (Finke & Kosslyn, 1980).

There are, however, also two notable differences. (1) Unlike visual perceptions, visual images do not depend on interpretative processes. They are not dependent on 'unconscious inferences', to use Helmholtz's phrase. They are 'pre-organized into objects and properties of objects', as Kosslyn has put it. (2) Mental images tend to be specified by categories rather than particulars. Hence my use of the phrase 'objects of a certain type' in my explanation of imaginative representations. Termini can be left open. Faces can be imagined without the colour of the eyes being 'mentioned'. Though the leopard may be imagined as a spotted animal, the spots are not indi-viduated. Instead, there is a readiness to meet just a particular type of surface structure, namely a *spotted* one. I shall describe such 'abstractive' representations as *conceptual* representations. An interesting case of a conceptual representation has been observed in the premotor cortex of the monkey. Cells were here found that gave a maximal response *both* if the monkey grasped a small morsel of food, *and* if it saw such a morsel being grasped (Gallese et al., 1996).

8.2. Concepts and their representations

As the word says, a concept is an entity that grasps things together (note also the German, *Begriff*). The concept of any object, be it a triangle or a spacecraft, is a representation in which certain properties are combined as criteria for the object falling under the concept in question. It is a process of categorization. Indeed, it is hard to think of perceptions without categorization. Seeing and understanding are indivisible. As Kant put it, perceptions without concepts are blind (*Critique of Pure Reason*, 1781).

All animals categorize the objects they encounter in the sense that they form *internal reactions that consistently generalize over particular selections of objects* – for example, when they distinguish between edible and inedible objects. Such generalized reactions may be innate or acquired, and they may also depend on some specific set of discrete criteria, as when we distinguish triangles from squares.

In the human case, these categorizations, as well as the criteria on which they may be based, can be either conscious or unconscious. The brain may have unconscious reactions that generalize over a range of stimuli or situations, such as the occurrences that make a person blush. Again, conscious categorizations may have unconscious criteria. You may love or hate someone without knowing why. As this example also shows, the criteria may be wholly subjective. In addition, of course, we have a capacity to form imaginative representations that satisfy some specific set of criteria, as when we imagine a unicorn.

Concepts may have a name attached, as has our concept of a house, fruit or car. Or they may not, as in many of the concepts artists seek to express. Occasionally one sees the notion of concepts restricted to the nameable kind. But that is not a practice I recommend.

Abstractive internal representations are often called *prototypes*, or *schemata*. Thus we can carry in the brain the concept of an aircraft or a fruit without having a specific kind in mind. But when we perceive an actual one, this will activate the concept in an associative manner as a supplementary reaction. This broadly accords with Kant's notion of 'schemata' which connect concepts with percepts in a synthesis that contributes to our understanding.

Concepts of *properties* are easier to understand as generalizing reactions than concepts of *relations*. Yet, the latter offer no special difficulties. Binary relations, for example, can be conceived as reactions that generalize over a class of ordered pairs. The concept of an object A being *above* an object B, for example, can be interpreted as a reaction that generalizes over cases in which a move of visual fixation from B to A requires an upward movement of the eyes. Depending on the case concerned, this may be internally represented as either a gravitational or a body-centred upward movement. However, it could also be object-centred, for example when we look at the drawing of a house and perceive a window as situated above the door.

In verbal communications an object of interest can be identified unequivocally either by a name, such as John Smith or the Albert Memorial, or, if it lacks one, by way of a description in terms of nameable categories or 'classes' according to a rule-governed syntax, as when we identify a certain object as 'the blue ball lying on the little table'. I have argued elsewhere that such a description requires a capacity of the brain to see the object as the logical **intersection** of a sufficient number of nameable classes of entities to narrow it down to a class that has only a single member – which is here foreshadowed by the definite particle 'the'. The nameable classes could be classes of objects ('ball', 'table'), properties ('blue', 'little') or relations ('lying on'). The rules of syntax map the logical intersections. I suggested in passing that a lack of this capacity to form the required logical intersections may be one of the barriers that prevent even the most highly trained chimps from learning more than a rudimentary sign language that is syntactically structured (Sommerhoff, 1974).

When concepts are formed by way of reactions that generalize over a set of sensory perceptions, the main cortical regions involved will lie in the parietotemporal field. However, studies of neural activity made with scalp electrodes have suggested that the *co-ordination* of concepts, hence thought, also critically implicate the prefrontal cortex (Krause et al., 1998). This accords fully with other known prefrontal functions [9.7].

Brain lesions can affect the formation of generalized reactions and their naming in various ways. An interesting case is cited by Rosenfield (1992) after Goldstein (1948). When a patient with parietotemporal lesions was shown a knife together with either a pencil, a loaf of bread, an apple or a fork, it was to her a pencil sharpener, a bread knife, an apple parer or knife-and-fork respectively. The word knife was never uttered spontaneously and when asked 'Could we not always call it simply a knife?' the patient promptly answered 'No.' Clearly, in this case, the lesion had destroyed one type of generalizing reaction.

8.3. More empirical pointers

The idea that the mental image of an object consists of brain processes amounting to a readiness to perceive that object is supported by empirical findings which showed that an object is more quickly recognized if it is first imagined. For example, Farah (1985) demonstrated that detection of a particular letter in a presented text is facilitated by concurrently imagining that letter as opposed to a different letter. Conversely, detection of faint visual stimuli can be made more difficult by imagining other stimuli of the same modality (Segal & Fusella, 1970; see also Finke, 1985). When I have to find a particular word on a printed page, I am often struck by the speed with which the eyes jump to it.

The readiness to perceive an object can be quite powerful. When people expect to see an object they often see it in advance of the critical sensory inputs, and may sometimes confuse the real and imagined object. This mutual influence of imagery and perception adds further evidence of a close relationship, as does the fact that the above observations about the manipulation of visual images also apply to the (nonvisual) mental images formed by congenitally blind subjects. As any author knows, the difficulty in finding misprints in one's own text lies in a tendency of the eyes to see what they expect to see.

The study of brain lesions has given further support to the idea of a close relationship between perception and imagery. Bisiach and Luzzatti (1978) demonstrated that brain injury producing visual neglect of specific regions in visual space impaired visual imagery in the same way. However, inquiries along these lines can be complicated by the fact that both the spatial relations of an image and the more specific visual information of the object's features may be differentially affected in some brain lesions (Farah et al., 1988). This may be due to the different brain regions in which the *where* and the *what* are processed [2.1]. According to the findings of this author and her associates, these two deficits are mainly associated with bilateral lesions in the superior parieto-occipital areas and the inferior temporal-occipital areas respectively. This agrees with the picture I have presented in Chapter 2, and also with the conclusion reached on different grounds by Roland and Gulyas (1994) that the parieto-occipital and temporo-occipital association areas are the main areas subserving visual imagery.

However, the primary visual cortex may also become involved in visual imagery. This has been shown by brain scans for a variety of tasks involving visual imagery, compared with similar tasks that did not. Only the former engaged the visual cortex (Farah et al., 1988). More recently, Kosslyn and his colleagues have shown through similar scans that the primary visual cortex is activated when subjects close their eyes and visualize objects (Kosslyn et al., 1995). This does not, however, imply that the visual image is actually realized in the primary visual cortex. According to our assumptions, mental imagery consists of states of readiness to perceive an object of the imagined kind. It could be that the activation of the primary cortex means no more than that the elements of the elicited states of readiness penetrate right down to this level. Cases have also been reported in which the memory recall of a visual stimulus activated the primary visual cortex.

Visual perceptions and visual imagery have different functional roles. If their implementation is followed up in the brain, a dissociation must, therefore, be expected at some stage. Servos and Goodale (1995) have reported case studies in which patients with bilateral occipital lesions lost visual perception but could still imagine the objects they failed to perceive. Similarly, lesions in the occipital lobe have been observed that caused severe loss of object recognition but did not interfere with the recall of visual images from memory (Behrmann et al., 1992).

As is to be expected, blindness caused by lesions on the visual input side, such as a failing retina, does not impair visual imagery, although visual memories of things seen before the blindness occurred may fade away with time – to the distress of patients who struggle to keep the face of a loved one alive in their mind's eye.

It is interesting to note that neural structures may also be shared in the field of motor images (Decety, 1996; Jeannerod, 1997). Motor imagery occurring in the premotor cortex appears to share neural systems with those involved in active motor control. Similar observations have been made in the higher subcortical structures such as the basal ganglia and cerebellum. This makes sense if, as we have assumed, motor images consist of a state of readiness (or preparation, in this case) for the motor acts – in this case elicited even when no execution is planned.

Since imaginative representations of possible motor acts occur regularly in a subject's review of options, Kosslyn has suggested that the imagery system may actually have evolved to mimic the sorts of gradual transformation that occur when one is physically manipulating objects.

8.4. Episodic memory recall

In connection with consciousness two kinds of memory function are of prime importance: (1) **episodic memory** recall: the return to consciousness (i.e. the IGR) of past experiences; and (2) the so-called **working memory**: traces that contribute to the RWM and maintain its continuity. Since this book focuses on the visual modality, I shall also in the discussion of episodic memory confine myself mainly to the recall of past visual experiences.

The notion of 'memory changes' covers many different kinds of enduring changes produced as the result of experience. There is, for example, a stark difference between the memory changes involved in learning a skill, the formation of habits, and certain kinds of conditioning, on the one hand, and, on the other, the memory record formed of something just seen, heard or done. These two types of memory function may conveniently be distinguished as *procedural* vs. **declarative** memory. Episodic memory recall clearly belongs to the latter. They are separate systems. Brain lesions that affect the one generally leave the other unimpaired. It is widely held that only *attended* experiences will be recorded in declarative memory.

The lasting effect of experiences that cannot individually be recalled is often distinguished as *implicit* knowledge vs. *explicit* knowledge. For example, the single presentation of a novel visual pattern may facilitate appropriate responses at subsequent presentations of the same pattern, without the original experience being recallable.

It is now widely accepted that in both cases of memory changes we are dealing with enduring, and sometimes widely distributed changes at the level of the neurons' synapses. Systems of synapses can evolve in both potency and number (see Appendix A). The potency changes may be changes either inside the synaptic knobs, even a restructuring of them, or changes in adjacent regions. Numerical changes may result from the sprouting of new **dendrites**. To explain basic learning changes, one notable suggestion was made by the Canadian psychologist Donald Hebb in 1949 and is now dubbed the 'Hebbian synapse'. Hebb suggested that synapses increase in potency if they are active at the time that the neuron discharges. This would lead to a strengthening of effective pathways and could result in functionally distinct neural assemblies (see again Appendix A). However, more complex mechanisms, some involving presynaptic contributions from an additional neuron, have since been suggested.

If both implicit and explicit memories reside in changes at the synaptic levels, where lies the difference? That is to say, what conditions must the memory record of a visual perception satisfy if we are to be able to recall that perception? In this connection it is important to realize what is really happening when the past perception of an object or event is brought back into consciousness. *It means that what occurred originally as a conscious perception, hence as an RWM part of the IGR, now reappears in the IGR in the form of an imaginative representation of a past event.* This implies that a population of enduring changes must be produced in the brain by the original perception which maps that part of the IGR and also include connections between them that enables them subsequently to re-enter the IGR *as a body* in their new representational role. This is obviously a very complex affair and very different from earlier conceptions of the records formed by visual perceptions as compact 'engrams', compact bands of neurons forming little capsules that lie dormant in the brain until reactivated.

Short-term and long-term memory

For some time it has been known that in declarative memory functions two systems need to be distinguished: short-term memory (STM) and long-term memory (LTM). The former actively maintains representations for brief periods only, up to 30 minutes at most; the latter can last throughout life, but the depth of its impression is a matter of growth over time, of a progressive *consolidation*.

It is still unknown what has to happen to transfer STM to LTM. Focused attention, repetition and internal rehearsal may all play a part. It is a complex process in which several nuclear structures appear to be critically involved, such as the amygdala, **mammillary bodies**, the medial thalamus and the hippocampus. But these are not the actual locations in which the memories are laid down. In the rare case of a patient in whom the hippocampus had to be removed because of a potentially lethal epilepsy, all memories laid down before the operation proved to have remained intact.

The complexity of the transfer from STM to LTM makes it a vulnerable process. Very tiny lesions can block it, such as lesions in the mammalian bodies or a small region of the hippocampus. It can also be disrupted by stimulation of the reticular formation and of the intralaminar nuclei of the thalamus (see Figure 9.3, p. 141). Both are parts of the brain's general activating and arousal system [9.2].

In contrast to LTM, STM has not only a limited life but also a limited stability throughout its life. Thus it may be wholly extinguished by shocks to the brain, as in concussion or electroconvulsive shock therapy. In this *retrograde amnesia* a period of up to 20 minutes before the shock remains a total blank. The brain's interpretation of its sensory inputs during that period appears to leave no trace. This contrasts with the deficits that occur when STM fails to transfer to LTM. A patient suffering from this *anterograde amnesia* may retain in the brain any task he has learnt in a series of laboratory experiments, but will not afterwards recall the experiments in which he learnt that task, or the laboratory equipment used. In a syndrome that can be caused by alcoholism and is known as the Korsakoff syndrome, after the Russian neuropsychiatrist who first studied it, anterograde amnesia occurs coupled with much confabulation and a general clouding of consciousness. Thus the patient may recognize his wife, but in her absence deny that he is married.

Where perceptual memories are located

The storage locations of the LTM are difficult to determine because loss of LTM through brain lesions appears to be mainly a loss of recall capacity. Nevertheless, it seems to be a general principle that both short-term and long-term memories of events are stored in the brain regions in which the remembered events were originally processed. Thus memory for object features appears to be mediated by a distributed system that includes the ventral parastriate cortex and the inferior temporal gyrus, whereas memory for spatial location is mediated by a system which includes the more dorsal parastriate cortex and also the posterior regions of the parietal lobe (Owen et al., 1996). This agrees with the two pathways shown in Figure 2.1 (p. 29). According to PET studies conducted by Faillenot et al. (1997) memories of object *shapes* may involve both pathways: the ventral one for the shape as such, and the dorsal one for 3D orientations.

Pictures of objects form a category of their own, and memories here seem to involve the medial temporal lobe (Grady et al., 1998). In recent fMRI studies conducted by Brewer et al. (1998), subjects were tested on how well they remember photographs in a series shown to them. The recorded magnitude of the regional activation in the right prefrontal cortex and bilateral parahippocampal cortex then permitted prediction of which photos would be remembered best. The parahippocampal cortex is part of the medial temporal lobe, and, as we shall see later, the right prefrontal cortex is generally implicated in the initiation of memory searches.

Positioning events in time

Consider the concrete case of episodic memory recall when an event I perceived in the recent past now returns to my consciousness. At the time of its perception the event was part of the conscious portion of the RWM, the portion that is included in the IGR. Now it reappears in the IGR in the narrowly focused form of an imaginative representation of a past perception. I can't go back in time. But my imagination can, and it can present me with representations (including the self-reference we discussed in Section 3.1) that are positioned in time and amount to a chunk of autobiography.

Does this positioning in time presuppose experiences to be recorded in the brain together with a time co-ordinate, perhaps one linked to some inner clock? I am certain that it does not. Rather, I subscribe to the view that experiences are recorded together with the *context* in which they occurred. Hence it is plausible to assume that in autobiographical representations it is the recorded context that fits the recalled experience into a time frame. I remember once as a child being lightly but painfully struck by a passing car, and I remember *when* that happened because I also remember that I was playing outside my primary school. I don't believe, therefore, that autobiographical memory recall forces us to introduce discrete temporal variables into our account of consciousness. This contextual reference also shows that autobiographical representations are fairly sophisticated achievements. Experimental work with children suggests that the ability to remember events autobiographically does not develop before the age of about four or five years (Perner & Ruffman, 1995).

Acquisition and retrieval

PET scans have shown that the acquisition and retrieval of episodic memory activate different brain regions (Shallice et al., 1994). Some studies have shown that the controlled recall of such memories is the result of a search initiated in the prefrontal cortex (Schacter et al., 1997), a region we have met before as the source of a top-down raising of regional activity levels. Closer studies have suggested that the encoding of episodic memory is under control of the left prefrontal (Cabeza et al., 1997), whereas the search for episodic memory recall is guided by the right anterior and posterior prefrontal areas (Nyberg, 1998). This prefrontally initiated recall of past events will typically start with a concept held in working memory, followed by a search for memory records that satisfy the object of the search. An example would be my trying to remember where I had previously met the person who had just greeted me across the street. Now this search need not be a conscious search and *serial* process. It can also be a set of parallel unconscious processes, not unlike those suggested in the case of the brain's subliminal review of the alternative possible responses in a given situation [2.4]. On this view, the brain here tentatively activates simultaneously a set of domain-relevant structures, with the winner taking all, so to speak. In either case, the final result will tend to be a reactivation of the cortical structures in which the recalled episode was originally processed (Rosler et al., 1995). This conclusion is supported by the brain regions at which physical stimulation can produce episodic memory recall [9.5]. I have described above the form in which this reactivation occurs.

Episodic memory recall is not necessarily faithful. When resurrecting a past event the imagination can fill gaps, add cohesion and certainly cause distortions to an extent that in some respects can make it a *reconstructive* rather than *reproductive* function. As long ago as in the early 1930s Frederic Bartlett studied this constructive element and drew attention to it. He showed that recalled memories are not facsimiles of the original experiences. They tend to fill in and distort the original information according to present beliefs or emotions. Thus the pure trace theory of episodic memory proved to be an over-simplification. Another point to note concerns the richness of the contents of episodic memory. Here what is recorded and retrieved consists not of the raw sensory data of the original experience, but of the conscious components of the brain's interpretation of those data, possibly including context and affective components. This very richness of episodic memory underscores that we are dealing here with widely distributed patterns of neural changes. It explains why local removal of brain tissue never produces loss of the memory of any single episode.

As regards the limits of episodic memory recall, our analysis suggests that (1) in a recallable experience, the neural changes that form the record of that experience must lie within the scope of the *potential* receptive fields of the networks of neurons that constitute the IGR; and (2) memory *recall* implies a top-down selective raising of neural activity that causes the influence of those neural changes to enter the *dominant* sphere in those receptive fields (see Appendix A).

8.5. Working memory

Working memory is commonly taken to denote the short-term storage and online manipulation of information necessary in action planning, language and problem solving. Although it is a species of STM it needs to be given a separate identity. In the light of our analysis I include notably the records of recent experiences that shape the current RWM and maintain its continuity, especially through the expectancies that recent experiences have created.

Whenever our eyes scan the surrounding world, or parts of it, they engage in a serial process, and serial processes need a buffer if they are to have a cumulative effect. In the present model it is provided by the cumulative effect of the contributions to the RWM that the scanning eyes make in confirming or updating it. This can be considered the most basic level of working memory.

Next we have the expectancies that result from recent experiences and figure as part of the current RWM. Examples were given in Section 2.3. To add yet another example: out of the window of an apartment I am visiting, I look at the garden. I then turn away again. The episode leaves several traces. It has expanded my brain's RWM of my location and environment. Part of this comes in the form of expectancies of what I would see if I returned to the window, or even if I were to enter the garden. If I return to the window, the sight will now be familiar, that is to say, it will no longer elicit the orienting reactions common to novel events. My awareness of this, as part of the qualia, amounts to a recognition that the sight has been met before.

Yet another form of working memory occurs when representations are kept alive 'in the mind' because of their relevance to current tasks, as in the so-called 'self-ordered tasks'. These are serial tasks in which the subjects have to see the responses that still have to be made in the light of the responses already made. But we need not look just at laboratory experiments. Even in ordinary language communications we have to remember, in starting a new sentence, what was said in the last one. Rodney Cotterill (1998) has aptly called this kind of working memory 'the blackboard of the mind'. Even rats appear to have this kind of working memory, as shown by ingenious experiments conducted by Beninger and colleagues (1974). These concentrated on four activities that the rats do naturally if left to their own devices: face-washing, rearing up, walking or remaining immobile. Four levers were provided, each relating to one of these activities. The rats could obtain food if they pressed the lever that corresponded to the last of these four activities that they had performed. The startling fact is that the animals could learn this.

One of the tests for working memory, often used with animals, is the *delayed response* task. In these arrangements the animal is tested for its ability to respond after an interval to a briefly presented stimulus. The results have shown the prefrontal cortex to play a critical role in this ability. For animals with lesion in this part of the brain, out of sight was out of mind.

9

WHERE DOES CONSCIOUSNESS RESIDE IN THE BRAIN?

9.1. No 'Cartesian Theatre'

In the dualist philosophy of Descartes (1596–1650) the mind was seen as a nonmaterial substance distinct from the material brain and interacting with it at just one location, the pineal gland. Descartes had picked on this organ because he saw it as the highest unitary brain structure below the two hemispheres. Dualism, as I have explained, now has few followers among neuroscientists; nor has the belief that at some obscure central location in the brain there is a *place* where 'it all comes together' and consciousness arises. Dennett (1991) calls it a 'Cartesian Theatre'. A great deal of his widely read and very substantial book is devoted to convincing us that this 'metaphorical picture of how consciousness must sit in the brain' is an illusion – as indeed it is.

In our model it 'all comes together' in quite a different sense, namely in the IGR, defined as an extensive internal representation of the current state of the organism which includes the total situation facing the organism in both the external and the internal world. Since we identify the primary consciousness with the IGR, the seat of that consciousness in the brain will be the seat of the IGR. My suggestions in this respect will be made in Section 9.8, and it will certainly not be a narrow location.

Dennett, of course, is a philosopher and his 'explanation' of consciousness is an attempt to clarify certain issues of interest to his profession. It is not a scientific explanation. It invites no criticism, therefore, that all his arguments are conducted on a metaphorical plane. But from a scientific standpoint this does make a big difference. He himself admits in retrospect that all he has done is to replace one family of metaphors with another. For a description of consciousness he introduces the metaphor of a 'virtual Joycean Machine'. This is a 'virtual machine' in the sense of a 'temporal structure made of rules rather than wires'. It is a 'Joycean' virtual machine in the sense that the underlying brain processes are able to produce a serial 'stream of consciousness' out of the 'parallel hubbub' of the brain – the stream of consciousness having been a characteristic literary technique of James Joyce. Unfortunately, Dennett clings here to likening the mind/brain relation to the relation between computer software and hardware. Add to this his dismissal of the qualia, and the gap between his treatment of consciousness and our biological approach becomes even more conspicuous.

However, there are also points of agreement, apart from his dismissal of the 'Cartesian Theatre'. We both agree on the essentially speculative nature of the brain's model of the world. In so far as the RWM is based on acquired what-leads-to-what expectancies, it is essentially a speculative interpretation of the sensory inputs on the basis of acquired knowledge. According to Dennett, at any point in time and at different places, the brain produces multiple 'drafts' of narrative fragments about the external world which are speculative and at various stages of being 'edited' in the light of the sensory inputs. Finally, I agree with Dennett when he demolishes the rather naive notion that if you could colour all afferent neural channels green and all **efferent** channels red, then you would find across the brain an interface strip between these colours that could be identified with the seat of consciousness.

9.2. Overview of the main structures involved in visuomotor responses

For the benefit of those readers who are not already familiar with the gross functional anatomy of the brain, I must start by drawing together what has already been said about the main players in the processes that lead from a visual perception to a considered response, and also fill some remaining gaps. Informed readers can skip this section. To keep it within reasonable bounds, I shall confine myself to the structures most relevant to consciousness. Even so, it can only be a thumbnail sketch.

Naturally we know most about the easiest accessible regions of the brain, the cerebral cortex. For its main divisions see Figures 9.1 and 9.2. This six-layered and crinkled surface structure of the brain is responsible for the highest brain functions due to the flexible way in which it is able to analyse, associate or integrate the information passed to it. It is only 3–5 millimetres thick, its inner surface consisting of the 'white matter', the massive neural fibres that form the links between the different cortical regions. Over 80 per cent of fibres leaving the cerebral cortex terminate in other cortical regions.

The main part of our story starts at the projection of the visual inputs to area V1 of the visual cortex (**Brodmann** area 17, Figure 9.2) – via the lateral geniculate body of the thalamus (see below, and Figure 2.3, p. 32). Here begins the analysis of the visual image at the lowest cortical level. The result is passed on to the areas V2–V6 (inside areas 18, 19) for analysis at more complex levels, as I have explained in Section 2.2.

Further processing on the way towards our visual perception of the world and the RWM then occurs along the dorsal and ventral pathways I have described in Chapter 2 and illustrated in Figure 2.1 (see p. 29).

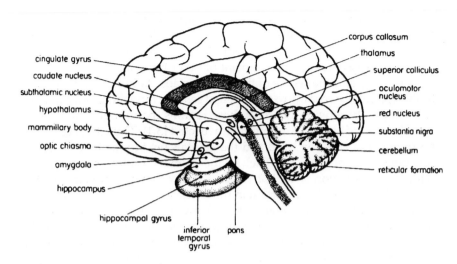

Figure 9.1   *Schematic section through the human brain (2)*

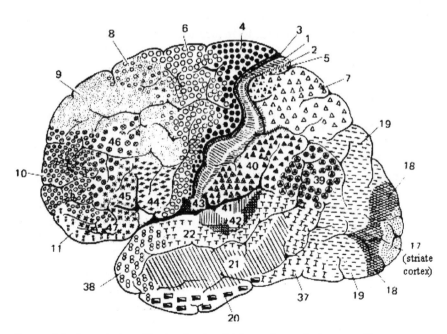

Figure 9.2   *Lateral view of brain, showing Brodmann's numbering according to perceived differences in cell structure. Note the size of the extrastriate visual processing area 19 and of area 21 implicated in object recognition*

Between the parietal cortex and the **central fissure** (the heavy line in Figure 9.2) lies the somatosensory cortex (area 5). Whereas the parietal cortex (area 7) is the main recipient of proprioceptive information, the somatosensory cortex is the recipient of other body information, such as body posture and the senses of the body surface. Although its regions are tidily separated according to the different sensory modalities, such as touch and temperature, within each of these regions the topography is not as straightforwardly simple as might be expected [3.1]. Thus the face may be represented next to the hand and the genitals next to the feet. One of its functions is to provide feedback to the **primary motor cortex** (area 4), whose main function is the fine regulation of voluntary movements. This close link is obviously important in the formation of somatic act–outcome expectancies. In fact, the interrelations between the primary sensory and motor areas are so close that they are often described jointly as the sensorimotor cortex. Jointly the somatosensory and parietal cortices are involved in the brain's internal representation of the body as a whole, the body schema, the very core of the RWM [3.1].

For the final stage in our cortical story we have to look at the large association areas of the frontal lobe. This lies forward of the central fissure that separates it from the somatosensory cortex. It consists of six main regions: the primary motor cortex (area 4), the premotor cortex (area 6), the **frontal eye fields** (area 8), the supplementary motor area (top of, and medial to area 6), the prefrontal cortex (areas 10 and 11) and Broca's area (named after Paul Broca, its discoverer) which is implicated in the production of words in phonic form (areas 44 and 45). For representations of the *meaning* of words we have to look to area 22 in the superior temporal lobe.

The prefrontal cortex has already been mentioned as a region of special interest, since it appears to harbour the highest level at which imaginative representations are brought into play, action plans are examined, attention is controlled and memory search initiated – all in response to both the currently perceived situation and the subject's current motivational state. I shall return to this region at some length in Section 9.7.

The activities of the cerebral cortex cannot be considered in isolation from those of subcortical structures, and especially the bundle of nuclei contained in the thalamus. Each cortical region receives from an associated thalamic nucleus and feeds back to it. In part, but only in part, the thalamus acts here as an upward relay station of sensory afferents to the respective reception areas of the cortex. In addition, different sensory fibre tracks are regrouped within its massive domain, and there are many opportunities here for the interaction and integration of different modalities. All regions of the thalamus receiving specific afferents are surrounded by nuclei that are actuated by diffuse multisynaptic and non-specific ascending and descending pathways. The *intralaminar region*, in particular, is held to perform crucial integrating functions, with vast projections to the cerebral cortex. The *centromedian nucleus*, too, is held to be a powerful integrator at the thalamic level. It receives from other thalamic nuclei and projects to them. It is a convergence centre for inputs from the **reticular formation** (a long tract of ascending and descending fibres that forms the core of the brainstem) and cerebellum and also affected by motivational factors through projections from the limbic system. In view of its close connections with the prefrontal cortex, the *dorsomedial nucleus* also needs to be mentioned.

The thalamus lies at the head of the *ascending reticular activating system* (ARAS), whose main body is formed by the reticular formation. The influence of the ARAS is paramount in controlling the overall level of activity or arousal in the major cortical areas and it also decides between sleep and wakefulness. Figure 9.3 shows the most relevant nuclei of the thalamus and their extensions (after Newman and Baars, 1993).

Another subcortical structure of considerable importance is the hippocampus, which I have already mentioned in connection with cognitive maps [6.5] and the transfer of STM to LTM [8.4]. It owes its name to its shape, which resembles that of a sea-horse. Folded into the medial (inner) temporal lobe and lying below the hippocampal gyrus and inferior

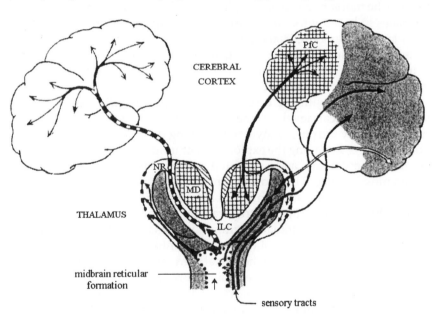

Figure 9.3 *Model of an extended reticular-thalamic activating system (ERTAS) showing a schematic coronal section through the midbrain and thalamus, illustrating projections (arrows) between them, and with the cerebral cortex (from Newman & Baars, 1993, with permission of World Scientific Publishing).*
The shaded areas represent classical sensory pathways (in the midbrain); the 'specific' nuclei of the thalamus; and the areas of the cortex (right side) with which these nuclei share projections. The crosshatched areas designate the medial dorsal (MD) nucleus and prefrontal cortex (PfC)

cingulate gyrus, it seems to draw upon a mass of processed information, receiving inputs from virtually all regions of the cerebral cortex. It plays a part in the processes of habituation to repeatedly occurring sensory or situational patterns. Anterior regions contain neurons specifically responsive to novelty in the sensory input, while in the posterior region neurons are found that respond specifically to familiar stimuli that have behavioural relevance (Strange et al., 1999). This seems a heady mixture of functions. Yet it does not seem to be essential for consciousness. It is perhaps best understood as a general supporting structure for the surrounding cortical areas.

Two main pathways are involved in the execution of action sequences: the **pyramidal** and the **extrapyramidal** tracts. The first originates mainly in the primary motor cortex (area 4), but also has inputs from the somatosensory cortex and motor association areas. It is topographically organized and local movements of face or limbs can be elicited by electrical stimulation. But it is not the originator of voluntary movements. Loss of area 4 does not impair the subject's general ability to execute fully goal-directed voluntary movements, but produces a loss of fine control. It runs straight down to the motor neurons of the spinal cord. The extrapyramidal pathway originates in broadly the same cortical areas but reaches the spinal cord only via the **basal ganglia** and an assortment of midbrain and brainstem nuclei performing a variety of organizational motor functions. It also includes nuclei connected with the cerebellum whose functions were briefly described in Section 2.3.

In conjunction with the cerebellum the basal ganglia constitute the highest subcortical level in the implementation of planned action sequences. They are deeply involved in laying down the gross features of motor patterns, including the exploitation or inhibition of built-in reflexes, and in such automatic and associated movements as those involved in maintaining balance. They collect sensory information from wide areas of the cerebral cortex and funnel it back to the frontal action planning centres. When these cortical centres are relieved through the development with practice of semi-automatic routines, the basal ganglia complex takes over as the key player, but not the sole one: unlike the pyramidal system, it has no direct connections to the spinal cord and its motor ganglia.

The motivational state of the brain is brought to bear on all of this through the activities of the limbic system. Its main subcortical constituents are hypothalamus, amygdala, mammillary bodies and parts of the thalamus. It also includes the hippocampal, **entorhinal** and cingulate gyri, and the periamygdaloid as well as prepyriform cortex. The bundle of nuclei composing the *hypothalamus* is of special importance because it forms the main region through which the physiological needs of the body, such as hunger and thirst, make themselves known. It controls body temperature, eating, drinking, sexual drive, maternal behaviour, hormonal balance, and to some extent also pain. The amygdala, on the other hand, seems to be more generally concerned with our well-being as a whole, including the social context and sexual arousal. Taken overall, the outputs from the limbic system govern the evaluation of the current situation in the light of the organism's needs. They add the affective dimension to what is perceived, connecting particular representations with particular gratifications and thereby influencing the attention they receive.

9.3. Evidence from brain lesions

In the next four sections I briefly want to review some information relevant to the IGR, and hence to consciousness, that can be gathered from four main methods of investigation: studying the effect of brain damage, the responses of individual neurons through microelectrode penetration, the effect of local physical stimulation, and regional brain activity as shown by modern imaging techniques such as PET and fMRI. The physical stimulation may be electrical, chemical or transcranial magnetic.

Some of the information reviewed below relates to memory recall, and here I must remind you that in our model *memory recall means that what occurred originally as a conscious experience, hence as a broadly distributed part of the IGR, now reappears in the IGR in the narrowly focused form of an imaginative representation, most commonly of an autobiographical nature.*

In connection with evidence from brain lesions, I must also remind you of the warning given in Chapter 1: if one removes a bit of the innards of a TV set and finds that the picture disappears, this does not mean that the picture is encoded in that part of the set. Similarly with the brain. Tiny lesions in the amygdala can disrupt a transfer from STM to LTM, but this does not mean that these small structures are part of the encoded LTM. Again, the perception of movement can be lost through lesions in visual area V5. Moving objects now appear as a succession of stills. But this does not mean that the movements themselves are encoded in V5. However, in the lesions discussed below the affected areas do seem to be part of the encoding process and shed light on the specialization or modularity of the structures concerned.

Whereas total loss of the primary visual cortex (area 17) causes blindness, localized lesions cause local blind spots, known as 'scotoma'. The effect of lesions in areas 18 and 19 depends on their location; they may, for example, interfere with optokinetic movements of the eyes, the movements in which the eyes automatically follow a moving object and remain fixed on it when it stops.

In view of its role in visually guided actions, lesions in the parietal cortex can cause deficits in the localization of targeted objects. I have mentioned the patient who could recognize a postage stamp but could not point to it. In others the control of actions in near extrapersonal space is impaired – the so-called *apraxias* (loss of skill). The affected processes are mostly unconscious and the defect shows itself in extreme clumsiness. The patient may know what movements are required in some practical skill, like peeling an apple, but has difficulty in executing them in a co-ordinated and integrated manner. Lesions in the parietal lobe may also impair the *imaginative* representation of spatial relations between objects. Patients suffering from this defect may be asked to draw a bicycle and quite contentedly go about the job, although they are, in fact, scattering its parts all over the page. Yet reality-centred representations still appear intact, at least in the unconscious portion of the RWM: the patient may have no problem in picking up that pencil to perform that task. None of these lesions have a direct bearing on the nature of consciousness. The opposite is true for the parietal lesions that have been described in Chapter 6 under the heading of 'neglect', when a whole limb or half the visual field may be lost from consciousness. These suggest that outputs from the affected parietal regions make an important contribution to the IGR. Alternatively, one might suppose that the affected structures are themselves part of the IGR network – the answer I shall defend below [9.8].

Lesions in the somatosensory cortex cause loss of fine discrimination between the stimuli to which the damaged region is receptive.

Lesions in the inferior temporal cortex can cause consistent impairment of visual discrimination and corresponding loss of object recognition, and what in more general terms may be described as vision-based deficits in the internal representations of external objects or events. Damage to the medial and inferior temporal lobes in man causes loss of recognition of complex shapes, words, faces, people or other objects, and may also cause emotional deficits. Lesions may also cause a loss of concepts, i.e. generalizing reactions of a specific kind. We are faced here with a loss of the kind of associations that contribute to the categorization of the sensory inputs, with a corresponding loss of meaning in what is perceived. Thus in some lesions the patient may show he is aware of a ladder by walking around it but has no idea what a ladder is for. In other cases he may see a flower just as a convoluted colourful shape with a green surround. You may also recall the case in which a brain lesion destroyed a very specific categorizing reaction, namely that to knives [8.2]. The subtlety of some such meaning systems is illustrated by known cases in which brain damage has been found to impair the recognition of living things significantly more than recognition of nonliving things. Complete removal of both the medial temporal regions (see Figure 2.1, p. 29) produces an amnesic syndrome: the patients may retain normal intelligence, learning ability and cognitive skills, but they cannot remember anything from one minute to the next. No lesions have ever been found that would remove a single discrete object from the RWM. We can see the reason for this in the fact that object recognition depends on the binding together of analyses conducted in different regions of the brain [2.6].

Total loss of consciousness may result from lesions in the ARAS. This includes the intralaminar nuclei of the thalamus, known to play a general activating role in supporting conscious awareness. Bilateral loss of these nuclei causes coma. This makes sense, since both have a cortical activating function.

In the frontal lobe two kinds of lesions are of interest from the organizational point of view: lesions in the motor association areas that can tell us where motor sequences may be formed, stored or imagined, and lesions in the prefrontal cortex, that can affect an important set of major functions. Both will be considered in Section 9.7.

9.4. Evidence from unit responses

The responses of individual neurons in different brain structures can be extensively investigated through microelectrode penetrations. This is one of the main tools of the bottom-up approach in neuroscience. A variety of results have been cited in Chapters 6 and 8, and need not be repeated here. Their main contribution lies in the information they give about the dominant receptive fields of neurons and their topographical organization. For example, as we move forward along the occipitoparietal-frontal pathway in the analysis of visual inputs (Figure 2.1, p. 29), we move into regions in which the visual inputs are analysed at higher and higher levels of complexity. Observed unit responses here show the topography of the visual field to be reproduced over and over again, but with a simultaneous expansion of the neurons' dominant receptive fields, and also a growing multimodal input.

No evidence has been found of single neurons in the brain being tuned to be responsive exclusively to a particular object. This is the myth of the 'grandmother cell', the cell that supposedly lights up only when grandmother is perceived (and not just as part of a general reaction to the lady). In view of what we know about the complexities of object recognition, it is hard to see how such single-cell responses could come about in the first place and how the brain might come to rely on the action of one single cell.

Given my earlier account of the role of act–outcome expectancies in the RWM, it is worth noting that both the parietal cortex and the medial superior area of the temporal cortex have been shown to contain cells that respond both to motor information about self-paced acts and to visual information about outcomes (Hietanen & Perrett, 1993). This is obviously relevant to the question of regional involvement in the formation of the RWM.

9.5. Evidence from physical stimulation

Electrical stimulation of the striate cortex produces the sensation of light flashes, and when applied to regions mapping the periphery of the retina it can cause movements of the eyes in the corresponding direction. Stimulation of the dorsal regions of areas 18 and 19 also produces eye movements. The effect changes when the stimulation is applied to the ventral regions of 18 and 19 where they pass into the inferior temporal lobe.

Stimulation in other parietal areas can result in uncontrolled movements in different parts of the body. As might be expected, stimulation of the somatosensory cortex produces sensations relating to different parts of the body. Stimulation of the primary motor cortex has already been mentioned. Although it elicits organized movements, it is not the area in which voluntary acts are initiated: the stimulation does not create a feeling of 'I want to' in relation to the elicited responses.

Stimulation in the inferior temporal cortex, notably area 21, can produce both sensations of visions *and* memories of such sensations. In the early 1950s Wilder Penfield discovered that electrical stimulation of the temporal lobe could on occasions produce in his patients the vivid recall of some past set of events, some episode in their life. One patient reported that she thought she heard a mother calling her boy – something that happened a long time ago. But Penfield also found that quite different memories might be evoked by the same stimulation on subsequent occasions. Nor is this kind of effect the sole property of cortical areas. Stimulation of the hippo-campus and amygdala can also produce recall of past events (Penfield & Jasper, 1954). The richness of what is here evoked suggests that stimulation produces these results through a spreading activation of regions beyond the immediately stimulated area.

In addition to evoking memories of past events, physical stimulation of locations in the temporal lobe has also produced illusions: objects may seem familiar when they are not, larger or nearer than they are, or receding when they are not. It can also result in hallucinatory experiences of complete scenes – occasionally in real time. Thus the temporal lobe appears to be involved also in the representation of temporal sequences. This has been confirmed by experiments in which subjects are asked to count. If a physical stimulus is then applied to the temporal lobe for a few seconds while they are counting, they will pause and then start again. If now asked why they stopped they may deny stopping (Ramachandran & Hirstein, 1998). Evidently, the disruption was not projected into the IGR. On the other hand, this work has also shown that seizures of the temporal lobe can have spreading hallucinatory effects that may cover everything we normally associate with consciousness: qualia, significance, body image, convictions of truth or falsehood and the unity of the person. As I have explained in Chapter 2, hallucinations can be interpreted as a case where purely imaginative representations are injected into the IGR as part of the RWM in a manner that seems to be beyond correction by sensory feedback.

9.6. Evidence from brain imaging

An obvious use for brain scans such as PET and fMRI is to look for local activity that is specifically related to conscious processes. However, interpretation of the data is limited by the fact that high regional activity may be caused by attentional processes rather than consciousness as such. And those attentional processes may cut across the division between the conscious and unconscious. Of course, the study of attention may be the very object of research. For example, PET studies have been used to study the changes in regional activity that occur when otherwise relaxed human subjects have been given an attention-demanding reaction task. This showed up the premotor and anterior cingulate cortex, the intralaminar nuclei of the thalamus and the reticular formation (Kinomura et al., 1996). Other work has shown the posterior parietal cortex to be active when the focus of attention is switched by way of a shift in the eyes' line of fixation. In both cases the results cut across the division between the conscious and unconscious brain processes.

Some PET studies have confirmed conclusions already reached by other means. For example, that novel events tend to engage the brain almost globally [7.1], but as suitable patterns of responses begin to be established, this falls away and activity contracts to whichever pathway most directly connects the sensory inputs with the appropriate representations or motor outputs. Similar studies have shown a diminished activity in the engaged frontal and parietal areas of the cerebral cortex when a task defined by arbitrary rules becomes a familiar one.

Blakemore and colleagues have investigated regional brain activity in response to tones that were either unpredictable, or predictable through self-generation. When tones were unpredictable, increased activity was seen in the inferior and superior temporal lobe bilaterally, the right parahippocampal gyrus and parietal cortex. Self-generated activity produced activity in a number of motor and premotor areas, including the dorsolateral prefrontal cortex (Blakemore et al., 1998). The involvement of the prefrontal region in self-generated activity is also shown by other brain scans. A simple example is the observation that self-paced finger movements will activate the prefrontal cortex, but not metronome-paced ones (Wessel et al., 1997).

PET scans uniformly show the prefrontal areas activated by simple willed actions, and the dorsolateral prefrontal cortex seems to be the hub of the actual decision-making processes. The region is known to have fibre connections to the motor association regions of the cortex involved in the execution of the willed acts. These may be activated even when a sequence of acts is merely imagined.

This brings me to the general question of imaginative representations. In Chapter 8 I mentioned the interesting fact that PET scans have shown the perception of an object and the imagining of the same object to activate similar areas in the visual cortex. As I pointed out, though, this does not imply that the activity of the visual cortex *mediates* visual imagery. Similarly, imagined motion as well as real motion of perceived objects activates visual area V5. So does the mere *illusion* of motion, such as that created by certain trick drawings. You may also recall my mentioning PET scans which showed that imagined grasping activates the left inferior and middle frontal cortex as well as the left frontal parietal cortex – all involved in actual grasping.

Also worth mentioning are the brain scans that have been designed to study tasks which demand something 'being held in the mind'. This occurs when a subject has to carry out a sequential task in which each step needs to take account of action taken at the preceding step or steps. These tasks showed an involvement both of the prefrontal cortex and of the posterior areas related to the kind of information that is being held in mind. It appeared to make no difference whether the associated information was internally generated or came from the outside world (Frith & Dolan, 1996).

PET scans performed on sleeping subjects have shown a decrease in neural activity in the orbitofrontal cortex during slow-wave sleep (Maquet et al., 1997).

9.7. The prefrontal cortex[1]

Several aspects of the prefrontal cortex have proved to be of interest so far: its involvement at the highest level at which the current situation is evaluated in the light of the subject's current motivational state and at which imaginative representations are co-ordinated, action plans are examined, attention is controlled and memory search initiated. Its role as a top level of control has been recognized by a number of writers: Shallice (1982) speaks of a 'supervisory attentional system' and Baddeley (1986) of a 'supervisory controlling system' which he calls the 'central executive'. In view of these high-level functions, the long-distance goals that humans can pursue and the possession of language, it is perhaps not surprising that, at 29 per cent, the portion of the brain occupied by the prefrontal cortex in humans greatly exceeds even that occupied in chimps (17 per cent) – although this is still very high compared with the 3 per cent occupied in cats, for example.

The effect of brain lesions has shown up some major regional divisions. Loss of the dorsolateral regions affects both cognitive and executive functions, and may increase aggressiveness. Loss of the orbitofrontal and orbitomedial regions results in emotional instability, distractibility, lack of social insight and loss of integration or initiation of emotional behaviour. Loss of mediofrontal regions results in loss of spontaneity, lack of motor behaviour, weakness of the lower extremities and increased response latency. It also seems that the ventral and cingulate regions of the prefrontal cortex are involved in affective, appetitive and/or aversive stimuli.

Action planning

By definition, all 'willed' or 'voluntary' actions are determined by conscious decisions, hence by the IGR. In view of what is included in the IGR, we can speak here of the highest level of action planning and of actions with the most richly informed goals. They are the most richly informed not only on account of how much information is covered by the IGR, but also because these frontal regions form the highest level at which received information is evaluated in the light of the subject's emotional and motivational state and appropriate action plans are explored in the light of current needs. These needs are brought to bear on the action planning through direct or indirect inputs from the limbic system. It is significant that even in the deepest state of mental relaxation the prefrontal cortex is more active than the rest of the brain. Some studies have shown that not only the prefrontal cortex but also the anterior cingulate cortex may be involved in learning major action sequences (Jenkins et al., 1994; Jueptner et al., 1996).

Cortical regions that deal with the examination of alternative action plans must be especially sensitive to act–outcome expectancies. As Ingvar has observed in a review of the cerebral correlates of wilful acts: 'The prefrontal activation accompanying volitional acts most likely corresponds to a wilful mobilization of inner representations of future events' (1994, p. 11). Masataka Watanabe (1996) has recorded reward expectancies in the prefrontal cortex of the monkey. Some cells fired selectively in accordance with an expected reward, while others fired in accordance with the location of that reward. A third group was influenced by whether the reward had actually been seen in the given test. Some of these neurons showed throughout a high level of activity in delayed reaction tasks in which working memory had to keep in mind the location of some food-wells while they were temporarily hidden by a screen.

Note that the frontal exploration of alternative action plans requires communication with the posterior regions in which the relevant act–outcome expectancies are encoded. PET studies have shown that when prefrontal regions are activated the contributory occipital regions tend to be co-activated. Thus we must expect to find both fronto-occipital pathways serving the neural distribution of the attentional set [6.2], and occipito-frontal pathways supplying the frontal regions with the necessary information about anticipated consequences of contemplated actions. Injections with tracers have shown, for example, that the mid-dorsolateral regions 9, 46 and 46/9 receive not only inputs from the frontal areas 6, 8, 9 and 11 and anterior cingulate, but also distant inputs from the retrospinal cortex, the ventral part of the medial parietal region, medial region of visual area 19, and from the superior temporal lobe (Pandya and Yeterian, in Roberts et al., 1998).

A number of studies have reported a dissociation in the prefrontal cortex between spatial processing and feature processing, the dorsolateral regions serving the first and the ventrolateral the second. Some action planning must, therefore, involve an integration of these two elements. PET studies have shown that the regions around area 46 are consistently activated as human subjects access visuospatial information from long-term storage and/or from the immediate experience of representation-based actions.

(Goldman-Rakic in Roberts et al., 1998). In monkeys, lesions in this region cause severe deficits in delayed response tasks.

The fact that the prefrontal cortex deals predominantly with distant goals and goals based on social awareness explains the paradox that the prefrontal cortex can be severely damaged without any immediately apparent effects on the subject's behaviour. This is true even when its connections with the thalamus are severed in prefrontal leucotomy. This paradox was startlingly brought to the notice of the medical world about 150 years ago in the famous case of Phineas Gage, an American mining engineer who was heedlessly tamping down dynamite with an iron bar when the resulting explosion drove this bar right through his prefrontal lobe. Yet he lost neither consciousness nor, it seems, any of the intellectual functions which at that time were still believed to be resident in the bulge of the cranium that so noticeably distinguishes us from the apes. However, strong personality changes soon became apparent, such as fitfulness, loss of social inhibitions and concern for others, loss of industriousness, and especially loss of foresight and in the capacity to adopt new goals. Similar side effects tend to follow prefrontal leucotomies. One immediate effect, and one reason for performing the operation, is to reduce anxiety. For example, awareness of pain does not cease, but it no longer arouses the patient. Even severe pains may be reported with a smile. Another effect is a diminished ability to do two tasks at once.

Imaginative functions

The ultimate goal of an action tends to generate a hierarchy of intermediate goals. If I want a cup of tea I first have to go to the kitchen. To get to the kitchen I have to leave the room, to leave the room I have to get up from my chair. More distant goals can be very abstract, resulting in complex action strategies. For example, I may be moved by a desire to renew a particular friendship and decide to visit the friend in question, also decide to go by car, to leave it until after lunch and first check whether he will be at home. In all such sophisticated processes of action planning, the mobilization and co-ordination of relevant imaginative representations plays a major part. Some of the imagined action plans will be rejected, others stored, and some passed on for execution via the premotor and **supplementary motor areas**. I deliberately said 'passed on', for, by contrast with areas 4 and 6, stimulation of the prefrontal cortex does not produce motor responses. PET records have shown that the primary motor cortex itself does not light up until the movements actually occur, whereas prefrontal and premotor areas do. Brain activity during stimulus-independent thought has been found to show increased regional activity in the medial prefrontal region (McGuire et al., 1996).

Both visual imagery and motor imagery [2.4] are deeply involved in most action planning. Frontal lesions have been observed that produced a unilateral neglect in visual imagery (Guariglia et al., 1993) and PET scans

have shown that imagined grasping activated the left inferior and middle
frontal cortex as well as the left frontal parietal cortex (Grafton et al., 1996).
EEG recordings of human prefrontal activity have also shown a greater
dimensional complexity when a moving object like a swinging pendulum
is *imagined* than when it is *perceived* (Schupp et al., 1994).

Memory functions

In connection with episodic memory, I have mentioned work which
showed that the acquisition and retrieval of a memory activate different
brain regions, left frontal regions being activated in the (attention-
supported) encoding and right frontal ones in the initiation of retrieval.
According to PET studies by Fink and colleagues, retrieval of autobiographical memory additionally involves the temporal cortex, the
posterior cingulate cortex and the **insula** (Fink et al., 1996). The latter is a
circular area of cortex at about the level of the thalamus, whose functions
are closely integrated with the prefrontal cortex. Andreason et al. (1995)
have pointed to differences between focused and random memory recall.
In these trials, focused memory recall involved the right inferior medial
frontal lobe and cingulate cortex plus several subcortical structures
including the thalamus and cerebellum. At the cortical level, random recall
also activated the parietal and posterior inferior temporal lobes.

A number of studies have suggested that the lateral prefrontal cortex is
essential for working memory, though it has other functions as well.
Different types of information will engage different locations. A letter
identification task involving working memory showed enhanced levels of
activity in areas 9, 10, 46 and 47 in both hemispheres (Kammer et al., 1997).

Controlled attention

All efficient behaviour needs selective processes in the brain that cause
relevant streams of information to be accentuated and irrelevant material
to be shut out. These attentional processes have been reviewed at some
length in Section 6.2. To avoid confusion between different kinds of
selective process, I have restricted the literal meaning of 'attention'
exclusively to changes of focus occurring at the conscious level, and I have
distinguished here between *controlled* attention and *captured* attention. The
first denotes the case when the subject's current state of attention is the
product of conscious decisions, the second when it is unwittingly captured
by, for example, the sudden occurrence of an unexpected event. It is only
natural to find that the cortical regions responsible for controlled attention
overlap with those involved in willed action decisions. This points to the
prefrontal cortex and anterior cingulate as the key players in controlled
attention, and therefore also as the source of outputs designed to raise the
influence of the relevant domain-specific posterior brain structures to
the required high level. I have called this the 'neural distribution of the

attentional set'. PET studies conducted at Oxford have shown visuospatial attention to be reflected in raised regional activities in the right anterior cingulate gyrus, in the intraparietal **sulcus** of the right posterior parietal cortex and in the mesial and lateral premotor cortices (Nobre et al., 1997).

9.8. The seat of consciousness: what our model suggests

Considerations

According to the first of our four main propositions, the brain forms an extensive internal representation of the current state of the organism, including the situation facing it in both the outer and the inner world. This was called the Integrated Global Representation, or IGR. In the third of these propositions consciousness was identified with the IGR. It follows that to find the seat of consciousness we have to find the seat of the IGR. What kind of neural network is this IGR? Broadly speaking, we are dealing in both the RWM and IGR with widely distributed functional units or 'modules' which are indirectly defined by the feedback that keeps them in trim. The distribution of the RWM was briefly discussed in Section 2.2 (point 10). For the distribution of the IGR, let us first look at its applications.

We have concentrated on four main areas of IGR-controlled activity: action planning, the top-level control of attention, the mobilization and co-ordination of imaginative representations and the initiation of memory search, all governed by the subject's motivational state as conveyed by the outputs of the limbic system. It follows, from our definitions, that the extent to which these actions can be correctly related to the total situation facing the organism depends on the extent to which the brain correctly relates them to the IGR as a whole , i.e. to the current activities of the IGR network as a whole. So the question turns on where this relationship is established. A number of considerations may help us answer this question.

Beginning with willed actions, we recall that by definition they are actions determined by conscious decisions, hence by the IGR. On the empirical evidence, the main regions implicated are the prefrontal cortex, frontal eye fields and anterior cingulate. It follows that the action-deciding assemblies of neurons in these regions are either members of the IGR network or receive massive inputs from its members. However, only the first suggestion makes sense. The second suggestion implies that these regions form a higher level of control than does the IGR, which is contrary to our basic assumptions. The same reasoning applies to the assemblies of neurons accountable in the top-level control of attention, the mobilization and organization of imaginative representations, and the initiation of memory search. Prefrontal lobotomy does not destroy the main prefrontal roles in all this, since only its connections with subcortical structures are severed, leaving intracortical connections intact. The loss of limbic inputs may possibly account for the main deficits caused in the patient's long-term and socially aware outlook.

Next we need to look at the parietal lobe, because of its involvement both in the body schema and in the representation of spatial relations in the visual field and extrapersonal space. The latter makes it a region of unique importance, because the very *presence* of objects in the brain's model of the external world hinges on the representations of spatial relationships. The importance of this involvement was demonstrated in the phenomenon of neglect which I described in Section 6.3. Here we had lesions that resulted in loss of awareness of the existence of entire limbs or of half of the visual field. Are the neurons whose missing activities caused that loss of awareness members of the IGR network? Or do they merely feed into it? Again, I lean towards the first answer. The gaps in awareness caused by the respective lesions, be this a missing limb or a missing half of the visual field, are absolute. If the lesions caused merely a loss of important information projected into the IGR, we should expect the effects to be a matter of degree. Slightly lesser lesions in the same regions might produce half-way conditions in which a limb is merely perceived in a dizzy, distorted or otherwise deficient fashion, or the visual hemifield is unstable or blurred.

In contrast to the parietal lobe, lesions in the medial and inferior temporal lobes do not cause loss of awareness, for these regions deal in the main with just the brain's categorizing reactions to what is perceived, i.e. with the *features* of perceived objects. Damage to these regions thus causes loss of *recognition* of complex shapes, words, faces, people or other objects. This suggests that these regions provide massive inputs to the IGR network, but are not themselves part of that network.

The primary sensory cortices, such as the V1 and the somatosensory cortex, are clearly *necessary* for conscious awareness but not *sufficient*. They are necessary because they are a link in the pathway along which information about the external world reaches the brain's main processing regions. That they are not sufficient is shown by such observations as the time delay that intervenes between the arrival at the somatosensory cortex of a stimulus applied to the skin and the subject's awareness of that stimulus [2.5]. This suggests that the primary sensory cortices are not part of the actual IGR network.

Since the IGR serves the emotional and motivational state of the organism, the IGR network of neurons must either extend over the limbic system or just receive massive inputs from it. Since lesions in this system cause loss of motivational forces, but not loss of awareness of such forces, I would exclude it from the IGR.

Since consciousness and the cycle between sleep and wakefulness is controlled by the ascending reticular activating system (ARAS) via the intralaminar nuclei of the thalamus, we must expect massive inputs to the IGR constellation from this system. However, it seems to me that this global activating input is more like the energizing input of the power pack in a

TV set, and I would not, therefore, list these regions as part of the IGR network as such.

Finally, I must add that some structures have proved to be inessential for consciousness, notably the hippocampus, and the motor executive structures, such as the primary motor cortex, the basal ganglia and the cerebellum.

Conclusion

So where does this leave us? Is the seat of consciousness in the brain? We have identified this with the seat of the IGR and the above considerations suggest that the IGR network of neurons is a widely distributed network that extends over the frontal, anterior cingulate and parietal cortices, including, of course, their associated thalamic nuclei. Yet it functions as a connected whole in the determination of IGR-based, hence conscious activities. This still leaves a lot of questions unanswered, notably about the precise way in which the IGR as a connected whole can determine the action-set and attention-set of the brain. The clarification of concepts, which has been my main aim throughout this book, and the simplicity of my abstract model of the primary consciousness cannot disguise the staggering complexity of the neural connections and processes involved in this sophisticated faculty of the brain. I nevertheless hope that I have had some success in lifting at least a corner of the veil.

Note

1 For most of this section I have been guided by the outstanding and comprehensive review found in Fuster (1997), to some extent supplemented by Roberts et al. (1998). Work in this field has become so massive that even a selection of references would be a huge undertaking. For the most part, the references given in this section merely supplement the extensive bibliography of these two books.

Appendix A

REAL AND ARTIFICIAL NEURONS

I. The neuron

Neurons do all the fast information processing work in the brain. In the human brain there are some 100 billion of them and they come in all shapes and sizes. But, with few exceptions, they have certain central features in common. Among these are treelike branches, called the *dendrites* on which are situated most of the *synapses*, the points at which a neuron receives inputs from other neurons. These afferent contacts come in many different forms (Figure A1), and there may be up to 100,000 synapses on a single neuron. The treelike formations of the dendrites can be of great complexity. Many have protrusions, called *dendritic spines*, on which afferent fibres form synapses. Synapses can also occur between dendrites; neighbouring dendrites can influence each other and their activities summate – to mention just some of the complications. In contrast, each neuron has only a single output fibre, called the **axon**, to carry messages away from it. This is a long and slender process that issues from the cell body of the neuron and is nourished by it. It can extend over considerable distances and will generally branch out extensively into the so-called *axon collaterals*, thus making synaptic contacts with a large number of other neurons. An excited neuron discharges through its axon and these impulses are all-or-nothing events. They consist of brief changes in the electrical potential across the axonal membrane. These may be recorded as *axon potentials*, also called **spikes**. They always have the same amplitude and this does not diminish as the impulses travel along the axon, but they can vary greatly in frequency. Each discharge is followed by an *absolute refractory period* of a few milliseconds in which no new discharge can be created, followed by a *relative refractory period* in which spikes can be generated but only at a reduced sensitivity. In this manner the frequency of the discharges comes to reflect the intensity of the total afferent stimulation that the neuron receives at the synapses. This is summed not only spatially but also temporally over 100 milliseconds or so. Human nerve fibres can transmit up to 1,000 spikes per second.

The synapses

The synapses are the junctions at which axon collaterals of one neuron impinge on the surface of another neuron or one of its dendrites and thus provide a site of information transfer. These terminals are of the nature of swellings or knobs at the afferent terminal, called *boutons*, which are separated from the body of the receiving (or 'postsynaptic') neuron by a minute cleft of only about a millionth of an inch. When a synapse is stimulated by spikes arriving in its afferent fibre, a *neurotransmitter* substance is released from the bouton. This diffuses across the synaptic cleft, where it acts on specific **receptors** on the membrane of the postsynaptic neuron, and opens gates of ion flow that in effect produce a local short-circuit and consequent electrical depolarization. This spreads electronically across the surface of the receiving neuron and sums with similar effects at other stimulated synapses. When this total depolarization, also known as the *excitatory postsynaptic potential* or EPSP reaches a certain critical point the neuron discharges through its axon. This is just a broad description of what is an extremely complex set of processes at the biochemical level. The responses of the receptors may also be influenced by what is happening at neighbouring synapses.

Neurotransmitters differ widely over different regions of the brain, and the receptors have to match the local transmitter. About 50 different ones have been identified. Some appear to be mainly involved in the rapid transmission of information, e.g. *glutamate*, others in the production of temporary brain states, such as *dopamine*, which is active in brain structures influencing our emotional life, and is notably associated with pleasurable sensations and feelings of euphoria. The transmitter substances are produced and stored inside numerous small bodies called *vesicles*, which are situated in the boutons and discharge individually.

There are also synapses whose transmitter substances have an opposite, *inhibitory* effect. Instead of a depolarization, they produce a hyperpolarization. Most of these tend to be situated on the body of the postsynaptic neuron rather than a dendrite. Figure A1 is a simplified composite that gives some idea of the various forms in which these basic arrangements may be realized in practice. Inhibitory synapses are shown in black.

The main significance of synapses in the context of this book lies in the fact that they can undergo lasting changes in their strength – or 'weight' as it is often called – as a transmitting medium, and that they can undergo these changes as the result of the activities in which they are involved. This is generally held to be the main site of learning changes and of lasting memory records. However, new dendrites can also grow and new synapses can be formed as the result of the ongoing activities. An early, and still sometimes suggested explanation of learning changes is the so-called 'Hebbian synapse'. This type of synapse was first hypothesized in 1949 by Donald Hebb, who suggested that a synapse would increase in strength if it was active at the time that the postsynaptic neuron discharged. This

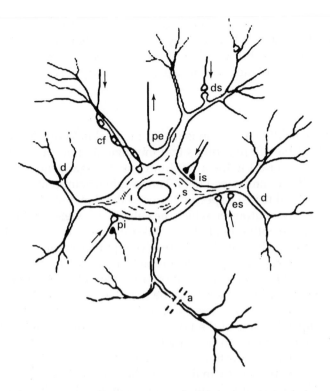

Figure A1 *Composite representation of neuron to illustrate different types of neural elements. a, axon; cf, climbing fibre; d, dendrite; ds, dendritic spine; es, excitatory synapse; is, inhibitory synapse; pe, presynaptic element; pi, presynaptic inhibition; s, soma*

would lead to a strengthening of active pathways which, in turn, could generate closely linked assemblies of neurons active at the same time (Hebb, 1949). However, as I mentioned in Chapter 8, this is not the only suggested mechanism of adaptive changes at the neural level. An interesting addition has been the recent discovery that in the presence of glutamate the receptors can also multiply, even to the point at which the effect of single afferent input can become strong enough to fire the postsynaptic neuron.

Work done by a team at Duke University with a brain-derived neural growth factor (BDNF) and neurotrophin (NT–3) has demonstrated the positive effect of the former on the growth of dendrites, and especially in layer 4 of the cerebral cortex, whereas NT–3 here inhibited that growth. To their surprise, the opposite was found in layer 6 (as reported in *Neuron*, **18**, p. 767). I mention this only to repeat the point that nothing is simple at this level of the brain's remarkable plasticity.

Most of the space between the brain's neurons is taken up by the *glial cells*, which perform a variety of physiological supporting functions, and these, too, may be involved in memory storage. Studies of RNA and DNA concentrations have shown both to play a part in memory functions, the former only transiently. But how all of this fits together to explain the complete mechanisms of memory storage remains a mystery.

Receptive fields

By the 'receptive field' of a neuron is meant the total field of stimuli that can activate it via the afferent fibres that impinge on it at the synapses. Peripheral neurons closest to the input from a sense organ tend to have a fixed and narrowly circumscribed field. Thus a spinal neuron in our sense of touch may respond to just a specific region of the skin. But higher up in the brain there will be neurons on which the outputs of lower-level neurons converge and the receptive fields thus coalesce. And when it comes to cortical regions in which neurons may receive inputs from up to 100,000 other neurons, the receptive fields may become both large and variable.

Some of the variations found are in the nature of long-term adaptations. This applies in particular to the size of the population of neurons which are receptive to a particular category of stimuli. In the somatosensory cortex, for example, the size of the population of neurons receptive to a particular limb will depend on the variety of movement patterns which that limb can execute. Thus the fingers have a relatively much larger population of neurons receptive to them than, say, the upper arm. And if one or more limbs are lost – a couple of fingers, for example – adaptive changes tend to occur in which the now redundant population is taken over by the neighbouring limbs. This can be a comparatively quick change, as a team at the National Institute for Neurological Disorder and Stroke, near Washington, DC has found (*New Scientist*, 14 February 1998). When the afferent fibres of the lower arm were inactivated by a tight tourniquet at the elbow, the brain's internal representation of the upper arm was found to have begun extensions into the former lower-arm representation after only 20 minutes (see also Section 4.2). In cases of blindness in which the eyes fail to deliver an input to the primary visual cortex, so that it is now redundant, this region has frequently been found in due course to be co-opted by other senses, for example hearing.

How is such transfer of function to be explained? Here, I think, we need to distinguish between the *potential* receptive field of a neuron and its *dominant* receptive field. By the *potential* receptive field of a neuron I mean the whole range of stimuli to which a neuron could in theory become receptive by virtue of the chain of connections that link this neuron to the stimulus sources concerned. But, although these connections exist, only the most powerful inputs they supply may in fact be effective. The sources of these powerful inputs I call the *dominant* receptive field. If for any reason these powerful inputs cease or are weakened, previously subdued inputs may now become effective. Hence we get the effect of *shifting* receptive fields, although it is only the dominance that shifts. Thus we must assume in the case of the strangled afferents of the lower arm that the lower-arm neurons already had upper-arm stimuli among their *potential* receptive fields, but the lower-arm stimuli formed the *dominant* group. When the 'amputation' of the lower arm caused these dominant inputs to vanish, the weaker voices of the upper-arm stimuli now began to have an effect and this was gradually strengthened by active engagement, either in the Hebbian way or by the growth of additional dendrites and synapses. The same applies in my earlier example of the cortical neurons that are responsive to inputs from the two fingers prior to their loss, and that now shift their receptive fields to the remaining fingers. It follows from the above that all fingers must have been wired to lie in the potential receptive field of the neurons in the cortical region concerned.

It is plausible to assume that this is also what occurs in the rapid shifts that have been observed at other cortical levels. In fact, it is difficult to explain them in any other way. Thus in the extrastriate cortex there are neurons whose receptive fields shift when the subject's gaze is shifted (Gur & Snodderly, 1997). Again, neurons in the parietal cortex may be responsive to tactile stimuli to the arm and also have a visual receptive field. And here it has been shown that in some of these 'bimodal' neurons the latter field can move in accordance with the movements of the arm (Graziano et al., 1997). In the monkey similar bimodal cells have been found in a parallel region whose visual receptive fields covered the monkey's hand, but when the monkey was given a rake as a tool, these fields expanded to cover the full length of the rake (Iriki et al., 1996). Moveable receptive fields are also known in subcortical structures, for example in the superior colliculus, a structure deeply involved in the movement of the eyes. On our present understanding, all these shifts are shifts in dominance.

When a given neuron is linked to a source of stimuli by a chain of intermediate neurons, it follows that its potential receptive field increases exponentially with the number of members in that chain. This shows the enormous plasticity possible in a system in which such chains exist and in which the dominant fraction of the inputs to a neuron can undergo adaptive changes.

II. Artificial neural networks

These networks can be created in either hardware or computer simulations and consist of individual units that mimic the basic features of real neurons by having a number of input channels but only a single output. The output is computed from the activity in the input channels according to weights attached to the separate input channels and can be distributed to any number of other units or 'nodes' in the system. The system is designed to undergo learning changes in the form of changes in the weights according to whatever formula the designer decides to adopt in order to achieve the desired results. The archetype of such systems is the three-layered system illustrated in Figure A2. It is an archetype in the sense that it was the first system to show remarkable capacities for trial-and-error learning and thus became the prototype for a great variety of modified and elaborated systems, distinguished by their trial-and-error learning capacities. Such

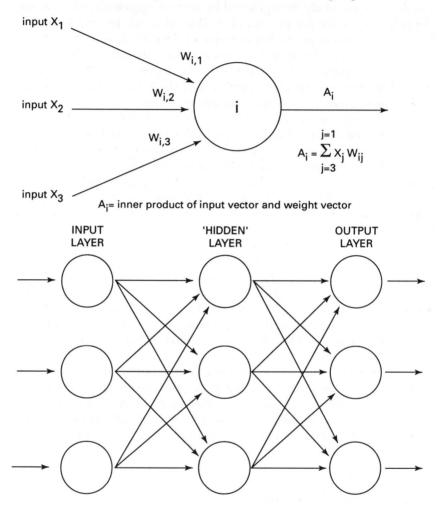

Figure A2 *Neural network and sample algorithms*

advanced networks can be 'trained' by presenting them with examples of a complex problem, such as identifying a car in the digital image of a street, and causing the weights to be adjusted until the network produces the desired output – which, in advanced cases, may even include drawing an outline around the car.

As a simple example of the algorithms adopted, consider the so-called *back-propagation* formula when applied to the three-layered system in order to get it to recognize some particular input pattern. The system is given as initial state a random distribution of weights, thus producing random outputs in response to the presented variety of inputs. It is then programmed so that whenever it happens to give an output in the right direction, all the pathways that contributed to this output are retrospectively strengthened. Even though an extremely large number of trials may be required, this has proved a very effective formula. However, the neural mechanisms involved in the brain's reinforcement of successful actions are not sufficiently well understood for us to decide whether any parallels can be drawn here.

Appendix B

MAIN PROPOSITIONS AND DEFINITIONS

I The scope

In this book consciousness is taken to have three main facets: *an awareness of the surrounding world, of the self as an entity,* and *of one's thoughts and feelings.* The explanations offered cover all three and also the fact that these components of awareness have both an objective aspect as particular faculties of the brain, and a subjective aspect as particular qualities of experience, often called the qualia. Both aspects are explained in terms of the functional architecture of the underlying brain processes. However, the theory concentrates exclusively on levels of consciousness that can also exist in creatures lacking a language faculty, such as the neonate, the deaf-mute and nonhuman animals. This subverbal level of consciousness is called the *primary* consciousness.

II The four main propositions

Proposition 1

The first conjecture:

> *The brain forms an extensive internal representation of the current state of the organism which includes representations of the total situation facing the organism both in the outer and the inner world.* This is called the brain's *Integrated Global Representation* or *IGR.*

Proposition 2

The second conjecture:

> *The IGR, however, is subject to capacity and/or access limitations.*

Proposition 3

The first identity statement:

> *The primary consciousness is the IGR.*

Proposition 4

The second identity statement:

> *The subjective or qualitative aspects of conscious experience, the qualia, consist of those components of the overall effect an event has on the organism which are included in the IGR and, according to Proposition 3, thus become part of our conscious experiences.*

III Main concepts

Structural representations

Definition:

> *The activity of a set N of neurons constitutes a* structural representation *of an entity X, if and only if it maps the structure of X – where 'mapping' is here to be understood as a one-to-one or many-to-one (but not all-to-one) correspondence.*

Functional representations

Definition:

> *The activity of a set N of neurons constitutes a* functional representation *of an entity X, if and only if responses that need to be correctly related to X in some particular way are treated by the brain as responses that need to be correctly related to the activity of N in some particular way.*

States of expectancy

Definition:

> *By a* state of expectancy, *conscious or unconscious, shall be meant a state of the brain that has two components:*
>
> *(a) a state of readiness for the occurrence of a particular event – that is to say, a state which facilitates or advances an appropriate reaction to that event, and*
> *(b) a state in which the occurrence of a significantly different event tends to elicit a characteristic reaction of surprise, technically known as an* orienting reaction. *Pavlov called it a 'What is it?' reflex.*

The Running World Model or RWM

The Running World Model is conceived as the brain's internal representation of the current state of the external world, including the body and its place in that world. Most of the properties of the external world are represented here by the way in which they affect the outcome of our actions, i.e. by acquired act–outcome expectancies. But more general what-leads-to-what expectancies also play a part. Not all of the RWM enters the IGR, hence consciousness.

Imaginative representations

Proposition:

> *To imagine an object of a certain type is for the brain to be in a state of readiness to perceive an object of that type without expecting the perception.*

Self-reference and self-awareness

In the present theory *self-reference* or *implicit self-awareness* denotes the fact that the contents of the IGR, hence of the primary consciousness, have the functional status of representations of the current state of the organism. *Explicit self-awareness* has three main levels:

1. The *basic experiential or 'apprehensive'* level. By this is meant how the above-mentioned self-reference manifests itself experientially and in the qualia of conscious experience.
2. The *conceptual/autobiographical* level. For example, when the self-reference is expressed in such statements as 'I have a toothache'.
3. The *conceptual/contemplative* level. This occurs when introspectively one engages in *thoughts* about what kind of object or person one is.

GLOSSARY

Accommodation. Adjustments in the curvature of the eye's lens that brings fixated objects into sharper focus.

Afferent. Conducting information towards the brain or individual neurons.

Alexia. Inability to read, sometimes caused by lesions in the temporal lobe*.

Amygdala. A walnut-sized knot of neurons deep inside the brain below the level of the thalamus which forms part of the limbic system* and is held to be especially implicated in social sensitivities, judgements and attitudes. If damaged on both sides, the patient will show impoverished memory for emotionally charged events and, for example, fail to read expressions of fear and anxiety on the faces of other people.

Axon. The single fibre and its branches (called **axon collaterals**) through which an excited neuron discharges in an all or nothing fashion and at frequencies which depend on the degree of excitation.

Basal ganglia. A set of important nuclei surrounding the thalamus*, comprising the caudate nucleus*, the putamen*, the globus pallidus*, the substantia nigra*, and the subthalamic nucleus*. They form part of the extra-pyramidal motor system*, and, in conjunction with the cerebellum* figure as the highest subcortical level in the control of motor functions.

Binocular disparity. The disparity in retinal inputs resulting from the different locations from which the eyes see the world.

Blind spot. A small circular area, called the *optic disk*, where the retina* is interrupted by the bundle of nerve fibres leaving it.

Blindsight. The unconscious detection of external visual stimuli and their direction or movement, when lesions in the visual cortex* have caused total blindness at the conscious level.

Body schema. Also called **body image**. A coherent structural representation in the brain of the spatial relations involved in body posture, body movement and body surface.

Brainstem. The structures between the spinal cord and the midbrain*.

Brodmann numbers. The numbering of different cortical regions introduced at the turn of the century by the German anatomist Korbinian Brodmann on the basis of cytoarchitectonic differences. Although his criteria are still a matter of some dispute, as are the functional implications of his divisions, his system has worked well on the whole, and has remained one of the most widely used ways of charting the cortex.

Caudate nucleus. One of the basal ganglia*, implicated in the implementation of action plans generated in the premotor* and supplementary motor cortex*.

Central fissure. A deep cleft at the centre of the cortex, between the primary motor cortex* and the somatosensory cortex*.

Cerebellum. A large brainlike structure with a three-layered cortex which surrounds the back of the brain stem and contains about half the neurons of the central nervous systems. It is deeply implicated in the smooth control and timing of complex movement patterns, largely achieved through its acquired powers to predict the consequences of motor commands on the overall posture and movement of the body and its limbs. This speeds up the movement sequences, because if the brain had to rely entirely on sensory feedback to control the movement of the limbs, we would have to move very much more slowly.

Cerebral cortex. The convoluted grey rind of the two cerebral hemispheres. Generally composed of six layers of tightly packed neurons arranged in vertical columns communicating vertically with each other. Long-distance connections from other cortical regions arrive via the outermost layer while sensory afferents* from the thalamus arrive at intermediate layers and outputs flow from the bottom layers via fibres that jointly constitute the 'white matter'. Often just called 'the cortex' where the context permits.

Cingulate gyrus. A part of the limbic system* implicated in emotion and especially aggression. It arches over the corpus callosum* and comprises Brodmann* areas 23, 24, 26, 29, 31 and 33.

Conditioning. A basic form of learning consisting of the formation of new stimulus–response or stimulus–stimulus associations. The concept was originally restricted to what is now called *classical* conditioning. The prototype of this was Pavlov's demonstration that if the presentation of food to a dog is regularly preceded by a bell, the dog will in due course start salivating simply at the sound of the bell.

Corpus callosum. The large bundle of about 800 million nerve fibres linking corresponding points in the two cortical hemispheres*.

Declarative memory. Memory of something that happened, as opposed to memory of how to do something.

Dendrites. The treelike outgrowths of neurons that receive afferents from other neurons.

Dorsal. On or towards the back of the body or (in upright species) the top of the brain.

EEG. Short for electroencephalographs, the readings of electrodes attached to the scalp which are sensitive to the bulk electrical activity of the underlying cortical cells.

Efferent. Conducting information away from the brain or individual neurons.

Entorhinal cortex. One of the polysensory associative regions in the medial cortex which both projects to the hippocampus* and receives inputs from it.

Episodic memory. The (not always faithful) part of the memory system that stores conscious personal experiences, including, for example, witnessed events.

Exteroceptive information. Information derived from the external senses, such as the eyes and ears.

Extra-pyramidal motor system. See **Pyramidal tract.**

fMRI. Functional Magnetic Resonance Imaging. A technique for mapping regional brain activity. It uses powerful magnetic fields to align the tiny magnetic dipoles of atomic nuclei in the brain. Carefully tuned radio pulses can then reveal changes in oxygen levels, which are indicative of blood flow, by measuring the frequencies at which the oxygen atoms resonate.

Fovea. An axially central region of the retina* in which the photoreceptors are extremely densely packed, permitting high resolution. It consists predominantly of wavelength-sensitive 'cones'.

Frontal. Towards the front of the body or an organ.

Frontal eye fields. A region in the frontal cortex involved in the voluntary control of eye movements.

Ganglia. Groups of neurons at the periphery of the nervous system that perform some basic operations such as the enhancement of contrasts in the retina. But see basal ganglia*.

Globus pallidus. One of the basal ganglia*, which receives mainly inhibitory inputs from the putamen* and caudate nucleus*, and acts on both the thalamus* and subthalamic nucleus*.

Gyrus (pl. gyri). A bulge or raised fold in the surface of the cortex.

Haptic. To do with the sense of touch.

Hemi-. Means 'half', as in hemisphere, hemifield.

Hemisphere. One of the two halves of the cerebral cortex* linked by the corpus callosum*.

Hippocampus. An older structure of the brain, shaped like a sea-horse (hence the name) which is folded into the temporal lobe below the hippocampal gyrus and inferior cingulate gyrus*. It draws upon a mass of inputs from other regions of the cerebral cortex*, and seems to be involved in a variety of supportive functions, including mediating the transfer of short-term to long-term memory, responding to novelty in the sensory inputs and containing cells that are sensitive to an organism's location.

Hypothalamus. Part of the limbic system* mainly concerned with the organism's physiological needs. It controls body temperature, eating, drinking, sexual drive, hormonal balance, and, to some extent, pain.

IGR or **Integrated Global Representation.** My name for a comprehensive internal representation* which I assume to be formed by the brain of the current state of the organism, which includes representations of the total situation facing the organism both in the **outer** and the **inner** world.

Insula. A cortical area hidden behind the temporal* and parietal lobes* and mainly implicated in the processing of visceral* information.

Internal representations. I distinguish a **structural** and **functional** sense of this phrase. Both are defined on pp. 17–21.

Interoceptive information. Information derived from the internal body sensors, such as those in muscles, tendons, joints and the vestibular system*.

Intersection and **union** (logic). The intersection of n classes of entities is the class of entities that are members of all, while the union of n classes of entities is the class of those that are a member of any one of them.

Lateral. Situated at or towards the side of a named structure.

LGN or **lateral geniculate nucleus.** One of the nuclei of the thalamus* which acts as relay station for the optical inputs.

Limbic system. A system of structures which governs the emotional and motivational forces in the determination of behaviour. It is not a very firm notion. Generally included are the hypothalamus*, amygdala*, septal nuclei, mammillary bodies*, parts of the thalamus*, and, at the cortical level, the cingulate gyrus*, the hippocampal gyrus*, including the entorhinal* region and the adjacent periamygdaloid and prepyriform regions.

Mammillary bodies. Distinct cell bodies involved in the processing of outputs from the limbic system*.

Medial cortical regions. Cortical regions on the inner side of the hemispheres (see Figure 2.1, p. 29). Some are important convergence zones which receive information of both the *what* and the *where*.

Microtubules. Fine longitudinal structures in the neuron that seem to be associated with the transport of substances.

Midbrain. The region containing the colliculi, red nucleus, substantia nigra* and regional reticular formation*.

Motion parallax. The way in which the position of nearby objects shifts against the background of more distant ones when the head moves sideways to the line of vision.

Neglect. The effect of brain lesions which cause sections of the brain's world model to vanish from consciousness.

Neurotransmitter. The chemical substance secreted by excited synapses*, which diffuses across the narrow cleft that separates the synapse from the membrane of the neuron it contacts. Through receptors* straddling that membrane it effects voltage changes that spread across the remainder of the neuron's surface (see Appendix A). The chemical composition of neurotransmitters can differ widely over different regions of the brain and needs receptors to match.

Nucleus. A tight group of functionally associated neurons.

Occipital lobe. The lobe at the back tip of the brain which hosts the visual cortex*.

Occam's razor. The admonition given by Bishop William of Occam (c. 1285– c. 1349), a scholastic philosopher of some note, that 'entities should not be multiplied without necessity'. In other words, the best explanations are those that make the fewest assumptions.

Optic chiasma. The crossover point in the optical tracts required because the right half of the visual field of both eyes is processed in the left hemisphere, and the left half in the right hemisphere.

Orienting reactions. A general class of original reactions to unexpected events, inhibited when familiarization comes to substitute more specific responses.

Parietal lobe. A cortical region and association area which lies between the visual* and somatosensory* cortex, heavily involved in the body schema* and in the visual control of movements.

PET or **Positron Emission Tomography.** A technique for mapping regional brain activity by measuring the local metabolic rate. It is based on administering radioactively labelled blood, blood sugars or important neurotransmitters*. A sphere of detector crystals placed around the skull measures the gamma rays emitted when positrons collide with electrons. It is a slow process since the scanner has to sift through 7 or 8 million signals every second to locate concentrations of the tracer.

Pons. Prominent part of the reticular formation*, including the parts that connect the cerebellum* to the midbrain*.

Prefrontal lobe. The part of the frontal lobe forward of the premotor* areas. Held to be the highest level at which the brain evaluates the current situation in the light of the organism's needs and desires, as conveyed by the limbic system*.

Premotor cortex. Motor association area in the frontal lobe anterior to the primary motor cortex*, and held to be implicated in the formation of patterns of movements and the learning of motor skills.

Primary motor cortex. A deep cortical strip in front of the central fissure*, which has direct connections to the motor nuclei (ganglia*) of the spinal cord and plays a dominant part in the fine adjustments of voluntary movements. Brodmann* area 4.

Proprioception. The senses in joints, tendons, muscles and the vestibular system* that inform about the position and position changes of the body and limbs relative to one another and to gravity.

Putamen. One of the basal ganglia*, situated at the level of the thalamus* and implicated in the processing of signals from the somatosensory* and motor areas of the cortex.

Pyramidal tract. A tract of efferent fibres originating in the motor cortex (mainly the primary*) and running straight down to the motor ganglia* in the spinal cord. It supplements the **extra-pyramidal** motor system which comprises the basal ganglia* and associated nuclei, as well as parts of the reticular formation*, and some of its work may be described as playing on the keyboard of built-in reflexes – activating some while inhibiting others.

Receptive fields. The field of stimuli that can activate a neuron via excitation in the totality of afferent* fibres that impinge on its synapses*. A distinction can be drawn between **potential** and **dominant** receptive fields, the latter being the effective portion of the former (see Appendix A). Neurons at the input end of a sensory receptor* tend to have a fixed and narrowly circumscribed field. Thus a primary neuron in our sense of touch will respond to just a specific region of the skin. But higher up in the brain there will be neurons on which the outputs of lower-level neurons converge and the receptive fields thus coalesce. At this level, too, the dominant fraction can undergo adaptive and sometimes rapid changes. In a **chain** of neurons the potential receptive field of the last one in the chain will depend exponentially on the number of neurons in that chain.

Receptors (on neural membranes). Protein molecules on the surface of a neural membrane which are responsive to the neurotransmitter* secreted by the contacting synapses*.

REM sleep. The **Rapid Eye Movement** phase of sleep, distinguished from the non-REM or slow-wave sleep. A periodic phase occurring about every 90 minutes and marked by jerky eye movements, dreams, and notable changes in the EEG* rhythms. PET* studies have shown that during dreaming the prefrontal* areas involved in action planning and self-reflection are turned off. On the other hand, structures involved in emotional reactions, such as the amygdala*, showed enhanced activity. Hence dreams are often fearful. Some occipital areas involved in vision and movement also showed high activity. This may account for the hallucinatory quality of dreams.

Representations. See **Internal representations**

Reticular formation. A complex network of ascending and descending neurons which runs the length of the brain stem and up to the thalamus*, through which it projects diffusely to the cerebral cortex*. Strongly implicated in sleep, arousal, visceral* functions like breathing and body posture. Also in consciousness: even partial damage can cause a coma.

Retina. A structured sheet covering two-thirds of the inner surface of the eyeball. It contains blood vessels, the eye's light-sensitive cells, and ganglia* whose output fibres leave it via the blind spot*. The light-sensitive cells , or **photoreceptors**, are of two types, the **rods** and **cones**. Only the cones are sensitive to specific wavelengths.

RWM or **Running World Model.** My name for the brain's internal representation of the current constitution and state of the external world and its properties, which the brain infers from its sensory inputs on the basis of past experience and other prior knowledge. It includes the body schema*.

Saccades. The eyes' rapid jumps from one point of fixation to another.

Somatosensory cortex. Region of the cortex receiving information from the mechanical sensors in muscles, tendons, joints and the skin. From Greek *soma* = body.

Spike. The brief all-or-nothing discharge of an excited neuron. Since the spikes are always of the same amplitude, the effective variable is their frequency, the number of spikes per second.

Substantia nigra. Part of the extra-pyramidal motor system*, situated at the upper end of the pons*. Degeneration here is held largely responsible for Parkinson's disease.

Subthalamic nucleus. A member of the basal ganglia*, which appears mainly to exercise a gain control over the globus pallidus*.

Sulcus. A groove in the convoluted surface of the cortex.

Superior colliculus. A nuclear structure deeply implicated in the control of eye movements. It contains both maps of the visual field and motor images of saccades*.

Supplementary motor area. A cortical motor association area lying on top of and medial to the premotor cortex*.

Synapse. The knob-like junction at which the outputs of one nerve cell via its axon* or axon-branch stimulate another nerve cell or a muscle fibre. The effect is mediated, generally by way of a chemical transmitter substance, across a narrow cleft that separates the knob from the receiving cell. However, electrical transmission is also known. The stimulus results in changes in the electrical potential of the cell which causes the cell to 'discharge' through its axon when the total effect of all active synapses reaches a certain critical level.

Temporal lobe. A forward-reaching lobe which occupies the lower middle part of the cortex between the visual and frontal* lobe and below the parietal*. Its inferior regions contain association areas heavily implicated in visual object recognition, but also auditory areas and some language areas.

Thalamus. A large integral body of nuclei* which lies as an intermediate station between the sensory inputs and the cortical areas where they are analysed. Each cortical region receives from an associated thalamic nucleus and feeds back to it. In part, but only in part, the thalamus acts here as an upward relay station of sensory and other afferents* to the respective reception areas of the cortex, for it has important functions of its own. Different sensory fibre tracks are regrouped within its massive domain, and there are many opportunities here for the interaction and integration of different modalities.

Topographical projections. Projections into a brain region of a system of sensory inputs, such as inputs from the retina, which maintain the spatial relations between the respective sensors.

Topography. The spatial relation of cells in a brain structure.

Union (logic). See Intersection* (logic).

Ventral. On or towards the front of the body or the base of the brain.

Vergence. Adjusting the angle between the eyes' line of vision to suit the distance of a fixated object (*convergence* if the angle is diminished, *divergence* if increased).

Vestibular system. The system in the inner ear and its semicircular canals that provides us with a sense of balance.

Viscera. The body's internal organs, in particular the abdomen.

Visual cortex. The convoluted cortical region in the occipital lobe* which receives the primary optical inputs and carries out the initial processing in a number of functionally distinct areas.

Working memory. Representations of recent events or experiences that maintain the continuity of the RWM*, including those that are kept alive 'in the mind' because of their relevance to current tasks, for example in serial tasks in which the subjects have to see the responses that still have to be made in the light of the responses already made.

REFERENCES

Anderson, J.R. (1978). 'Arguments concerning representations for mental imagery.' *Psychological Review*, **85**, pp. 249–77.

Anderson, R.A., Essik, G.K. & Siegel, R.M. (1985). 'Encoding of spatial locations by posterior parietal neurons.' *Science*, **230**, pp. 456–8.

Andreason, N.C., O'Leary, D.S., Cisadlo, T., Arndt, S., Rezai, K., Watkins, G.I., Ponto, L. & Hochwa, R.D. (1995). 'Remembering the past: two facets of episodic memory explored with positron emission tomography.' *American Journal of Psychiatry*, **152** (11), pp. 1576–85.

Baars, B.J. (1988). *A Cognitive Theory of Consciousness*. Cambridge, UK: Cambridge University Press.

Baars, B.J. & Banks, W.P. (1992). 'On returning to consciousness.' *Consciousness and Cognition*, **1** (1), pp. 1–6.

Baddeley, A.D. (1986). *Working Memory*. Oxford: Oxford University Press.

Baillargeon, R. (1993). 'The object concept revisited. New directions in the investigation of infants' physical knowledge.' In C.E. Granrud (ed.) *Visual Perception and Cognition in Infancy*. Hillsdale, NJ: Lawrence Erlbaum.

Barlow, H.B. (1987). 'The biological role of consciousness.' In C. Blakemore & S. Greenfield (eds) *Mindwaves*. Oxford: Basil Blackwell.

Barlow, H.B. (1991). 'Vision tells you more than "what is where".' In A. Gorea (ed.) *Representations of Vision: trends and tacit assumptions of vision research*. Cambridge, UK: Cambridge University Press.

Behrmann, M., Winocur, G. & Moscovitch, M. (1992). 'Association between mental imagery and object recognition in a brain-damaged patient.' *Nature*, **159** (6396), pp. 636–7.

Beninger, R.J., Kendall, S.B. & Vanderwolf, C.H. (1974). 'The ability of rats to discriminate their own behaviours.' *Canadian Journal of Psychology*, **28**, pp. 79–91.

Beritashvilli (Beritoff), I.S. (1963). 'The characteristics and origin of voluntary movements in higher vertebrates.' *Progress in Brain Research*, **1**, pp. 340–8.

Berlyne, D.E. (1960). *Conflict, Arousal and Curiosity*. New York: McGraw-Hill.

Bisiach, E. & Geminiani, G. (1991). 'Anosognosia related to hemiplegia and hemianopia.' In G. Prigitano & D.L. Schacter (eds) *Awareness of Deficit after Brain Injury*. New York: Academic Press.

Bisiach, E. & Luzzatti, C. (1978). 'Unilateral neglect of representational space.' *Cerebral Cortex*, **14**, pp. 129–33.

Blackmore, S. (1992). 'The nature of consciousness.' Lecture given in February to the Cambridge University Science Society.

Blakemore, C. (1977). *Mechanics of Mind*. Cambridge, UK: Cambridge University Press.

Blakemore, C. (1990). 'Understanding images in the brain.' In H.Barlow, C. Blakemore & M. Weston-Smith (eds) *Images and Understanding*. Cambridge, UK: Cambridge University Press.

Blakemore, C. & Greenfield, S. (eds) (1987). *Midwives*. Oxford: Basil Blackwell.

Blakemore, S.J., Rees, G. & Frith, C.D. (1998). 'How do we predict the consequences of our actions?' *Neuropsychologia*, **36** (6), pp. 521–9.

Blumenthal, A.L. (1977). *The Process of Cognition*. Englewood Cliffs, NJ: Prentice-Hall.

Boden, M. (1988). *Computer Models of Mind*. Cambridge, UK: Cambridge University Press.

Borsook, D., Becerra, L., Fishmaan, S., Edwards, A., Jennings, C.I., Stojanovie, M., Papinicolas, L., Ramachandran, V.S., Gonsalez, R.G. & Breiter, H. (1998). 'Acute plasticity in the human somatosensory cortex following amputation.' *Neuroreports*, **9** (6), pp. 1013–17.

Bower, T.G.R. (1971). 'The object in the world of the infant.' *Scientific American*, **225**, pp. 30–8.

Brewer, J.B., Zhao, Z., Desmond, J.E., Glover, G.H. & Gabrieli, J.D. (1998). 'Making memories: brain activity that predicts how well visual experience will be remembered.' *Science*, **281**, pp. 1185–7.

Broadbent, D.E. (1952). 'Listening to two synchronous messages.' *Journal of Experimental Psychology*, **44**, pp. 51–5.

Brotchie, P.R., Anderson, R.A., Snyder, L.M. & Goodman, S.J. (1995). 'Head position signal used by parietal neurons to encode locations of visual stimuli.' *Nature*, **375**, pp. 232–5.

Cabeza, R., Kapur, S., Craik, F.I.M., Mcintosh, A.H., Houle, S.A. & Tulving, E. (1997). 'Functional neuroanatomy of recall and recognition: a PET study of episodic memory.' *Journal of Cognitive Neuroscience*, **9**, pp. 254–65.

Carpenter, R.H.S. (1988). *Movement of the Eyes*. London: Pion.

Carpenter, R.H.S. (1996). *Neurophysiology*. London: Arnold.

Carpenter, R.H.S. (1999). 'A neural mechanism that randomises behaviour.' *Journal of Consciousness Studies*, **6** (1), pp. 13–22.

Chalmers, D.J. (1995). 'Facing up to the problem of consciousness.' *Journal of Consciousness Studies*, **2** (3), pp. 200–19.

Chalmers, D.J. (1996). *The Conscious Mind*. New York: Oxford University Press.

Churchland, P.S. & Sejnowski, T.J. (1992). *The Computational Brain*. Cambridge, MA: MIT Press.

Cohen, M.S., Kosslyn, S.M., Breiter, H.C., DiGirolamo, G.J., Thompson, W.I., Anderson, A.K., Brookheimer, S.Y., Rosen, B.R. & Belliveau, J.W. (1996). 'Changes in cortical activity during mental rotation. A mapping study using functional MRI.' *Brain*, **119**, pp. 89–100.

Colby, C.L., Duhamel, J.R. & Goldberg, M.E. (1995). 'Oculocentric spatial representation in parietal cortex.' *Cerebral Cortex*, **5** (5), pp. 470–81.

Cotterill, R.M.J. (1998). *The Enchanted Loom*. Cambridge, UK: Cambridge University Press.

Craik, K. (1943). *The Nature of Explanation*. Cambridge, UK: Cambridge University Press.

Crick, F. (1994). *The Astonishing Hypothesis*. New York: Simon & Schuster.

Damasio, A.R. (1994). *Descartes' Error*. New York: G.P. Putnam & Sons.

Damasio, A.R. (1998). 'Investigating the biology of consciousness.' *Philosophical Transactions of the Royal Society*, Section B, **353**, pp. 1879–82.

Davis, K.D., Kiss, Z.H., Luo, L., Tasker, R.R., Lozano, A.M. & Dostrovsky, J.O. (1998). 'Phantom sensations generated by thalamic microstimulation.' *Nature*, **391**, pp. 385–7.

Decety, J. (1996). 'The neurophysiological basis of motor imagery.' *Behavioral Brain Research*, **77** (1–2), pp. 45–52.

Deiber, M.P., Wise, S.P., Honda, M., Catalan, M.J., Grafman, J. & Hallett, M. (1997). 'Frontal and parietal networks for conditional motor learning: a positron emission tomography study.' *Journal of Neurophysiology*, **78** (2), pp. 977–99.

Dennett, D.C. (1991). *Consciousness Explained*. Boston: Little, Brown.

Dennett, D.C. (1997). 'The unimagined preposterousness of zombies.' *Journal of Consciousness Studies*, **2** (4), pp. 322–5.

Deubel, H. & Schneider, W.X. (1996). 'Saccade target selection and object recognition: evidence for a common attentional mechanism.' *Vision Research*, **36** (12), pp. 1827–37.

Ducom, J.C. (1999). 'Lights, sounds, action! Report on the work of Ducom and his colleagues.' *New Scientist*, **2183** (24 April), p. 6.

Duncan, J. (1998). 'Converging levels of analysis in cognitive neuroscience of visual attention.' *Philosophical Transactions of the Royal Society*, Section B, **353**, pp. 1307–17.

Eccles, J.C. & Popper, K.R. (1977). *The Self and its Brain*. Berlin: Springer International.

Edelman, G.M. (1992). *Bright Air, Brilliant Fire*. London: Allen Lane.

Faillenot, I., Sakata, H., Costes, N., Decety, J. & Jeannerod, M. (1997). 'Visual working memory for shape and 3D-orientation: a PET study.' *Neuroreport*, **8** (4), pp. 859–62.

Farah, M.J. (1985). 'Psychophysical basis for a shared representational medium for mental images and percepts.' *Journal of Experimental Psychology: General*, **114**, pp. 91–103.

Farah, M.J. (1997). 'Consciousness of perception after brain damage.' *Seminar Neurology*, **17** (2), pp. 145–52.

Farah, M.J. , Peronnet, F., Gonon, M.A. & Girard, M.H. (1988). 'Electrophysiological evidence for a shared representational medium for visual images and visual percepts.' *Journal of Experimental Psychology: General*, **117**, pp. 248–57.

Felleman, D.J. & Van Essen, D.C. (1991). 'Distributed hierarchical processing in primate cerebral cortex.' *Cerebral Cortex*, **1** (1) (Jan.–Feb.), pp. 1–47.

Ffytche, D.H., Howard, R.J., Brammer, M.J., David, A., Woodruff, P. & Williams, S. (1998). 'The anatomy of conscious vision: an fMRI study of visual hallucinations.' *Nature Neuroscience*, **1** (8), pp. 738–42.

Fink, G.R., Markowitsch, H.J., Reinkemeier, M., Bruckbauer, T., Kessler, J. & Heiss, W.D. (1996). 'Cerebral representation of one's own past: neural networks involved in autobiographical memory.' *Journal of Neuroscience*, **16** (13), pp. 4275–82.

Finke, R.A. (1985). 'Theories relating mental imagery to perception.' *Psychological Bulletin*, **98**, pp. 236–59.

Finke, R.A. & Kosslyn, S.M. (1980). 'Mental imagery acuity in the peripheral visual field.' *Journal of Experimental Psychology: Human Perception and Performance*, **6**, pp. 244–64.

Fodor, J.A. (1975). *The Language of Thought*. Hassocks, UK: The Harvester Press.

Földiak, P. (1992). 'Models of sensory coding.' Dissertation, Department of Physiology, University of Cambridge.

Frith, C. & Dolan, R. (1996). 'The role of the prefrontal cortex in higher cognitive functions.' *Cognitive Brain Research*, **5** (1–2), pp. 175–88.

Fuster, J.M. (1997). *The Prefrontal Cortex* (3rd ed.). New York: Lippincott-Raven.

Gallese, V., Fadiga, L., Fogassi, L. & Rozzolatti, G. (1996). 'Action recognition in premotor cortex.' *Brain*, **119**, pp. 593–609.

Gallistel, C.R. (1989). 'Animal cognition: the representation of space, time and number.' *Annual Review of Psychology*, **40**, pp. 155–89.

Gardner, M. (1996). 'Computers near the threshold?' *Journal of Consciousness Studies*, **3** (1), pp. 89–94.

Gazzaniga, M. S. & LeDoux, J.E. (1978). *The Integrated Mind*. New York: Plenum.

Georgopolous, A.P., Lurito, J.T., Petrides, M., Schwartz, A.B. & Massey, J.T. (1989). 'Mental rotation of the neuronal population vector.' *Science*, **243**, pp. 141–272.

Gibson, J.J. (1979). *The Ecological Approach to Visual Perception*. Boston: Houghton-Mifflin.

Gobnik, A., Meltzoff, A.N. & Kuhl, P. (2000). *How Babies Think: the science of childhood*. New York: Weidenfeld and Nicolson.

Goldstein, K. (1948). *Language and Language Disturbances*. New York: Grune and Statton.

Goodale, M.A., Jacobson, L.S. & Keiller, J.M. (1994). 'Differences in visual control of pantomimed and natural grasping movements.' *Neuropsychologia*, **32**, pp. 1159–78.

Goubet, N. & Clifton, R.K. (1998). 'Object and event representation in 6-month-old infants.' *Developmental Psychology*, **34** (1), pp. 63–76.

Grady, C.L., McIntosh, A.R., Rajah, M.N. & Craik, F.I. (1998). 'Neural correlates of the episodic encoding of pictures and words.' *Proceeding of the National Academy of Science*, **95**, pp. 2703–8.

Grafton, S.T., Arbib, M.A., Fadiga, I. & Rizolatti, G. (1996). 'Localization of grasp representations in humans by positron emission tomography. 2. Observation compared with imagination.' *Experimental Brain Research*, **112** (1), pp. 103–11.

Graziano, M.S.A., Hu, X.T.A. & Gross, C.G. (1997). 'Visiospatial properties of ventral premotor cortex.' *Journal of Neurophysiology*, **77** (5), pp. 2268–92.

Greenfield, S. (1998). 'How might the brain generate consciousness?' In S. Rose (ed.) *From Brains to Consciousness?* London: Allen Lane.

Gregory, R.L. (1970). 'On how little information controls so much behaviour.' In A.T.Welfod & L. Housiadas (eds) *Contemporary Problems in Perception*. London: Taylor & Francis.

Gregory, R.L. (1987). *The Oxford Companion to the Mind*. Oxford: Oxford University Press.

Gregory, R.L. & Wallace, J.G. (1963). *Recovery from Blindness: a Case Study*. Cambridge, UK: Cambridge University Press.

Grossberg, S. (1980). 'How does the brain build a cognitive code?' *Psychological Review*, **87**, pp. 1–42.

Guariglia, C., Padovani, P. & Pizzamiglio, L. (1993). 'Unilateral neglect restricted to visual imager.' *Nature*, **383**, pp. 78–81.

Gur, M. & Snodderly, D.M. (1997). 'Visual receptive fields of neurons in the primary visual cortex (V1) move in space with the eye movements of fixation.' *Vision Research*, **37**, pp. 257–65.

Gyr, J., Willey, R. & Henry, A. (1979). 'Motor-sensory feedback and geometry of visual space: an attempted replication.' *Behavioral and Brain Sciences*, **2**, pp. 59–94.

Haith, M.M. (1993). 'Future-oriented processes in infancy. The case for visual expectations.' In C.E. Granrud (ed.) *Visual Perception and Cognition in Infancy*. Hillsdale, NJ: Lawrence Erlbaum.

Halligan, P.W. & Marshall, J.C. (1993). 'The history and clinical presentation of neglect.' In L.H. Robertson & J.C. Marshall (eds) *Unilateral Neglect: clinical and experimental studies*. Hove, UK: Lawrence Erlbaum.

Hameroff, S.R. (1994). 'Quantum coherence in microtubules: a neural basis for emergent consciousness?' *Journal of Consciousness Studies*, **1**, pp. 98–118.

Hayhoe, M., Lachter, J. & Feldman, J. (1991). 'Integration of form across saccadic eye movements.' *Perception*, **20** (3), pp. 393–402.

Head, H. (1920). *Studies in Neurology*, 2. London: Frowde, Hodder & Stoughton.

Hebb, D.O. (1949). *Organization of Behaviour*. New York: John Wiley & Sons.

Heijden, A.H.C. van der (1992). *Selective Attention in Vision*. London: Routledge & Kegan Paul.

Held, R. & Hein, A. (1963). 'Movement-produced stimulation in the development of visually guided behaviour.' *Journal of Comparative and Physiological Psychology*, **56**, pp. 872–6.

Helmholtz, H. von (1867). *Handbuch der Physiologischen Optik*, Vol. III. Leipzig: Leopold Voss.

Hietanen, J.K. & Perrett, D.I. (1993). 'Motion sensitive cells in macaque superior temporal polysensory area. Lack of response to the sight of the animal's own limb movement.' *Experimental Brain Research*, **93** (1), pp. 117–28.

Hochberg, J. (1968). 'In the mind's eye.' In R.N. Huber (ed.) *Contemporary Theory and Research in Perception*. New York: Holt, Reinhart & Winston.

Hofstadter, D. (1989). *Gödel, Escher, Bach: An Eternal Golden Braid*. New York: Basic Books.

Holst, E. von & Mittelstaedt, H. (1950). 'Das Reafferenz Prinzip.' *Naturwissenschaften*, **37**, pp. 465–76.

Hubel, D.H. & Wiesel, T.N. (1962). 'Receptive fields, binocular interaction and functional architecture in the cat's visual cortex.' *Journal of Physiology (London)*, **166**, pp. 106–54.

Humphrey, N. (1992). *A History of the Mind*. London: Chatto & Windus.

Ingvar, D.H. (1994). 'The will of the brain: cerebral correlates of willful acts.' *Journal of Theoretical Biology*, **171** (1), pp. 7–12.

Iriki, A., Tanaka, M. & Iwamura, Y. (1996). *Neuroreports*, **7** (14), pp. 2325–30.

Jackendoff, R. (1987). *Consciousness and the Computational Mind*. Cambridge, MA: MIT Press.

James, W. (1890). *Principles of Psychology* (2 vols). New York: Dover.

Jaynes, J. (1976). 'The origins of consciousness.' In *The Breakdown of the Bicameral Mind*. Boston: Houghton Mifflin.

Jeannerod, M. (1994). 'The representing brain: neural correlates of motor intention and imagery.' *Behavioral and Brain Sciences*, **17**, pp. 187–245.

Jeannerod, M. (1997). *The Cognitive Neuroscience of Action*. Oxford: Blackwells.

Jenkins, I.H., Brooks, D.J., Nixon, P.D., Frackowiak, R.S.J. & Passingham, R.E. (1994). 'Motor sequence learning: a study with positron emission tomography.' *Journal of Neuroscience*, **14**, pp. 1775–90.

Johnson-Laird, P.N. (1983). *Mental Models*. Cambridge, UK: Cambridge University Press.

Jueptner, M., Stephan, K.M., Frith, C.D., Brooks, D.J., Frackowiak, R.S.J. & Passingham, R.E. (1996). 'The anatomy of motor learning. The frontal cortex and attention to action.' *Journal of Neurophysiology*, **77**, pp. 1313–24.

Kammer, T., Bellemann, M.E., Guckel, F., Brix, G., Gass, A., Schlemmer, H. & Spitser, M. (1997). 'Functional MR imaging of the prefrontal cortex: specific activation in a working memory task.' *Magnetic Resonance Imaging*, **15** (8), pp. 879–89.

Kellman, P.J. (1993). 'Kinematic foundations of infant visual perception.' In C.E.Granrud (ed.) *Visual Perception and Cognition in Infancy.* Hillsdale, NJ: Lawrence Erlbaum.

Kellman, P.J., Geltiman, H. & Spelke, E.R. (1987). 'Object observer motion in the perception of objects by infants.' *Journal of Experimental Psychology: Human Perception and Performance,* **13,** pp. 586–93.

Kellman, P.J. & Spelke, E.R. (1983). 'Perception of partly occluded objects in infancy.' *Cognitive Psychology,* **15,** pp. 483–524.

Kinomura, S., Larsson, J., Gulyas, B. & Roland, P.E. (1996). 'Activation by attention of the human reticular formation and thalamic intralaminar nuclei.' *Science,* **274,** pp. 512–15.

Kinsbourne, M. (1988). 'Integrated field theory of consciousness.' In A.J. Marcel & E. Bisiach (eds) *Consciousness in Contemporary Science.* Oxford: Clarendon Press.

Kinsbourne, M. (1995). 'The intralaminar thalamic nuclei.' *Consciousness and Cognition,* **4,** pp. 167–71.

Kohler, I. (1964). 'The formation and transformation of the perceptual world.' (Fiss, H., Trans.). *Psychological Issues,* **3,** pp. 1–173.

Köhler, W. (1925). *The Mentality of Apes.* New York: Harcourt Brace.

Kohonen, T. (1984). *Self-organization and Associative Memory.* New York: Springer.

Kornhuber, H. & Deecke, L. (1965). 'Hirnpotentialänderungen bei Wilkürbewegungen und passiven Bewegungen des Menschen: Bereitschaftspotentiale und Reafferente Potentiale.' In *Pflüger's Archiv der Gesamten Physiologie. Menschen – Tiere,* **284,** pp. 1–17.

Kosslyn, S.M. (1978). 'Imagery and internal representations.' In E. Rosch & B.B. Lloyd (eds) *Cognition and Categorization.* Hillsdale, NJ: Lawrence Erlbaum.

Kosslyn, S.M. (1983). *Ghosts in the Mind's Machine: creating and using images in the brain.* New York: W.W. Norton.

Kosslyn, S.M.,Thompson, W.L., Kim, I.J. & Alpert, N.M. (1995). 'Topographical representations of mental images in primary visual cortex.' *Nature,* **378** (6556), pp. 496–8.

Krause, W., Gibbons, H. & Schack, B. (1998). 'Concept activation and coordination of activation procedure require two different networks.' *Neuroreport,* **9** (7), pp. 1849–53.

Krechevski, I. (1932). '"Hypotheses" in rats.' *Psychological Review,* **39,** pp. 516–32.

Krushinski, L.V. (1965). 'Solutions of elementary problems by animals on the basis of extrapolation.' In N. Wiener & J.P. Schade (eds) *Cybernetics and the Nervous System.* Amsterdam: Elsevier.

Lacquantini, F. & Maioli, C. (1965). 'The role of preparation and tuning anticipatory to reflex responses during catching.' In N.Wiener & J.P.Scade (eds) *Cybernetics and the Nervous System.* Amsterdam: Elsevier.

Legerstee, M. (1998). 'Mental and bodily awareness in infancy: consciousness of self-existence.' *Journal of Consciousness Studies,* **5** (5–6), pp. 627–44.

Libet, B. (1993). 'The neural time factor in conscious and unconscious events.' In *Experimental and Theoretical Studies of Consciousness.* CIBA Foundation Symposium 174. New York: John Wiley & Sons.

Libet, B. (1994). 'A testable field theory of mind-brain interaction.' *Journal of Consciousness Studies,* **1** (1), pp. 119–26.

Libet, B., Wright, E.W. & Gleason, C. (1982). 'Readiness potentials preceding unrestricted "spontaneous" vs. pre-planned voluntary acts.' *Electroencephalography and Clinical Neurophysiology,* **54,** pp. 322–35.

Luria, A.R. (1959). 'Disorders of "simultaneous perception" in case of bilateral occipitoparietal brain injury.' *Brain*, **83**, pp. 437–49.

McGinn, C. (1991). *The Problem of Consciousness*. Oxford: Basil Blackwell.

McGuire, P.K., Paulesu, E., Frackowiak, R.S. & Frith, C.D. (1996). 'Brain activity during stimulus independent thought.' *Neuroreport*, **7** (13), pp. 2095–9.

Maguire, E.A., Frackowiak, R.S.J. & Frith, C.D. (1997). 'Recalling routes around London: activation of the right hippocampus in taxi drivers.' *Journal of Neuroscience*, **17** (18), pp. 7103–10.

Maquet, P., Degueldre, C., Delfiore, G., Aerts, J., Peters, J.-M., Luxen, A. & Franck, G. (1997). 'Functional neuroanatomy of human slow wave sleep.' *Journal of Neuroscience*, **17** (8), pp. 2807–12.

Marr, D. (1982). *Vision*. San Francisco: Freeman.

Marshall, J.C., Halligan, P.W. & Robertson, I.H. (1993). 'Contemporary theories of unilateral neglect: a critical review.' In L.H. Robertson & J.C. Marshall (eds) *Unilateral Neglect: Clinical and Experimental Studies*. Hove, UK: Lawrence Erlbaum.

Melzack, R. (1990). 'Phantom limb pain.' *Trends in Neuroscience*, **13** (3), pp. 88–92.

Melzack, R. & Wall, P.D. (1996). *The Challenge of Pain*. London: Penguin.

Meredith, S. (1991). As reported in *New Scientist*, 5 September, p. 52.

Milner, A.D. & Goodale, M.A. (1995). *The Visual Brain in Action*. Oxford: Oxford University Press.

Minsky, M. (1986). *The Society of Mind*. New York: Simon & Schuster.

Mountcastle, V.B., Lynch, J.C., Georgopolous, A., Sakata, H. & Acuna, C. (1975). 'Posterior parietal association cortex of the monkey: command functions for operation within extrapersonal space'. *Journal of Neurophysiology*, **38**, pp. 871–908.

Nagel, T. (1974). 'What is it like to be a bat?' *Philosophical Review*, **38**, pp. 435–50.

Neisser, U. (1976). *Cognition and Reality*. San Francisco: Freeman.

Newman, J. & Baars, B.J. (1993). 'A neural attentional model for access to consciousness. A Global Workspace perspective.' *Concepts in Neuroscience*, **4** (2), pp. 255–90.

Nobre, A.C., Sebestyen, G.N., Gitelman, D.R., Mesulam, M.M., Frackowiak, R.S. & Frith, C.D. (1997). 'Functional localization of the system for visuospatial attention using positron emission tomography.' *Brain*, **120** (3), pp. 515–33.

Noton, D. & Stark, L. (1971). 'Scanpaths in saccadic eye movements while viewing and recognising patterns.' *Vision Research*, **11**, pp. 929–41.

Nyberg, L. (1998). 'Mapping episodic memory.' *Behavioural Brain Research*, **90** (2), pp. 107–14.

O'Keefe, J. (1976). 'Place units in the hippocampus of the freely moving rat.' *Experimental Neurology*, **51**, pp. 78–109.

Olsen, C.R. & Gettner, S.N. (1995). 'Object-centered direction selectivity in the macaque supplementary eye fields.' *Science*, **269**, pp. 985–8.

Olson, E.T. (1998). 'There is no problem of the self.' *Journal of Consciousness Studies*, **5** (5–6), pp. 645–57.

Olton, D.S. (1979). 'Mazes, maps and memory.' *American Psychologist*, **34**, pp. 588–96.

Owen, A.M., Milner, B., Petrides, M. & Evans, A.C. (1996).'Memory for object features versus memory for object location: a positron-emission tomography study of encoding and retrieval processes.' *Proceedings of the National Academy of Science, USA*, **93** (17), pp. 9212–17.

Pani, J.R. (1982). 'A functional approach to mental imagery.' Paper presented at the twenty-third annual meeting of the Psychonomic Society, Baltimore, MD.

Penfield, W.G. & Jasper, H. (1954). *Epilepsy and the Functional Anatomy of the Human Brain*. Boston: Little, Brown.

Penrose, R. (1989). *The Emperor's New Mind*. Oxford: Oxford University Press.

Penrose, R. (1994). *Shadows of the Mind*. Oxford: Oxford University Press.

Perner, J. (1991). *Understanding the Representational Mind*. Cambridge, MA: MIT Press.

Perner, J. & Ruffman, T. (1995). 'Episodic memory and autonoetic consciousness: developmental evidence and a theory of childhood amnesia.' *Journal of Experimental Child Psychology*, **59**, pp. 516–48.

Perrett, D., Harries, H., Mistlin, A.J. & Citty, A.J. (1990). 'Three stages in the classification of body movements by visual neurons.' In H. Barlow, C. Blakemore & M. Weston-Smith (eds) *Images and Understanding*. Cambridge, UK: Cambridge University Press.

Piaget, J. (1954). *The Child's Conception of the World*. London: Routledge & Kegan Paul.

Piaget, J. & Inhelder, B. (1956). *The Child's Conception of Space*. New York: Humanities Press.

Pinker, S. (1997). *How the Mind Works*. New York: W.W. Norton.

Pribram, K.H. (1999). 'Brain and the composition of conscious experience.' *Journal of Consciousness Studies*, **6** (5), pp. 19–42.

Pylyshyn, Z.W. (1973). 'What the mind's eye tells the mind's brain.' *Psychological Bulletin*, **80**, pp. 1–24.

Quine, W.V. (1960). *Word and Object*. Cambridge, MA: MIT Press.

Ramachandran, V.S. & Hirstein, W. (1998). 'The perception of phantom limbs.' The D.O. Hebb lecture. *Brain*, **121** (9), pp. 1603–30.

Rader, N. & Stern, J.D. (1982). 'Visually elicited reaching in neonates.' *Child Development*, **53**, pp. 1004–7.

Rieser, J.J., Guth, D.A. & Hill, E.W. (1986). 'Sensitivity to perceptive structure while walking without vision.' *Perception*, **15**, pp. 173–88.

Rizzolatti, G., Fadiga, L., Fogassi, L. & Gallese, V. (1997). 'The space around us.' *Science*, **277**, pp.190–1.

Roberts, A.C., Robbins, T.W. & Weiskrantz, L. (eds) (1998). *The Prefrontal Cortex*. Oxford: Oxford University Press.

Rochat, P. & Hespos, S.J. (1996). 'Tracking and anticipating invisible transformations by 4- to 8-months old infants.' *Cognitive Development*, **11**, pp. 3–17.

Roelfsema, P.R. (1998). 'Solutions for the binding problem.' *Zeitung für Naturforschung*, **53** (7–8), pp. 691–715.

Roland, P.E. & Gulyas, B. (1994). 'Visual imagery and visual representation.' *Trends in Neuroscience*, **7**, pp. 2373–89.

Rose, S. (1973) *The Conscious Brain*. London: Weidenfeld & Nicholson.

Rosenfield, I. (1992). *The Strange, Familiar and Forgotten: An anatomy of consciousness*. London: Vintage.

Rosenthal, D. (1993). 'Thinking that one thinks.' In M. Davies & G.W. Humphreys (eds) *Consciousness: psychology and philosophical essays*. Oxford: Blackwells.

Rosler, F., Heil, M. & Hennighausen, E. (1995). 'Exploring memory functions by means of brain electrical topography: a review.' *Brain Topography*, **7** (4), pp. 301–13.

Ryle, G. (1949). *The Concept of Mind*. London: Hutchinson.

Schacter, D.L., Uecker, A., Reiman, E., Yun, L.S., Bandy, D., Chen, K., Cooper, L.A.

& Curran, T. (1997). 'Effects of size and orientation change on hippocampal activation during episodic recognition: a PET study.' *Neuroreports*, **8** (18), pp. 3993–8.

Schilder, P. (1935). 'The image and appearance of the human body.' *Psychological Monographs*, **4**. London: Kegan, Trench & Trubner.

Schupp, H.T., Lutzenberger, W., Birbaumer, N., Miltner, W. & Braun, C. (1994). 'Neurophysiological differences between perception and imagery.' *Brain Research*, **2**, pp. 77–86.

Seager, W. (1995). 'Consciousness, information and panpsychism.' *Journal of Consciousness Studies*, **2** (3), pp. 272–88.

Searle, J.R. (1990). 'Consciousness, explanatory inversion, and cognitive science.' *Behavioral and Brain Sciences*, **13**, pp. 585–642.

Searle, J.R. (1992). *The Rediscovery of the Mind*. Cambridge, MA: MIT Press.

Searle, J.R. (1997). *The Mystery of Consciousness*. London: Granta Books.

Segal, S.J. & Fusella, V. (1970). 'Influence of imagined pictures and sounds on detection of visual and auditory signals.' *Journal of Experimental Psychology*, **83**, pp. 458–64.

Servos, P. & Goodale, M.A. (1995). 'Preserved visual imagery in visual form agnosia.' *Neuropsychologia*, **33** (11), pp. 1383–94.

Shallice, T. (1982). 'Specific impairment in planning.' *Proceedings of the Royal Society*, **298**, pp. 199–209.

Shallice, T., Fletcher, P., Frith, C.D., Grasby, P., Frackowiak, R.S.J. & Dolan, R.J. (1994). 'Brain regions associated with the acquisition and retrieval of verbal episodic memory.' *Nature*, **386**, pp. 633–5.

Shepard, R.N. (1984). 'Kinematics of perceiving, imagining, thinking and dreaming.' *Psychological Review*, **91**, pp. 417–47.

Shepard, R.N. & Metzler, J. (1971). 'Mental rotation of three-dimensional objects.' *Science*, **171**, pp. 701–3.

Sommerhoff, G. (1974). *Logic of the Living Brain*. London: John Wiley & Sons.

Sommerhoff, G. (1990). *Life, Brain and Consciousness*. Amsterdam: Elsevier.

Spelke, E.S. & Van de Walle, G.A. (1993). 'Perceiving and reasoning about objects: insights from infants.' In N. Eilan, R. McCarthy & W. Brewer (eds) *Spatial Representation*. Oxford: Basil Blackwell.

Sperry, R.W. (1987). 'Split brain and the mind.' In R. Gregory & O.L. Zangwill (eds) *The Oxford Companion to the Mind*. Oxford: Oxford University Press.

Standing, L. (1973). 'Learning 10,000 pictures.' *Quarterly Journal of Experimental Psychology*, **25**, pp. 207–22.

Stoet, G. (1998). 'The role of feature integration in action planning.' Unpublished dissertation. University of Munich.

Strange, B.A., Fletcher, P.C., Henson, R.N., Friston, K.J. & Dolan, R.J. (1999). 'Segregating the functions of the human hippocampus.' *Proceedings of the National Academy of Science*, **96** (7), pp. 4034–9.

Strawson, G. (1997). 'The self.' *Journal of Consciousness Studies*, **4** (5–6), pp. 405–28.

Sutherland, S.(1989). *The Macmillan Dictionary of Psychology*. London: Macmillan Press.

Taube, J.S., Muller, R.U. & Ranck, J.B. (1990). 'Head-direction cells recorded from the postsubiculum in freely moving rats.' *Journal of Neuroscience*, **10**, pp. 420–35.

Tolman, E.C. (1932). *Purposive Behavior in Animals and Men*. New York: Appleton Century.

Tolman, E.C. (1948). 'Cognitive maps in rats and men.' *Psychological Review*, **55**, pp. 189–208.

Tulving, E., Markowitsch, H.J., Kapur, S., Habib, R. & Houle, S. (1994). 'Novelty encoding in the human brain: positron emission tomography data.' *Neuroreport*, **5** (18), pp. 2525–8.

Umeno, M.M. & Goldberg, M.F. (1997). 'Spatial processing in monkey frontal eye field. (1) Predictive visual responses.' *Journal of Neurophysiology*, 78 (3), pp. 1373–83.

Van der Meer, A.L.H., van der Weel, F.R. & Lee, D.N. (1950). 'The functional significance of arm movements in neonates.' *Science*, **267**, pp. 893–4.

Walter, W. Grey (1964). 'Slow potential waves in the human brain associated with expectancy, attention and decision.' *Zeitschrift für die gesamte Neurologie*, **206**, pp. 309–22.

Watanabe, M. (1996). 'Reward expectancies in primate prefrontal cortex.' *Nature*, **382**, pp. 629–32.

Weiskrantz, L. (1997). *Consciousness Lost and Found*. Oxford: Oxford University Press.

Wessel, K., Zeffiro, T., Toro, C. & Hallett, M. (1997). 'Self-paced versus metronome-paced finger movements. A positron emission tomography study.' *Journal of Neuroimaging*, **7** (3), pp. 145–51.

Wilkins, K.L., McGrath, P.J., Finley, G.A. & Katz, J. (1998). 'Phantom sensations and phantom limb pain in child and adolescent amputees.' *Pain*, **78** (1), pp. 7–12.

Wurtz, R.H., Goldberg, M.E. & Robinson, D.L. (1982). 'Brain mechanisms of visual attention.' *Scientific American*, **246** (6), pp. 100–5.

Wynn, K. (1992). 'Addition and subtraction by human infants.' *Nature*, 358 (6389), pp. 749–54.

Zaporozhets, A.V. (1965). 'The development of perception in the pre-school child.' *European Research in Cognitive Development*, **30** (2). Chicago: University of Chicago Press.

Zeki, S. (1993). *A Vision of the Brain*. Oxford: Basil Blackwell.

INDEX